A HOUSE FOR SPIES

SIS Operations into occupied France from a Sussex farmhouse

Edward Wake-Walker

SAPERE
BOOKS

A HOUSE FOR
SPIES

Published by Sapere Books.

20 Windermere Drive, Leeds, England, LS17 7UZ,
United Kingdom

saperebooks.com

ISBN: 978-1-913518-01-1

ACKNOWLEDGEMENTS

At the top of my list of those I would like to thank for their help and encouragement are Barbara and Tony Bertram's family. Their eldest son, Tim, gave me access to Barbara's wonderful monologue, *C'est On, C'est Off*, and allowed it to be published for the first time in this book. His daughter, Tasha, who has been working on a film script based on her grandparents' experiences in parallel to but independent of my own project, has been equally supportive. And the sadly now deceased, Father Jerome Bertram, Barbara's other surviving son, who allowed me to paint what I hope is an accurate picture of his parents' background and to use a number of very relevant photographs.

Jerome was also responsible for introducing me to Colin Cohen, son of Kenneth Cohen who had such a leading role in running SIS missions in France during the war. I am extremely grateful to Colin, who has fed me intriguing snippets of his father's memories as well as some photographs which appear in this book.

I spent a fascinating twenty-four hours with Gilbert Pineau, son of the network chief, Christian, who was twelve years old when his father was arrested by the Gestapo and who kindly put me up in his Paris apartment and provided invaluable insights into that traumatic period. My thanks go also to Jean Novosseloff of the organization *Mémoires et Espoirs de la Résistance*, who put me in touch with Gilbert Pineau.

I will also not forget the help Elspeth Forbes-Robertson gave me in pointing me in the direction of useful sources at the beginning of my research and I am equally grateful to those who gave me spontaneous assistance as I retraced the footsteps of some of the leading players in this story. Ann Dennis, the current owner of Bignor Manor, is one example and members of the de La Bardonnie family, close to the Dordogne, are another. Guy de La Bardonnie, in particular, eldest son of the pioneering *Résistant*, Louis, has provided me with useful family memorabilia.

Lastly, I should like to thank my wife, Fiona, companion on some of my research expeditions and sounding board for a number of draft passages and also Martha Dancy, my niece, whose original idea set me thinking about writing the book in the first place.

TABLE OF CONTENTS

INTRODUCTION

Barbara Bertram always said she felt sick when the moment came for her guests to leave for the aerodrome at Tangmere. It must have felt as though she were standing over a dark, dizzying abyss into which they were disappearing. These were young Frenchmen and women of her own age, many of whom she had come to know well during their shared anxious days and nights waiting for the message, '*c'est* on' or '*c'est* off'. And they were heading off to an existence about which she was allowed to know nothing other than that many would encounter torture and death. Even after the war, when she wrote and lectured about the bizarre role she played, she kept her audiences rapt mainly by the account of her own daily routines, only occasionally giving anecdotal glimpses of what it was like for the pilots and the agents they served.

So the book you are holding is an attempt to place my great aunt Barbara's efforts into a broader context, to shed light on the dingy world that awaited her guests and to demonstrate how her contribution, although far from the front line, provided a crucial, revitalizing link in the often murderous chain of wartime intelligence gathering. Although there are chapters which describe life at Bignor Manor, this story is not so much about Barbara Bertram but because of her. It is also a reminder that the agents of the Secret Intelligence Service and its Free French equivalent had as great, if not as explosive, an impact on the liberation of Europe as their more celebrated counterparts in the Special Operations Executive.

My greatest regret is not having begun this study fifteen years earlier when many of the main protagonists who survived the war were still alive. But despite being unable to ask them now how they felt at the crucial moments of their adventures, there has been a wealth of highly readable autobiographical material to draw upon, particularly from the French. Their accounts of their relations with officers of the SIS are likely to be the only publicly accessible record of such encounters, the Official Secrets Act and MI6 security (even over events of eighty years ago) being what they are.

I make no apology for having produced a chronicle rather than an analysis of this intriguing aspect of the war. By following a handful of individuals through their extraordinary experiences, I leave it to the reader to draw conclusions about the magnitude of their achievements. The story poses other questions too. What persuaded some of these individuals to expose not just themselves but their loved ones to such danger, especially in the early days of the occupation when help from abroad seemed so remote? Are people who are prone to extreme political standpoints greater risk takers? Did a paucity of schooling in intelligence-gathering techniques help or hinder the likes of Renault and Fourcade in their prodigious network building? And how much more difficult or simple would the SIS's task have been without General de Gaulle and what he stood for? Please ponder at your leisure.

And you might want to ask yourself what sort of effect the sight of a tiny British aeroplane, bumping down into a moonlit field after its lonely plod over a hostile land mass, had on a man about to make his escape from occupied France. Many such Frenchmen and women who survived would go on to follow important careers in public life after the war. Most of them had very mixed feelings about the British and their apparent desertion of France in 1940. Some would even harbour a degree of jealous hatred for a nation that had so far escaped the Nazi jackboot through no show of strength or courage — or none that was obvious to them, at least. How much did the skill and daring of the Lysander pilot that delivered them to safety, or the homely and heartfelt welcome encountered on the doorstep of Bignor Manor, help to dispel their Anglophobia and seal long-lasting international friendships?

CHAPTER 1: RAF OPERATION BACCARAT II

Bignor Manor, Wednesday 26 March 1942

This had been a comparatively simple departure for Barbara Bertram. Only one man to see off from the starkly moonlit driveway, one more with whom the words '*au revoir*' carried far more hope than certainty. She knew him only as Rémy and had no idea what kind of existence awaited him in France. She guessed he must be of particular value to 'The Office' as his escort from London had included another somewhat po-faced intelligence officer in addition to her husband Tony. But he was gallant too, for, despite the intense apprehension he would have been feeling for the journey ahead of him, he had still been able to express a charmingly Gallic appreciation of her efforts. Then, as he had walked towards the car, laden with belongings, he had turned back towards her and, with a smile, had lifted a hefty, rounded package by its string to shoulder height and bowed his head in apparent reverence. They had both laughed.

She imagined there would be little conversation during the short drive to the aerodrome at Tangmere. Rémy had taken the front seat of the black Chrysler, probably to savour the last few moments of proximity to the fragrant Jean, one of the indefatigably amiable FANY (First Aid Nursing Yeomanry) drivers who had brought the three men down from London. Before supper, she and Barbara had carried out the customary procedure of unpacking the Frenchman's suitcase and checking every item for makers' names or other signs of British origin. They had mirthfully admired some very fine pink silk pyjamas but, before Barbara could begin to rub away at the label with Milton fluid, Rémy had snatched them away, protesting that he had bought them in Paris before the occupation and he would not have them defaced in any way.

Bignor Manor, near Petworth, West Sussex, in 1933. (*The Bertram Family*)

Now it was time to prepare for the return passengers. She expected them in about seven hours, which would be about four o'clock the next morning. She knew that with only one person flying out that night, it would be a single Lysander operation with no more than two French to feed and provide a bed for — that was if the whole operation hadn't been cancelled and the same quartet returned. She would get the 'reception pie' prepared but saw no point in changing the sheets until the 3 a.m. call came about how many to expect.

On her way through to the kitchen, Barbara heard a faint sound coming from the sitting room.

'Duff?' she called. No dog came padding through to the hallway so she put her head round the door. A boy in pyjamas stood on a chair, his upper half hidden by a wide piece of plywood with a dartboard mounted at its centre, which was swung open on its hinges above a stove. As he looked round guiltily at his fast approaching mother, he clasped to his chest an assortment of articles including a toothbrush, soap, matches, Gauloises cigarettes, a penknife and a pair of compasses.

Having re-installed her six-year-old in bed alongside his now wakeful and inquisitive older brother, Barbara returned to the kitchen in a daze of bewildered self-chastisement. By an inexcusable lapse in her normally fastidious routine, she had failed to close up the secret store of specialist supplies which, apart from everyday utensils of apparently French origin, also contained maps of France printed on fine silk, fountain pens which released tear gas and cyanide tablets which, if they asked for them, she would sew into the cuffs of departing agents.

The cottage, RAF Tangmere, the same evening

Flying Officer Guy Lockhart was bent over a green and mauve chart, oblivious to his neighbours' conversation or anyone entering or leaving the room when Gilbert Renault, codename Rémy, was escorted into the dining quarters in 'The Cottage' outside the main gates of Tangmere RAF station. The serious and somewhat sad expression on the face of this slim, striking-featured pilot masked an impish, risk-taking streak which made him a very enthusiastic and successful poker player but which had also played havoc with his flying career. His brief peacetime commission with the RAF had ended in a court-martial after he had performed an over-exuberant low pass over the airfield, forcing the Air Officer Commanding to fall flat on his face.

The declaration of war had given Lockhart a second chance. The RAF needed all the skilful pilots it could muster and he was readmitted, first as a Flight Sergeant, but soon once again with a commission and an invitation to perform the very special duties demanded of 161 Squadron.

In a few moments, he would be embarking on only his second operation with the squadron and, as with many natural risk takers, he was putting in the work necessary to ensure that the odds did not get the better of him. The mission would take him into occupied France and involve a 400-mile round trip, during which he would have to find his own way in moonlight to a small patch of pasture a few miles south of the Loire, near Saumur. One 'Joe' was to be delivered, two to be brought back. He wanted to memorize as much of his route as possible. The weather was clear and unlikely to be a problem but his path was further to the west than that of his first mission when he had successfully collected two agents sixty miles south of Orléans. Tonight, he was going to have to pick his way past different flak defences and enemy aerodromes.

When one of his fellow officers tapped him on the shoulder to present Renault, Lockhart stood up, smiled, shook hands, introduced himself and then sat down again to finish his chart work, leaving his passenger to be entertained by the others around him. Then, indicating finally that he was ready, he folded up the chart and stood up to go. In his right hand, he clutched the laces of a tiny pair of child's white suede shoes.

'Hey, Guy, are you sure those are big enough for you?' joked one of the officers who was nearby. Showing no reaction whatsoever, Lockhart walked out of the room and shut the door behind him. He did not hear the sharp rebuke aimed by another at the man who had just spoken, informing him that he had just lost his son and that he carried the shoes as a mascot.

With the single propeller a roaring transparent disc a few feet in front of him, Lockhart went through his pre-flight checks. He had just helped to install the rounded shape of Renault, somewhat comically encumbered by a fur-lined flying suit, a Mae West, a self-inflating rubber dinghy and a parachute, into the rear compartment of the fuselage. Now he was ready to taxi across the moonlit tarmac to the end of the runway. A female voice came over the radio as the Lysander trundled towards her point of departure:

'"J" for John, "J" for John, do you hear me, do you hear me?'

'"J" for John, "J" for John speaking. I hear you loud and clear.' Lockhart replied.

Clearance was given for take-off and, after only a few seconds of full throttle, he levered the plane into the air. As they crossed the coastline, there was a final message from the homely-sounding Tangmere radio operator:

'"J" for John, "J" for John, good luck to you, good luck!'

The plane climbed steadily over the silvery English Channel into the vastness of the night. The moon's distorted reflection, their only companion, hurried along over the uneven surface of the sea beneath them.

Lockhart suddenly became aware of another voice in his headphones, although it was barely audible. It could only be his passenger who had an intercom link with him. He had been told to keep an eye out for any aircraft. When it became clear that it was just a friendly 'hello' from Renault, Lockhart brusquely informed him to make contact only if he saw something.

Visibility was extraordinarily clear as the Lysander plodded on at 3,000 feet over the Normandy countryside. It may have been night but anyone out and about on the ground could easily have picked out her dark silhouette against the paler sky. With no cloud to escape into, the sense of vulnerability was acute for both pilot and passenger.

A series of lights, some red, some green, passed below them. They were the signals of a railway line which Lockhart had been following as it led him conveniently towards his target. Eventually, ahead, a glistening ribbon appeared, snaking extravagantly into the distance both to the east and the west. They had reached the Loire and, even under a blackout, Saumur, with its two bridges and its château, was unmistakeable. Lockhart began his descent.

Then, over to his right, he was alarmed to see what appeared to be a small town lit up with hundreds of electric lights. If he was where he thought he was, there was nothing of that nature marked on his map. In any case, why on earth was it not blacked out? With a sudden crisis of confidence in his own navigation, he turned the aircraft through 180 degrees and retraced his route as far as Saumur. Reassured by the town's landmarks, he turned again for his target and this time ignored the distracting patch of illumination (which, unbeknown to him, was a large German prison camp for gypsies, its perimeter fence floodlit in case of escape attempts).

Now the aircraft was low, circling a wide tract of farmland, and both pilot and passenger peered down at the ground. Both felt a surge of relief as a light pierced the darkness — two short flashes and a long one — the letter 'U', the one they were expecting. Lockhart immediately signalled back 'S' and, after a few seconds, three uninterrupted lights appeared marking out an inverted L-shape, denoting their rudimentary landing strip.

Lockhart learned just how rudimentary it was very soon after his plane touched down. At a safe taxiing speed, he turned right along the shorter length of the 'L' and then back towards the point where they had landed and where the passenger exchange would take place. The Lysander came suddenly to a jarring halt, throwing him painfully against his harness. He opened the throttle to a full bellow but the plane would not budge. He tried again, this time with a longer blast until the vibrations seemed to threaten the very integrity of the aircraft. Still there was no movement.

He threw open his cockpit canopy and gestured to his passenger to do the same.

'We're stuck! Mud!' he shouted.

Renault took what seemed an age to struggle out of his safety gear and jumped from the plane. Shadowy figures were now running to join him. In a mixture of broken English and French, they shouted to Lockhart that his tail-wheel had disappeared into the mud. All seven men and Renault positioned themselves around the tail-plane and began to haul upwards. With the reluctance of a cork leaving a bottle, the wheel came slowly up out of the mud and the Lysander was able to move forward once more, apparently undamaged. Lockhart knew that these extra minutes on the ground would have added greatly to the risk of the whole mission, not just for him and his returning passengers but for Renault and his reception party who needed to be clear of the landing area as quickly as possible. The sound of the revving of the engine would have travelled miles on such a still night. Sensing the urgency, Christian Pineau, one of the two returning 'Joes', clambered aboard as soon as the aircraft had reached the take-off position, back at the top of the 'L'.

Renault shouted at him to pass him his luggage which was still stashed in the cockpit. Then, as he and others were carrying it away from the plane, he turned and shouted again, realizing that there was still a package of his on board, extremely fragile and wrapped in paper and string.

Then the second man for the journey home ran up to the plane. This was François Faure, alias Paco. He stopped at the figure of Renault and threw his arms around him. They exchanged half a dozen words before he climbed swiftly up the ladder and into his seat beside Pineau.

The plane began to lumber forward. Renault ran after it, waving and shouting. Faure waved back. Renault gesticulated and shouted more wildly, 'The canopy! Shut the canopy!'

With the plane now at full tilt, the message at last got through and the cockpit slid shut seconds before the Lysander lifted clear of the field.

Parc du Champ de Mars, Paris, Tuesday 25 March 1942

Christian Pineau had much of the afternoon and the evening to kill in Paris before he was due for his rendezvous at the Gare d'Austerlitz whence he would be taking the night train to Tours. This was the city he had fled only a few weeks earlier, after the Gestapo had called at his apartment, fortunately while he was out. Then, he had managed to get away to Vichy in the free zone and his wife and children had been able to follow him there. Another from his resistance group, his good friend René Parodi, had not been so fortunate. He had been arrested in the same police operation and now he was dead, officially having hanged himself in his cell; in other words, he had died at the hands of his torturers.

Now, unbeknown to his family, Pineau was back among the Nazi uniforms, many of whose off-duty wearers sauntered along the grand boulevards of the capital, taking in the sights with a detached enjoyment no different from any peacetime tourist.

Pineau knew to avoid the Metro stations and cinemas, where random searches were most likely. Instead, he sat on a park bench under the chilly but clear March sky, close to the Eiffel Tower and thumbed a Paris newspaper with an air of some distaste. He wondered how many of his fellow citizens in the Occupied Zone were influenced by such blatant propaganda. Even the Vichy government was criticized for being too reactionary and for its over-tepid relations with the occupiers. It called for a united effort between the occupied and the occupiers to mount a crusade against communism, the only way Europe could be saved from Soviet subversion. There were condemnations of the British on nearly every page.

A couple sat down on the bench next to him; a young French girl and a German NCO. The girl pressed herself against the tall, blond soldier with a genuine look of love in her eyes. She was clearly not a prostitute and Pineau realized that if anyone had talked about treachery to her, she would have looked at them with wide-eyed amazement. To her, the German was simply a man she adored and there was nothing wrong in that. Pineau moved to a bench further away.

When, at last, the time came to go to the station, his meeting with François Faure, alias Paco, Renault's right-hand man in the Confrérie de Notre Dame network, whom he had only met for the first time that morning in Pierre Brossolette's bookshop basement, was very brief. One of the two young men accompanying Paco slipped Pineau a train ticket with the words:

'Get out at Tours. We're travelling separately.'

Tours was only the first stage of the journey. From there, after spending much of the night in the waiting room, they took another train and, at Loudun, boarded a bus from which they disembarked after about half an hour at a remote crossroads on the road to Montreuil-Bellay. A man, who was a farmer if one were to judge by his clothes, was waiting for them and, after brief introductions, everyone using pseudonyms, he led them off along the road.

They reached his farmhouse after about fifteen minutes and were ushered into the main room with its smoke-blackened beams, where a very young man greeted them warmly. This was Robert Delattre, alias Bob, a radio operator in Faure's network in charge of the landing operation, who was able to tell them that, as long as the weather held, the pick-up was on for that night, sometime between midnight and one o'clock. The nearest German unit, he assured them, was based at Saumur, about fifteen kilometres away, and they seldom sent patrols along the road past the farmhouse.

In spite of a night entirely without sleep, Pineau and his travelling companions felt far from tired. They were further enlivened by a sumptuous breakfast laid on by their host, Georges Geay, alias René, consisting of potted meats, saucisson, soft white bread and butter and real coffee — a far cry from the Vichy diet of carrots and chickpeas. After the meal, Geay took Pineau and Faure on a tour of his land. Neatly cultivated fields, where green shoots of corn were just beginning to show, stretched into the distance. Lines of denuded vines covered the hills, ready for their annual pruning — Geay's next job, once he had his visitors safely on their way.

He proudly informed them that his wine came under the Saumur appellation and suggested they went back to the farmhouse to taste some. He did not want them out in the open for too long, in any case, because, although the landscape appeared empty of people, he knew the locals had eyes like hawks and gossip, however innocent, could be lethal.

Geay emerged from his cellar and deposited two bottles on the long oak table. Ignoring his guests' protests at his generous pouring, he informed them that they were sampling his 1941 wine. Pineau found the new wine fruity, slightly acid and highly drinkable. The second bottle, a 1934, was spicier and mellower and altogether excellent. Geay assured him that there were even better growers in the region and promised the two men a taste of the Brézé and the Coteaux du Layon with their lunch. Relaxing under the early spring sunshine in a wicker armchair in the farm courtyard, Pineau found it difficult to believe that in only a few hours he was somehow to be spirited away from this beautiful but treacherous French countryside and would be feeling, instead, the safe soil of England under his feet.

The only thing to concern Mme Geay as she calmly laid a lavish lunch of fresh chicken and other meats, goats' cheese and cream with chocolate before Pineau and Faure was how much they were enjoying it. She uttered not a word about why they were there. The promised white wine, followed by some red Champigny '21, finally took its toll and the two men dropped thankfully into bed for the afternoon.

Geay woke them at 5 p.m. to find them looking somewhat groggy. He assured them that the only cure for white wine was white wine and that they were going to have to taste his 1904. Pineau could not refuse as that was the year he was born. They then found yet another meal set before them, after which it was time to listen to the BBC's French language broadcast. First, distorted by German jamming but just decipherable, came the news; then came the reading of 'personal messages'. A succession of random phrases wobbled across the airwaves, none eliciting any reaction from their host. Then, when they thought they had heard them all, came '*le lion a deux têtes*'. Geay stood up, switched off the radio and, rubbing his hands, smiled at his two guests. It was on for that night.

Mme Geay could only express her regret that they would not be able to sample the food she had lined up for them for the next day.

In the cold, clear night, Pineau and Paco sat under a blanket in the shelter of a small thicket, while Delattre, Geay and their helpers took up their positions on the field, torches at the ready. The cloud that had appeared at sunset had now dissipated and moonlight probed every corner of the darkness. There was utter silence; any approaching plane would be audible miles away. The minutes ticked by. They had been ready at 11 p.m. Now it was midnight.

Suddenly Pineau felt himself being shaken. It was Faure, astonished that he needed to inform his fellow passenger that the plane had landed. The effect of the Geays' hospitality had allowed Pineau to sleep through the entire episode of the Lysander's arrival, immobilization and eventual release from the mud.

As Pineau ran up to the plane, Guy Lockhart shouted from the cockpit that he had never heard of someone sleeping through a landing before and urged them to get going. Pineau tried to adopt an air of modesty, hoping that his somnolent behaviour would be taken as a sign of extreme sangfroid rather than excessive consumption of white wine.

There was precious little space in the Lysander's narrow fuselage for the two men, their belongings and all the packages of courier from their two networks bound for London. As the plane climbed northwards back over the Loire, Pineau found himself listening out for the sound of hostile aircraft, fully realizing that their own engine would drown out any other noise.

His watch told him eventually that nearly two hours had passed and that they must therefore be near the coast. At that moment, what looked like a rocket rose from the ground beneath them, just failing to reach their height. There was a thud, this time clearly discernible above the noise of the engine. Another streak of light shot towards them almost immediately, followed by another thud.

'Flack,' murmured Faure.

Several more shells exploded around them, then nothing more. They were clear of the French coast and could see only the Channel stretched out below.

At last, after an apparent eternity, the English coastline came into view. Almost immediately, the engine changed its tune and they began to lose height. In the distance, three runway lights were visible. Within minutes, they were on the ground; not a rough field this time but a proper aerodrome with a long runway, hangars and the silhouette of several other aircraft.

They had no idea where they had landed but it felt extremely reassuring. Willing hands helped them from the plane and took care of their luggage. Moments later, they plunged into the dazzling light of an officers' mess and were surrounded by friendly young men in blue uniforms, proffering glasses of whisky to celebrate their safe delivery to a free country.

Both men were speechless with joy and fatigue and could scarcely find answers to questions about the strength of the resistance in France and what conditions were like in the country they had come from. They were soon joined by a man in the uniform of an Army lieutenant colonel who introduced himself as the man charged with looking after them. He explained that they would be driving to London later that day but before then he would ensure that they got some sleep.

The atmosphere of welcome in the officers' mess was so intoxicating to Pineau and Faure that they could not resist one more whisky in spite of their tiredness. Eventually, though, they were on the move again, this time in the back seat of a comfortable car, nosing its way past high hedges along narrow winding lanes and through a rolling landscape.

Moonlight still lit the seventeenth-century fascia of Bignor Manor as the two passengers, enchanted by its rustic beauty, stepped from the Chrysler onto the driveway. A man in civilian clothes was waiting for them on the doorstep and welcomed them in French without a trace of an accent. The Lt Colonel introduced him as Anthony Bertram and explained that he would be putting them up for what was left of the night. Bertram led them indoors, commenting that they must be starving and that there was some supper ready for them before bed.

Barbara Bertram, with some ceremony, placed a steaming casserole in front of the two men. They looked at each other and then back at the generous portions she had doled out to each of them. To her, they were starving French fugitives, deprived of all nutrition by the strictest rationing in a destitute country. She could not possibly have suspected that her largesse would have found such a formidable rival on the other side of the Channel. Pineau and Faure slunk off to bed pleading tiredness and over-excitement as the reason for scarcely touching their reception pie.

CHAPTER 2: THE BERTRAMS AND BIGNOR MANOR

There was little in the early lives of either Anthony or Barbara Bertram to mark them out as likely recruits into the clandestine world of the Secret Intelligence Service during the four war years leading up to the liberation of France in 1944.

Barbara was born, the youngest child of seven, to Felton and Emily (Lily) Randolph in March 1906, in Chichester. Her father, originally a barrister, had moved to West Sussex to remain part of the coterie surrounding the 3rd Baron Leconfield of Petworth House — an association, costly to both pocket and liver, which had begun while the two men were up at Cambridge. Whatever Randolph earned as the managing director of Henty's Brewery in Chichester, it was clearly not enough to keep pace with the heady life at Petworth and when he died, aged 52, in December 1906, he left his wife with seven children under the age of ten and with gambling debts far in excess of any assets.

Lily Randolph was a resourceful and determined character, however, and her connections with the Sussex gentry prevented disaster. For a peppercorn rent, the family were housed in a four-bedroom cottage in the grounds of Bignor Park, near Fittleworth, the home of the Johnstones who were old friends of Lily's. Life was spartan for Barbara and her older brothers and sisters — there was neither running water nor other modern conveniences such as a bathroom — but they revelled in their rural surroundings, running wild through woods and over the common, fishing in the local pond, climbing trees and seeking out birds' nests.

Again, it was their mother's connections with the well-to-do which provided an education for the seven children. Lord Leconfield sponsored the three boys' attendance at Christ's Hospital School, while Barbara found herself packed off to a country mansion in Lincolnshire to share a governess with the only daughter of the house. Very similar arrangements were made for her two older sisters in other parts of the country, while the eldest was first a pupil, then a teacher at a school run by some cousins. Thus, for seven years, Barbara lived a strange double life, spent in stylish grandeur during the term and returning with the rest of her siblings to the humble, rural hurly-burly of family life in the holidays.

A sudden loss of fortune by her Lincolnshire guardians in 1920 forced them out of their house and ended Barbara's time with them. Instead, she went to a school in Eastbourne, thanks to the munificent Lord Leconfield, and, although her teachers there tried to persuade her to continue studies at university, she considered herself a home girl, wanting to return to her mother's house and run a smallholding. She attended a domestic economy school, beating egg whites on a plate with a knife, creaming butter straight from the fridge and peeling potatoes from ice-cold water out of doors in winter. Once installed at home, she learned how to keep bees and put her domestic training to use as well as taking on captaincy of the Sutton Girl Guides and providing companionship for her widowed mother, all the other children having found spouses or employment or both.

But, like her mother, Barbara enjoyed the society of the surrounding landed gentry and even if the only means available to get to a local ball was astride a boy's bicycle in full evening dress, she was not deterred. Tennis parties were another social opportunity and it was at one of these that Barbara met a quiet academic and writer in his early thirties, Anthony Bertram. The relationship blossomed and when, in the midsummer of 1928, they became engaged, Barbara chose to give her mother — who expected all her daughters to marry earls — all the bad news about her intended husband first.

'He's a lapsed Catholic, of no particular family and no money,' she told her. Fortunately, her mother took it on the chin and a low-key wedding was arranged for the following January.

Tony Bertram, by contrast to his wife, had been an only child. His mother was a Dollond, descendant of the eighteenth-century telescope maker and optician, and his father, who changed his name from Bresslauer to Bertram, was of Prussian Jewish descent. Born in 1897, Tony was educated at the Benedictine Douai Abbey School and at the Jesuit school in Wimbledon. He also learned to speak French at an early age thanks to childhood visits to Paris where his maternal grandfather lived prodigally off his shares in the family business.

At the age of 18, Tony joined the York and Lancashire Regiment to fight in the Great War. In 1917, he was sent to France and, in November of that year, was badly wounded in the stomach during the first wave of the attack on Cambrai. He owed his life to a group of German prisoners who were being escorted back across the battlefield, one of whom was a doctor. Bertram asked him to inspect the wounded men who lay around him. When the doctor eventually came to him, he saw that he needed operating on urgently and, with the help of two more prisoners, he was stretchered on a greatcoat slung across two rifles without further delay to receive the vital treatment.

After the war, Tony Bertram attended Pembroke College, Oxford, and when he graduated with a degree in English in 1921, he began to travel widely in Europe, studying art in the principal galleries of France, Italy, Belgium and Germany. This led to his appointment as art critic, first for the *Spectator*, then for the *Saturday Review*. He had also published three novels by the time he was married and would go on to write six more as well as several books about artists and the history of art.

The newly-weds had signed a lease on an Elizabethan farmhouse, Bignor Manor, just down the road from Barbara's mother's cottage and moved into it in bitter weather with the water supply frozen and oil lamps the only means of lighting. This somewhat basic but distinguished house would remain their home for the next thirty years. It was built of stone and had the unusual feature of a baked clay animal perched on the apex of each south-facing gable. It lay at the centre of the sparsely-built hamlet of Bignor, tucked beneath the line of Downs to the south. To the west of the house was the church; to the east, farm buildings used by the farmer who owned the Manor; and across two fields beyond these lay the remains of a Roman villa for which Bignor is still renowned. Northwards, there were fields dropping down to Bignor Brook and Bignor Park.

Electricity was brought to the village two years after Barbara and Tony moved in and they introduced further improvements during that time, installing a bathroom and basins in three of the four bedrooms and creating a study off the drawing room for Tony's writing. However, when Tony's widowed father was invited to stay, the enhancements clearly did not impress him. On leaving, he told his son, 'I don't think I can rough it again. You must find me somewhere else to stay next time.'

Barbara and Tony Bertram c. 1930. (*The Bertram Family*)

When he was not writing, Tony spent much of his early-married years away from their Sussex home giving Oxford extra-mural lectures. Barbara would sometimes accompany him and she became very well acquainted with many of his literary and artist friends, who included Ford Madox Ford and Paul Nash. Nash twice drew Barbara's portrait and was the subject of one of Tony's most important biographies. In the early 1930s, the Bertrams spent three summers climbing peaks in the Austrian Alps where Barbara became the first woman to reach the 3,002 metre summit of the Gigelitz. On one of these trips to Europe, they went on to Potsdam to stay with the German family of one of Tony's lecture students. One evening, their hostess asked them to choose between going to a fireworks display and attending an address by 'that funny little man Hitler'. Afterwards, they always rather regretted choosing the fireworks.

The arrival of two sons, Tim in 1934 and Nicky in 1936, curtailed Barbara's travels to some extent, but she still managed to get away with Tony to Czechoslovakia while he researched early German painting, to a summer holiday in south west France and a skiing holiday in Austria in 1937. The outbreak of war put an end to the travelling and, in September 1940, Tony was called up and Barbara turned her attention to the war effort, volunteering to recruit blood donors, working with the Women's Voluntary Service and offering sanctuary to child evacuees.

Tony had been called up to join his old regiment, the York and Lancaster. His application to be transferred to the Royal Sussex Regiment so as to be close to home resulted, perversely, in an order to join the Durham Light Infantry where, because he was 43, he was posted to the regiment's depot at Brancepeth, seemingly for the duration of the war. However, a young subaltern in the regiment, Stephen Joseph, sympathetic with Tony's predicament, decided he would contact his brother-in-law, one Kenneth Cohen at the War Office, asking if he could use an old chap who was bored with being stuck at the depot and who spoke fluent French.

Tony knew nothing of this letter and was surprised when a summons from the War Office in London appeared in his pigeonhole. Hopeful that some action might be coming his way, he reported in full fighting kit, complete with canvas bucket. He must have been somewhat taken aback by the brass plaque at the entrance to the address he had been given — Broadway Buildings, opposite St James's Park underground station — which gave it as the head office of the Minimax Fire Extinguisher Company. When he realized he was being recruited by the Secret Intelligence Service to work with the

French, he told his interviewer he did not want to do it. The idea of a life of deceit appalled him and it was only when the officer asked him if lying was really any worse than killing that he reluctantly accepted the post.

He could not help but be amused when washing before lunch with his new CO to find hot water running from the cold tap and cold from the hot. He turned to a senior-looking gentleman beside him and joked that he presumed it was to get them used to secrecy. The response — a sharp, 'not funny, young man' — filled him with foreboding for his new occupation.

His very first assignment in the autumn of 1941, to take a party of French for parachute training at RAF Ringway near Manchester, was equally inauspicious. He insisted, despite the instructors' misgivings about his age, to be put through all that his men had to do. On their fourth parachute jump, Tony misjudged his landing and broke his pelvis. The 'Office' rang Barbara the same day to tell her, mysteriously, that he had fractured his ankle.

Recovering from his injury, Tony returned to London and began his work as Conducting Officer. This entailed escorting French agents working with the SIS while they were in England, overseeing their training, especially where it involved working with the RAF in undercover operations, and ensuring their punctual arrival at important rendezvous. It included preparing them to leave the country to return to occupied France and getting them down to Tangmere near the Sussex coast for a night flight by Westland Lysander.

Although many agents were dropped into enemy territory by parachute, there was also a need to land aeroplanes in France, particularly by the SIS, embarking agents and their sacks of courier to bring them back to England with minimum delay, so that the intelligence they had gleaned remained as current as possible. Thus a moonlit shuttle service was formed, carrying agents back into the field and returning with men, women and sometimes even children, some for debriefing or training, but others as fugitives from the Gestapo's clutches.

The successful operation of such a shuttle relied on the tenuous combination of favourable weather, the outstanding skill and courage of pilots and a coded communications system between France and London, which in itself was fraught with difficulties and danger. No agent could be sure whether or when their passage would succeed and the uncertainty of every mission provided a logistical problem on both sides of the Channel. What the SIS required on the English side was a secret stop-over close to Tangmere, where agents could be fed, watered and made ready for their mission and where, should the flight out be cancelled or turned back, they could be given a bed for the night. For successful operations, there was a similar requirement for returning agents.

Tony Bertram knew that Barbara was not exactly relishing her role as foster mother to the evacuees — she had been severely bitten by one of her charges — but the offer he made to his superiors to use his own Bignor Manor as the secret staging post showed remarkable confidence in the forbearance of his wife and children. But his confidence was well placed; Barbara, who was invited to lunch in London by 'The Office', signed the Official Secrets Act and was delighted to be asked to give up her evacuees and WVS work and make her house ready, although what it should be ready for, no one would tell her. She had been asked to send a description of her house and to say how many she thought she could accommodate. Although her estimate was four or five, she had some concerns that the one bathroom and one lavatory would be enough for that number of guests. The water supply, pumped up from a stream at the bottom of Bignor Hill, was temperamental and the tiny kitchen was only really suitable for a small family. 'The Office' seemed not to share her concerns, however, and offered rent of £5 a week for the periods they needed the house, said they would pay for all the food Barbara would need to serve and gave her a weekly wage of £2.

For three weeks after these arrangements had been made, nothing happened. Barbara began to feel embarrassed as the village could see that she had rid herself of her evacuees and was now apparently doing nothing for the war effort. Then, at about seven o'clock one moonlit evening, a car drew up in front of the house. A Royal Navy officer got out, followed by a female driver in FANY uniform and three Frenchmen in civilian clothes. The officer stated that they would like dinner in half an hour and, when Barbara asked where she was to find food at such short notice, told her that was her job. During the makeshift dinner, the phone rang. Barbara answered it and a voice told her, '*C'est* off.' Mystified, she relayed the message to John, the naval officer, who said nothing except to ask for beds to be provided for his party. He and the driver left the next morning for London, leaving Barbara to entertain the three Frenchmen. She took them for a walk in the local countryside, discovering that one of them owned a chain of brothels in the south of France, another had a passion for fossils and the third had recently escaped from a German prison camp.

It was only after she was asked to drive them all back to London the next day that Tony was allowed to explain to her why she was being asked to play hostess in this way. Until then, she knew nothing of the night flights in and out of France, of the need to carry them out during the second and third quarter of every moon and of the terrifying and sometimes fatal missions of the men and women she would do her utmost to make comfortable during their last few hours on British soil.

As it transpired, physical comfort was probably not the most memorable aspect of a stay at Bignor Manor. Even when it was not crowded with Frenchmen and their escorts, there was an austere air about the house. This was partially induced by the modern, somewhat minimalist furniture Tony had chosen to install in the place of the more traditional pieces he had inherited from his family. Some items he and Barbara had even made themselves.

A routine evolved whereby Barbara received a terse message from London, either from Tony or his opposite number, John, to say, 'We're coming with three' (or any number up to eight or nine). The number signified how many French she should expect and each group of three required a conducting officer and a driver, so house parties of nine or twelve were common and occasionally, Barbara had eighteen in the house and once, she had twenty-one. And if a large party were being sent out to France — using three Lysanders in the same operation sometimes, or occasionally the larger Hudson — then there was likely to be as large a party returning to Tangmere, all of whom would need a bed for the remainder of the night. Camp beds supplied by the Office littered the house and often three slept in every bedroom while Barbara and the conducting officers slept on the sofa, in armchairs or on camp beds in the drawing room. As for the two boys, Tim, eight, and Nicky, six, they had to stay over at school as weekly boarders and in the holidays during moon periods, would often sleep in a tent in the garden or with neighbours when the weather was cold.

Understandably, the boys were less than enthusiastic about the disruption to their home life and referred to the French as the 'Hullabaloos' — their approximation of the unintelligible sounds issuing from their lips. Some consolation came when the agents, before their departure, searched themselves fastidiously for any signs that they had just left England. All British money had to be left behind and the Bertram boys were grateful recipients of numerous sixpences and occasional florins and half-crowns found in the corners of coat pockets. One agent, on his return to Bignor, told Barbara that on his last visit he had forgotten to search his overcoat and discovered, to his horror, that he was carrying a copy of the *Daily Telegraph* in the inside pocket while on a crowded Metro train in Paris. The German officer, against whom he had been pressed, must have been astonished to find the newspaper protruding from his own coat pocket once the crowd had subsided and the agent had long since left the train.

As the only other females with whom she could share the stresses and burden of her clandestine housekeeping, the FANY drivers came as a godsend to Barbara. They were, she found, without exception, hugely outgoing, sympathetic and co-operative. As Barbara put it,

> They had been chosen because they spoke French well or were utterly unselfconscious about their schoolgirl French. As well as their official duties they were expected to amuse the French, which they did admirably. They also helped me wash up but they weren't supposed to. They were all young, some married and some already war widows. They were immensely popular with everyone and must have made all the difference to the French waiting to go out.

Together with Barbara, they would go through the luggage of the departing agents to check nothing was marked 'Made in England'. They would remove waistcoat buckles, wrench off glove buttons, rub at shirt labels with Milton fluid and confiscate newly-purchased hats whose leather band inside was stamped and could not be removed. At the same time, all the essentials for their mission in France were distributed. They received their forged identity and ration cards and wads of French banknotes. The door of the secret cupboard in Tony's study was swung open, revealing its cornucopia of equipment and supplies. For those who wanted one, there was a revolver, a cosh which could be hidden up a sleeve, a tear-gas device disguised as a fountain pen and a poison tablet that Barbara would sew into the cuff of those who would sooner die than risk talking under torture.

There were miniature compasses, knives, pencils, magnifying glasses and maps of France printed on fine silk. Then there were everyday items which had to appear French, such as imitation Gauloise cigarettes, matches, soap, toothbrushes, combs and razor blades. To begin with, the cigarette packets were too well made and did not disintegrate in the way of the genuine article and the soap produced too much lather to have been made in occupied France, but these inaccuracies were soon rectified.

Tony Bertram's study at Bignor Manor, c. 1941, with the secret cupboard covered by a dartboard. (*The Bertram Family*)

Barbara was always given a time, not usually before 9 p.m., at which an outbound party was required to be at Tangmere, about a thirty-minute drive away. This depended on the state of the moon, the time of year and the distance they were flying into France. The routine was to give them a drink and dinner after the searches and provisioning session and to set them on their way with a tot of rum inside them. However much Barbara and the drivers tried to lighten the mood, these dinners were tense affairs. The agents knew that at any moment the telephone would ring with a '*c'est* on' or a '*c'est* off'. Barbara always felt physically sick at their moment of departure, knowing the fate of many of them would be far worse than that of an ordinary soldier going off to war. She was also extremely anxious that they set off in good time for Tangmere. The drivers had permission to defy the blackout and use headlights if they were late. For such occasions, the conducting officer kept a revolver on his lap to dissuade any policemen who might stop and question them about their lights en route from detaining them any further. Fortunately, they were never stopped.

There was little time to relax when a party had just left Bignor. Assuming the mission was going to be successful, Barbara needed to clear away and wash up and then prepare another meal for her new arrivals, due at three or four o'clock in the morning. She might sometimes snatch a few hours' sleep on the sofa before the telephone woke her and Tony or another conducting officer would tell her how many were coming. Tony did allow her to know how many of each sex, but John would not on the pretext of security, although she suspected he enjoyed, on his arrival, seeing her untangle the unintentionally indecorous sleeping arrangements she had made.

For the new arrivals in England, Bignor seemed like the Promised Land. Coupled with the euphoria of having escaped their occupied country cramped in the rear fuselage of a tiny and vulnerable aeroplane, came the delight of being greeted at the door of a quintessentially English farmhouse by an attractive young mother who, with bustling charm and energy, offered them wholesome food, a glass of whisky and a bed for undisturbed sleep. They marvelled at her ability to produce what seemed sumptuous meals, in spite of rationing. 'The Office' told her to cheat on her Food Office returns, but she seldom dared and instead worked tirelessly in her fruit and vegetable garden and with chickens, rabbits and a goat called Caroline to supplement the food and milk she bought. Without exception, all the guests of Bignor Manor who survived the war and wrote of their experiences recalled the outstanding hospitality of 'Madame Barbara' and the effect it had on their morale, both on arrival and departure and when their stay was prolonged through adverse circumstances.

Sometimes, the 3 a.m. arrivals turned out to be the same people Barbara had seen off the night before. There was no euphoria then, rather utter exhaustion and dejection after a six- or seven-hour round trip with the aircraft unable to land in France for one reason or another. Barbara knew she would have a house full of dispirited individuals who would need breakfast, lunch and dinner for at least another day, as well as calls on her remaining energy to distract them from their gloom with games of darts, table tennis or bridge. The stress of providing this service was immense — akin to single-handedly running a country house party of often incompatible individuals, for two weeks out of every four, for an uninterrupted period of more than three years.

Adding to the strain was the need to keep what she was doing secret from everyone she knew. It was, of course, impossible to hide the fact from locals that she was keeping a very unusual house. The cover was that this was a convalescent home for French officers and, in the early days, 'The Office' sent two agents who had genuinely broken a leg to stay at Bignor and hobble around on crutches to make the story convincing. It meant that guests could roam reasonably freely around the farm and the village and they became a familiar sight in the nearest pub, the White Horse in Sutton, often challenging the locals to a game of darts.

If the comings and goings in the middle of the night were thought strange by the villagers, they never remarked upon it to Barbara. Even when a Frenchman decided once to test fire his pistol out of one of the bedroom windows, the lady who had happened to come to the door, collecting for the Red Cross, dismissed Barbara's abject apologies with the kindly assurance that she expected anything to happen in war. None of Barbara's wider family ever suspected the real reason for her wartime work. Her mother could not understand why she saw so little of her daughter and grandchildren, and a cousin who was used to calling frequently resented Barbara's uncharacteristically obstructive habit of standing in the doorway, ready to shut the door on her as soon as she could.

Even among the French and their traffickers, there could not be full candour. Barbara never knew the real names of her guests and could only guess at the nature of their missions. For her part, she was never to let them know precisely where they were. If they did not know the name of the village, they could not divulge it under torture. She was helped in this by the removal of all local signposts, although on occasions when she was allowed to take some on outings to Chichester or

Brighton, they must have gained a reasonably accurate idea of their location. Barbara also had the task of keeping guests from different intelligence networks apart from each other, again to limit what and who they knew if captured. In such confined quarters and with the natural fellowship of brothers and sisters in arms, she did not always succeed.

In spite of the necessary secrets, a bond of mutual admiration grew up between all the people involved. At times of bad weather when she had a houseful of stranded guests, Barbara and Tony would help to strengthen the bond further by inviting the Lysander pilots over from Tangmere for high-spirited evenings of games and singsongs. As well as forming true friendships with many of the young men of 161 Squadron, they built up a unique rapport with some of the most influential names in French intelligence gathering, who, by dint of their responsibilities, were visitors to Bignor Manor on several occasions. But whether it was Passy himself, head of the French intelligence bureau (who made his own very risky visit to Paris at one stage), network heads such as Renault, Pineau and Fourcade, or the hugely courageous radio operators, it made every departure an ordeal for Barbara.

CHAPTER 3: THE QUEST FOR INTELLIGENCE FROM FRANCE

To appreciate the urgent need for an SIS air ferry service in and out of Tangmere, it is necessary to return to the early summer of 1940, which marked the abrupt end of the phoney war and the onset of a trauma of unprecedented breadth and depth throughout northern Europe. France was still recovering from the 1914-18 war, a conflict which had devastated its northern regions and killed or wounded one in twenty of its population. But then, at least, the theatre of war had been confined to a limited area. Now, inhabitants of towns, villages and countryside hundreds of kilometres from any previously disputed borderland were fleeing ahead of a German army that had burst through all their defences and which was advancing across their homeland at alarming speed.

It had taken only six short weeks from the moment Hitler, on 10 May, had launched his three-pronged attack on Holland, Belgium and France to the ignominious signature of an armistice with Germany by Marshal Philippe Pétain's hastily-formed Vichy government on 22 June. With Paris swathed in swastikas, grey uniforms in control as far west as Brest, Nantes and La Rochelle, and the French army in disarray with nearly 300,000 killed or wounded and seemingly abandoned by their allies, most French could see little alternative other than to make peace with the invaders.

The terms of peace included annexing the majority of Alsace and Lorraine to the Reich as well as placing the Nord and Pas de Calais *départements* under direct German rule. The rest of France would be divided by a demarcation line subjecting three fifths of the country to German occupation, including all the major financial and industrial centres and the entire Channel and Atlantic coast. France was still allowed to control the area to the south and east of the line, where the remnants of her army and air force were to be withdrawn and demobilized. Meanwhile, 1,600,000 French troops, captured during the invasion, would remain indefinitely as prisoners of war in German camps. Only the French navy, the fourth most powerful in the world, was still at large, its Atlantic-based ships having sailed for North Africa (and a few to England) before the Germans had reached Brittany.

A whole range of emotions swept the French nation at the signing of the armistice. There was impotent rage, despair and widespread fear at how the German occupiers would behave. To many, there was also a sense of relief; the fighting was over and their interests would now be in the care of a hero of the previous war, Marshal Pétain, who, they believed, would have the strength and guile to protect them from the worst effects of their country's violation. Some felt that France almost deserved a period of humiliation following two decades of weak and corrupt inter-war government and that, once Great Britain was defeated — a foregone conclusion in the opinion of most — the occupiers would withdraw. The sense that the British had betrayed them with the evacuation of its troops at Dunkirk was almost universal in France.

There remained in France, however, numerous sparks of defiance amid the submissive gloom, and however much animosity those who could not accept defeat felt towards perfidious Albion, they understood that while Britain was still free, she offered a lifeline for resistance against Hitler. Many thousands of French servicemen had fetched up there not through choice but because they were part of the Dunkirk evacuation or had been diverted from their return from the Norway campaign to avoid surrender. Others, though, civilians and servicemen alike, made a conscious decision to leave France, feeling that the only way to save their country was to offer their services to the only European power still holding out against Germany. Many more stayed put in France and hoped, as the occupation continued, that they would find an effective way to subvert and weaken the enemy regime.

Brigadier General Charles de Gaulle was a man whose pride would never countenance the defeat of France. This 49-year-old cavalry officer had led one of the few successful counter-attacks on the German advance in May 1940 and was afterwards sent to London by the Paul Reynaud-led government to broker, in desperation, a declaration of union with Churchill, whereby Britain and France would become a single power with a united army to combat Hitler. When, having secured an agreement, he returned to Bordeaux (the government's temporary home), he found Reynaud had been replaced by Pétain and an armistice with Hitler about to be signed.

His defiant attitude was now utterly unwelcome in government circles, so, on 17 June, accompanied by several cases of secretly acquired confidential files, he boarded an RAF aircraft bound for London. He felt that Britain, for the time being, was the only practicable platform from which to carry on the fight. Bereft of any meaningful resources and any legitimate claim to lead a French retaliation, he was nonetheless already planning his campaign to rally his fellow exiled servicemen under a Free French flag, and eventually to set up an alternative to the Vichy government in one of the African colonies, whence liberating forces could be launched onto the

French mainland. At the same time, he would, through any means at his disposal, begin the task of encouraging and harnessing the sentiment of defiance against the occupation wherever it existed across the political spectrum inside France, and to build a strong resistance ready to complement the efforts of the liberators when they arrived. His famous, if sparsely received, radio broadcast from London on the day after his arrival there, deploring Pétain's dishonourable capitulation and assuring his countrymen (with meagre evidence at that time) that the immense forces of the free world would soon be drawn into the war and crush the enemy, marked the beginning of his obsessive war-long crusade to ensure France played a creditable part in her own deliverance.

If the shock felt in Britain at the fall of Holland, Belgium and France was less traumatic than for those who actually found themselves under Nazi rule, the realization that no bulwark of defence other than the English Channel now lay between them and the might of the German army was a new and frightening sensation. At least, unlike the French, the majority of the British army was not behind German barbed wire thanks to the miraculous evacuation of 198,000 troops of the British Expeditionary Force, together with 140,000 French and Belgian servicemen from the beleaguered beaches of Dunkirk in the last days of May 1940. But any comfort drawn from such a triumph of muddling through soon dissipated as the real threat of a German invasion settled on every citizen. If France felt betrayed by Britain, the British were generally equally outraged at the willingness of the French to make a deal with Hitler, allowing him to turn his undivided and hostile attention towards their shores.

Even so, there was an element of public feeling, echoed within the corridors of power at Westminster, so impressed by the ferocity of the German war machine, that an armistice of their own with Hitler appeared the only possible way to avoid catastrophe. However, this option was never remotely entertained by the newly appointed prime minister of the all-party government, Winston Churchill. He had constantly opposed all efforts at appeasement prior to the declaration of war, telling Neville Chamberlain in the House of Commons, 'You were given the choice between war and dishonour. You chose dishonour, and you will have war.'

He was under no illusion, however, about the growing vulnerability of his country; all means of attacking Britain's defences and supply lines had been massively strengthened by the fall of France, Belgium and Holland. Forward Luftwaffe bomber and fighter bases in these occupied territories would now bring cities other than just those in the south east under the threat of bombardment. The German U-boats, already proving a scourge to British merchant shipping in the Atlantic, would now have far greater range, stepping off, as they could, from west coast ports of France. The same ports would also offer much greater freedom of activity for Germany's new and ferocious battleships such as the *Bismarck* and the *Tirpitz*.

The mood of stubborn national defiance against these adversities, aroused in part by Churchill's remarkable oratory and bulldog bearing, emboldened the young pilots of the RAF as they fought the crucial battle for air supremacy through the heat of the summer. It also steadied Londoners, bereaved and homeless, when the long-awaited blitz was eventually unleashed in September and it persuaded many citizens that they could play a part in the defence of their country, be it through donning a Home Guard uniform at the age of fifty or by turning a lawn into a vegetable patch.

That is why, on 14 July 1940, when a small but proud parade of General de Gaulle's Free French soldiers progressed down Whitehall, past the Cenotaph, to mark Bastille Day, they were heartily cheered by onlookers who recognized, in spite of catastrophe in France, that the spirit of 'never surrender' was still alive in some of its countrymen. It was for the same reason that Churchill had agreed to give financial and practical support to de Gaulle when he was approached by him a few weeks earlier with his supremely optimistic proposal to begin the battle to regain France from a suite of scruffy offices on the Thames Embankment. The British prime minister recognized the need of those with fight still in them to rally under a flag unsullied by capitulation and understood how de Gaulle's vision of a strong and co-ordinated resistance movement would at least disrupt the Nazi occupation and could greatly assist any eventual invasion.

More immediately, there was a desperate need for intelligence. By its hasty abandonment of France, Britain had lost nearly every means of discovering where Hitler was assembling troops, preparing embarkation points and building forward airfields. Lack of such information would make defending against a German invasion even more difficult. Aerial reconnaissance could never supply sufficient detail and although, in May 1940, the geniuses at Bletchley Park had achieved their first triumph by decrypting the Luftwaffe's version of the Enigma code, military intelligence from occupied France was very difficult to come by.

The Secret Intelligence Service, known also as MI6, faced some dire challenges when France fell. The service's reputation among the military and government ministers was not good. They had doubted and failed to pass on intelligence received about Hitler's imminent invasion of Belgium and Holland and also ignored accurate warnings of the Germans' attack on France via the Ardennes. Even when first class intelligence became available to them through their Bletchley decrypts, their chief, Colonel Stewart Menzies, so successfully disguised the source of the information that its recipients took it to be coming from just another dubious SIS agent on the continent and gave it very little credence. This obviously changed once they knew the source, but the misunderstanding did little to enhance the credibility of the SIS in spite of their breakthrough with the Enigma code.

The Nazi advance had also deprived the SIS of most of its well-established stations and intelligence networks in the European capitals. Their operations were thus confined to the neutral countries with Madrid, Lisbon, Berne and Stockholm offering the only means of passing information in and out of the continent. But next to nothing was coming from these stations about what was happening in France during the early days of the German occupation. The service made attempts to collate information brought back by British servicemen who, for one reason or another, had missed the Dunkirk evacuation, but who had evaded capture and got home by their own initiative. There was some assistance from the Polish intelligence service which, from their headquarters-in-exile in London, was running an embryonic network in the unoccupied south of France. They would later set up a successful second network in Paris, codenamed *Interallié*, but for the moment their operation consisted of little more than two military wireless operators who had escaped the invasion of Poland and who had managed to build a rudimentary transmitter with which they made regular contact with their Madrid embassy.

The shared information wasn't much, but it was the sum total of the SIS's radio links with France.

It fell largely to Colonel Menzies' assistant chief, Claude Dansey, to re-establish undercover lines of communication from France and other occupied countries. Already well into his sixties at the outbreak of war, Dansey, calloused by a career in espionage and counter-espionage since the 1914-18 war, carried an air of hostile secrecy and harboured a deep mistrust in and contempt for most human beings, not least the agents he ran, all of whom, he believed, had their price. He constantly clashed with his opposite number, Valentine Vivian, who ran the service's counter-espionage section and also contributed to the rancour which existed between the SIS and its more glamorous independent offspring, the Special Operations Executive.

The idea of setting up a 'dirty tricks' department within the SIS first occurred in the build-up to war in 1938, when the need to attack an enemy other than by conventional military means was identified. D (for 'destruction') section was duly formed and, by July 1940, it boasted a complement of 140 officers, almost twice the number in the main body of the SIS. Several of their attempts to sabotage the German advance on Scandinavia and the Balkans had come to naught, but that did not deter Churchill and the war cabinet from wishing to strengthen their subversive arm in Europe. The result was the creation, in July 1940, of a new, independent 'instrument of war', the SOE, to come under the direct jurisdiction of the Labour politician, Hugh Dalton, minister of economic warfare in the coalition government. To the considerable resentment of its chiefs, the SIS had lost control of its sabotage department and therefore its monopoly of clandestine work overseas. This meant that in France, for instance, agents for both organizations would be operating in the same territory with very conflicting objectives. While an SIS agent wished to disturb the authorities as little as possible as he quietly gathered intelligence, the SOE, especially later in the war, was creating havoc through sabotage and assassination — setting Europe ablaze, to use Churchill's metaphor.

Both organizations had very similar requirements in getting personnel in and out of enemy territory and would necessarily share the various methods of clandestine transportation set up by the RAF and Royal Navy. However, considerable care was taken to keep agents of the two organizations apart, with individual missions dedicated either to SIS or SOE. The same separation was observed during training in Britain, much of which, such as parachuting and encryption, was given at the same establishments. This is also why different arrangements were necessary for agents waiting for their opportunity to fly back into Europe.

If the SIS felt emasculated by the loss of its D section, its officers knew that they still had a massive task ahead if they were to satisfy the war cabinet's insatiable demand to know what Hitler was up to, especially in occupied France. Dansey was faced with a particular dilemma with the fall of France: should he attempt to re-establish contacts with individuals from the pre-Pétain French intelligence service, many of whom were now attached to the Vichy government? Or should he assume that these were all now agents of collaboration and instead invest in a completely new network recruited from those Frenchmen and women who had fled the occupation, so demonstrating their moral opposition to Nazi rule? In the event, he decided to do both.

Before the war, Dansey had been asked to lead a top secret intelligence network, known as the 'Z' network, which, unknown even to senior SIS personnel, was running a parallel effort to gather information from inside Nazi Germany, using commercial enterprises rather than diplomatic functions as a cover. His second-in-command in this organization had been a former Royal Navy torpedo officer, Kenneth Cohen, and it was he whom Dansey now appointed to form and operate new networks, some of which would work directly for the SIS and others via de Gaulle's Free French movement. Cohen, who had left the navy in 1935 and was recruited into the 'Z' network in 1937 after a short spell of working for an electrical contractor, was of a calm, tactful disposition, the perfect foil to his abrasive boss. Meanwhile, the task of reviving the Vichy contacts was assigned to Commander Wilfred ('Biffy') Dunderdale, formerly the SIS's station chief in Paris who was well acquainted with the old French intelligence regime and in a good position to pick up the threads now connected to Vichy. Dunderdale was an urbane individual, fond of the luxuries of life, who had apparently so impressed Ian Fleming when the future author visited Paris as a new recruit to the SIS, just before the city fell, that he immortalized several of his traits in the character of James Bond. Kenneth Cohen was perhaps a little less in awe of his opposite number and described him as 'a genial expense-account salesman'.

The division of labour was not an easy one to keep and led inevitably to friction between Cohen and Dunderdale over who had first call on whom among French intelligence officers. If problems of demarcation led to disputes in the SIS French section, they were nothing in comparison with the mistrust, the conflicting purposes and personal animosity which coloured the dealings between the British and Free French intelligence services. The fact that they needed each other in order to function at all was the only thing that kept them together.

Charles de Gaulle may have found London to be the most convenient base for his Free French cause, but he never gave his British paymasters any sense of being a comrade in arms in the fight against Germany. He would not necessarily have shared the view of many in occupied France that it was only a matter of time before Great Britain fell in the same way that France had fallen, as he had observed the pugnacious attitude of his hosts at first hand. But he knew very well that Britain could not defeat Nazism unaided and that she relied on American involvement almost as much as France did to ensure her freedom. De Gaulle's greatest fear of all was that Frenchmen would play no part in their country's eventual liberation, leaving a population tainted by submission and collaboration and bereft of all self-respect. Such a wasteland would be a breeding ground for left-wing extremism, as he saw it, especially if the only spontaneous resistance against the occupiers had come from the communists.

With these concerns uppermost, de Gaulle set about establishing the intelligence wing of his Free French administration. Although he was to rely entirely upon the British Foreign Office for the wherewithal for its operation, his objective was already diverging from that of his SIS sponsors. Both envisaged the establishment of networks of resistance in France, but, whereas the SIS saw the networks' role simply as one of intelligence-gathering to help the British armed services defend their country and plan an eventual offensive, military espionage was of secondary importance to de Gaulle. In spite of his army background, his motive for building a resistance movement was political as well as practical. His networks would encourage strong anti-collaborationist sentiment in France and ensure that, come the liberation, the Free French banner was held high by the heroes of the maquis.

The man de Gaulle chose to run the *2e* and *3e bureaux* (intelligence and counter-espionage) of his administration was the 29-year-old army engineer, Captain André Dewavrin. It was an extraordinarily bold appointment considering he knew nothing about this man other than what he had gleaned from him during a brief and typically icy interview at his St Stephens House headquarters. It seemed to be enough for de Gaulle to know the man had been trained at the prestigious Ecole Polytechnique in Paris, had fought in the Norway campaign prior to the fall of France, happened also to be qualified in law and spoke fluent English. The fact that he was an innocent in the world of intelligence-gathering did not deter the general from making the appointment on the spot.

The truth was that experience of any kind was extremely scarce among those volunteering to join the Free French. Of the 50,000 French soldiers who found themselves in Britain after the armistice, only 1,000 opted to join de Gaulle. Most of the rest, including nearly all the senior officers, preferred to return to their families in Vichy France and undergo demobilization. Dewavrin himself, hereafter referred to by his widely-used codename, Passy, had wavered until the last minute between offering his services to de Gaulle and sailing with a corps of French soldiers, led by General Emile Béthouart, to carry on the fight from Casablanca. As he sat at his desk in a tiny office on his first day as chief of intelligence, he must have wondered whether he had made a foolish choice.

All he knew of secret services was what he had read in novels. De Gaulle could afford him nothing to pay for men or equipment and he knew very little about the motley collection of volunteers from whom he was to choose his personnel. He began by recruiting officers and NCOs who, like him, had fought in Norway and whose morale was therefore less damaged as they had not been in France to experience defeat. One of his very first recruits, Lieutenant Maurice Duclos, a genial giant, gourmand and womanizer, would soon distinguish himself by his courageous undercover work in France. However, he and another swashbuckling early appointee, Captain Pierre Fourcaud, had, before the war, both belonged to an outlawed fascist movement known as the *cagoulards*, whose tactics included subversion and political assassination. Duclos had even been imprisoned for his involvement. Their past would weigh heavily on Passy and, indeed, de Gaulle later in the war, when detractors of the Free French would accuse the movement of far right-wing motivation, preparing to impose draconian rule on the newly liberated France.

André Dewavrin, alias Passy, head of de Gaulle's intelligence service. (*Musée de l'Ordre de la Libération*)

Whether by accident or design, however, de Gaulle had found a smooth, if ruthless operator in Passy. The latter was quick to realize, when the SIS made their first approach to the Free French to ask if they could use some of their men as intelligence agents, that he had an invaluable bargaining counter with which to advance his general's cause of building networks. He had the French-speaking manpower while the British had the means in the form of money, radios, false papers, transport and operatives in the neutral countries. Even when a marriage of convenience was agreed, Passy had to persuade the British of the value of networks. The SIS was all for sending agents into France to go themselves, unaided, to observe and gather intelligence. Passy argued, on the whole successfully, that the information would be far more accurate and valuable if it were acquired by network members, such as port officials, whose everyday jobs took them close to sensitive areas. It meant, of course, a longer wait for intelligence, which did not worry de Gaulle, and it served his purpose admirably of building a resistance movement.

Passy did make some elementary mistakes as well, even if they were only to harm his dignity. He knew it was important that his real name and that of his early recruits should be hidden, not least to protect their families back in France. But he did not know the golden rule that you kept the initial the same when you gave someone a code name, so the choice of random Paris Metro stations such as Passy, St Jacques (Duclos' code name), Barbès (Fourcaud), Bienvenue and Corvisart seemed bizarre to his British counterparts. So did the civilian disguise Passy chose for himself: a morning suit and shiny bowler hat from Moss Bros, something he quickly realized made him appear like a grotesquely overdressed bank clerk and far more incongruous in the hot July sun than he was in his French army uniform.

In his memoirs, Passy is full of praise for his 'Uncle Claude' Dansey, who, he says, guided him through many other potentially more damaging pitfalls during his formative weeks and months as head of French intelligence. It was probably just as well that this unlikely friendship grew up between two such wintry personalities as there would be several occasions during the war when the two services might otherwise have ceased to co-operate. In his role of helping to build new sources of intelligence from France, Kenneth Cohen was the person with whom Passy dealt on important matters. Again, considering their purposes were often at odds, the two men understood each other well, Passy particularly respecting Cohen's discretion, intelligence and analytical ability.

That is much more than can be said for his opinion of the man Cohen put in charge of the day-to-day running of his French section, an English salesman who had been living in Bordeaux and whom Passy referred to as 'Crayfish'. It is very likely that he was the same man as the Major 'J' whom Renault and Pineau would later find so tiresomely controlling. Passy remarked on him that, 'Never in my life have I met such a narrow-minded, misguided and Francophobic individual. He would lie to us incessantly, trying always to corrupt our agents and forever sowing divisions and chaos.'

Maybe this is why Passy had no compunction in exploiting the demarcation dispute between Cohen and Dunderdale by working closely also with the latter. He saw this as a means to gain additional resources and influence which would not have come his way via a single SIS intermediary, particularly not Crayfish.

General Charles de Gaulle with the pioneer Free French intelligence agent, Pierre Fourcaud. (*Musée de l'Ordre de la Libération*)

The greatest cause of friction between the Free French and British intelligence services was the battle for control over agents. To the British, Passy and his embryonic service only represented one somewhat shaky potential source of information from France. Both Dunderdale and Cohen were briefed to look elsewhere for French agents who could work directly under their control as officers of the SIS. Much to the dismay of Passy and de Gaulle, they did this by a sifting process instituted at the old Royal Victoria Patriotic School on Wandsworth Common, MI5's interrogation centre for foreign refugees. Any likely candidates among the 'cleared' French nationals, unless they insisted on being put in touch with the Free French, were passed to an SIS representative and offered the opportunity to join the war effort back in France, working for His Majesty's Secret Service.

Kenneth Cohen also successfully moved in to take direct control of what would become the *'Alliance'* intelligence network in France, one of the most widespread and successful of the war. It was particularly galling to Passy that it was one of his first agents into France, Pierre Fourcaud, who had established contact with its founder, Commandant Georges Loustaunau-Lacau, who was first to see such a vigorous organization bypass the offices of the Free French. Loustaunau-Lacau, well connected with many in Vichy who had also been at army college with de Gaulle, sent details back to London via Fourcaud, not only about his nascent network, but also how he intended to whip up anti-German feeling in France through a movement he called *Spirale*. With the professed connivance of Pétain himself, he would circulate subversive literature and asked for similar leaflets to be dropped by air over France under the Free French banner. De Gaulle bridled at his old comrade's involvement with Vichy and also at his unrealistic request for 20 million francs to help him execute his plans. Loustaunau-Lacau's reaction to the news of de Gaulle's unwillingness to support his movement was to sever all links with the Free French and deal only with the British, who were only too keen to nurture his intelligence network.

If such manoeuvres led Passy and his team to mistrust the British, the feeling was mutual. The SIS, with its obsessive secrecy, looked upon de Gaulle's intelligence service as an amateurish band of misfits whose cavalier attitude to security threatened every one of their joint operations. Cohen's post-war recollections described them as:

> ... gossip-ridden but informative characters. This very much mixed bunch both in politics and merit, ranged from burning and saintly patriotism (e.g. Rémy, and St Jacques) to the brave, able but distinctly unsaintly Passy. But they included also, alas, adventurers and the odd traitor, i.e. 'Howard', who was housed to our shame by 'Biffy' Dunderdale, and which led to the Muselier scandal and eventual imprisonment for Howard (de Gaulle would have had him shot. Passy's remedy was, probably, torture).

The Muselier scandal followed de Gaulle's abortive expedition to Dakar on the West African coast. The General was determined to establish his Free French headquarters on French colonial soil sooner rather than later and had identified Dakar as the optimum place, not least because the gold reserves of the Banque de France were stored there. There were indications that, unlike most other French African colonies, French West Africa might be persuaded to change her Vichy allegiance and join the allies. Thus, in September 1940, de Gaulle set off with 8,000 troops and an escort of eighteen Royal Navy warships, including an aircraft carrier and two battleships. The attempted peaceful landing and negotiations of 23 September ended in a bloody sea battle between the British and Vichy French navy, the latter of which had been given wind of the attempted surprise expedition and bolstered their defences with six extra warships prior to de Gaulle's arrival.

The mission's failure was put down largely to loose talk by the French involved in its planning, which reached Vichy in time for them to forearm. Clearly, the British were furious and even more so when, three months later, they were shown documents which established that the head of de Gaulle's own armed services, Admiral Emile Muselier, had deliberately leaked the expedition's plans to Vichy. Churchill immediately ordered Muselier's imprisonment, only to learn a few days later that the incriminating documents had actually been forged by the same two men, 'Howard' and Colin, working in Passy's department, who had originally reported the supposed treachery to MI5. As these two men had been originally recommended to Passy by the SIS, the French assumed that they were agents of the British, bent on disrupting the Free French organization for some inexplicable reason. To the British, who denied any such duplicity, it was just another example of the ill-discipline and divided loyalties which existed in the Free French camp.

The vexatious affair led to one of de Gaulle's many short-lived embargoes on dealing with British intelligence and made him all the more determined that any intelligence coming back from his agents in France should be channelled through his officers first. However, he soon had to accept that his networks relied entirely on British facilities, and operating compromises were reached. These included an agreement that while agents' reports of a political nature could be in a code decipherable only by the French, military intelligence transmitted via the Bletchley listening post was to use the

British codes for instant decryption and use by the armed services. Kenneth Cohen kept a vivid recollection of this horse-trading episode:

> I remember one 'fencing match' with de Gaulle in particular, where I think I was insisting on our right to hold the Free French codes, which he vehemently denied. At this stage there was a good deal to be said for our view. The FF *Deuxième Bureau* was hardly in existence, and partly suspect. We had to carry all the operational tasks — parachuting, false papers, submarines, MTBs [Motor Torpedo Boats], W/T55 etc. and might be expected to wish for some say in the choice of objectives and personnel, (*i.e.* Vichy squabble or RAF targets!). Finally, there were risks of leakage such as *may* have occurred over Dakar. De Gaulle would have none of this and practically threw me out of his room saying that my stand '*atteint notre souveraineté*' [violated our sovereignty]. (He was a cashiered one-star general at the time)! I could not help a slight smile. '*Vous me prenez à la légère*' [You do not take me seriously], he remarked as we parted, '*mais vous verrez*' [but you will see].

But by the end of 1941, in spite of all the mistrust and struggle for control between the two secret services, their joint achievement had been to send twenty-nine intelligence agents into the field with twelve radios making regular contact, six of which had been established by the incomparably dynamic agent, Gilbert Renault (Rémy), whose story unfolds later in the book.

CHAPTER 4: THE LIZZIE

A dumpy black aeroplane, barely visible in the fading autumn moonlight, but highly audible, circles a desolate patch of French farmland at a height of about 300 feet. The silhouette of its pilot's rounded head can just be seen through the cockpit glass craning towards the ground, scouring the terrain. The plane makes another circuit, then another. Lights begin to appear in the windows of one or two of the neighbouring farmhouses — it has been overhead now for more than fifteen minutes. Finally, its wings level out, the throttle opens and it begins a climb towards the north. Almost immediately, the engine revs fall again and the plane banks sharply to the right. Nearly a mile from where it had been circling, a light on the ground is flashing a regular dash, dash, dot — the letter 'G'.

There are two short bursts on the throttle from the aircraft, now making straight for the light and, in response, the light switches to a steady beam, then two more lights appear, completing a flare path. After one circuit of what appears to be a very small grass field with a road and a line of tall trees at the windward end, the pilot makes his approach, dropping almost vertically from the sky. The plane thumps down onto the turf just to the right of the first torch, bounces forward drunkenly over the heavily pitted surface and halts abruptly after scarcely fifty yards. With its propeller still tearing at the night air, the aircraft turns and taxis back to the marker light furthest from the line of trees. In an instant, one man has clambered out of the rear cockpit and another is installed, strapping himself into his harness as the revs pick up.

The engine is now screaming as if in panic as the pilot tries to gather speed on the rough terrain. Each bump checks the acceleration and the trees at the end of the field are now only 100 yards away. The wheel hits yet another hummock but this one throws the plane into the air. It climbs at an improbable angle but the trees seem to have grown in height. Then there is a blinding flash and the aeroplane wobbles for a second in its trajectory. But its engine roars on and, with the undercarriage thrashing through the treetops, heaves itself clear. As the plane climbs northwards and disappears into the blackness, hanging limply from a nearby pole, a severed high-tension electricity cable and a finer telephone wire snake among the fresh leaves and broken twigs that now litter the field beneath the trees.

An hour and a half later, the same aeroplane is 14,000 feet above the north coast of France. Its sedate progress is suddenly broken as it makes a tight diving turn to the left. Passing about 300 feet overhead are two German night-fighters on patrol, their green starboard navigation lights clearly visible. As they reach the end of their patrol line, they turn in neat formation through 180 degrees and retrace their original route. The unlit black aeroplane, which had initially headed evasively back into France, has turned now once more towards the Channel as it makes a steep dive towards the water, pulling out when just a few feet above the waves. Only when the pilot is certain he has remained undetected does he pull up to 2,000 feet and head for home.

Home is not welcoming. A low-lying fog covers the runway, but the approach lights are just visible on the ends of their poles above it. The plane sinks into the fog, nose high, feeling for the ground so the tail wheel touches the tarmac first. A jeep escorts the aircraft to a safe parking place and when the pilot descends stiffly from his cockpit — he has been in the air for five hours and forty minutes — he peers at the undercarriage and disentangles a length of telephone wire and puts it in his pocket to keep as a souvenir.

The aircraft in this, the first clandestine operation of No. 138 Special Duties Squadron, on the night of 4 September 1941, was a Westland Lysander Mk III SCW, or a 'Lizzie' as they became fondly nicknamed. The pilot, Flight Lieutenant John Nesbitt-Dufort, had skilfully demonstrated in his very first trip just how well-suited the Lysander was to the business of ferrying secret service agents in and out of France during the occupation. On this occasion, its ability to land and take off in a confined space was tested to an unreasonable extreme. The incoming agent and his assistant had been delayed in leaving their hotel by a police inspection of all the guests' papers. When still a mile from the pre-selected landing field, they could hear the Lysander circling it and guessed that it was unlikely to stay around long enough for them to get there on their bicycles. They therefore chose the nearest likely field and began their signalling. No one had spotted the power lines in the darkness.

The history of the Westland Lysander, prior to its adoption by 138 and later 161 Special Duties Squadrons, had not been a particularly happy one. If not precisely a camel invented by Air Ministry committees, the aircraft certainly did not fulfil the purpose for which it was primarily intended. The idea had been to replace the aging Hawker Hector biplane which had been used by the RAF as an army co-operation aircraft, spotting artillery, collecting messages by scooping bags off the ground and occasionally dropping small bombs on the enemy.

Four companies were invited to submit designs for the new plane in 1934 and it was Westlands of Yeovil, a company which had developed from an agricultural engine manufacturer to an aircraft builder in the run-up to the First World War, which came up with the winning bid. Their chief designer, W.E.W. (Teddy) Petter, grandson of the firm's founder who went on in later years to design English Electric's Canberra and Lightning jets, spent considerable time talking to RAF pilots about their requirements. At the top of their somewhat inconclusive list was a plane with good all-round vision for pilot and observer, which could handle well at low speeds and which could land and take off on rough ground in as short a distance as possible.

By June 1936, Petter's prototype was ready to take her maiden flight. Considering that the sleek forms of the Hawker Hurricane and the Supermarine Spitfire had already taken to the air, the carrot-shaped fuselage of the Lysander, with its hefty fixed undercarriage and its high wing, gave it an awkward and antiquated appearance. But there were innovatory aspects to the design, not least the slats which extended automatically from the leading edge of the wing as the aircraft slowed towards stalling speed. The slats controlled automatic flaps which made landing approaches at slow speed much simpler for the pilot and allowed him to pull up in less than fifty yards. The angle of the entire tail plane was also adjustable to assist short take-off and landing. The undercarriage was a single inverted V-shaped piece of virtually unbreakable alloy, imported specially from Switzerland and built to withstand the impact of heavy, steep landings on uneven terrain. Perhaps the design's most visually characteristic feature was the pair of bulbous aerodynamic spats which covered the wheels and these, along with a machine-gun mounted in the rear cockpit, carried the Lysander's means of attack — forward-facing machine-guns and optional stub wings for dropping bombs. The single radial engine was an 870 hp, 9-cylinder Bristol

Mercury which allowed the aircraft a very modest maximum speed of 212 mph.

A Westland Lysander Mk III SCW of RAF special duties Squadron 161 fitted with the additional fuel tank slung under the fuselage and a ladder for rapid embarkation of passengers.
(*The Bertram Family*)

It was for the want of speed that the Lysander largely failed in the role for which it had been built. Four squadrons were sent to France and Belgium to assist the British Expeditionary Forces but when, in May 1940, Germany launched the *Blitzkrieg*, the lumbering Lysanders were no match for the 400 mph Messerschmitt 109s. Although records show that one Lysander crew destroyed a Messerschmitt 110 during an air battle and returned safely to base while another accounted for a Henschel 126 and a Stuka on the same sortie, the contest was dreadfully one-sided. As the BEF retreated to the beaches of Dunkirk, the depleted Lysander squadrons were withdrawn to British soil when some were deployed on missions back over the Channel to supply the beleaguered army. In one of these operations, sixteen Lysanders were sent and only two returned. All told, of the 174 Lysanders used in the battle over France and Belgium, eighty-eight were lost in air combat while thirty were destroyed on the ground. Between September 1939 and May 1940, 120 Lysander crew members lost their lives.

The RAF had also sent Lysanders to other parts of the world such as Egypt, Palestine and India, where they all played a front-line role to a greater or lesser degree. Even here, though, they were fairly soon replaced by fighters such as the Hurricane and the last offensive action seen by Lysanders was in 1943 over the jungles of Burma. Back in Britain, apart from some air-sea rescue work for downed pilots, the aircraft was relegated to the prosaic task of target towing, a far cry from the critically tight manoeuvring for which it had been so carefully designed. It was thus a fortunate coincidence when the RAF discovered that they possessed in the Lysander the perfect vehicle to carry out the clandestine task which, since the fall of France, they were increasingly asked to perform by the SIS and SOE.

The practice of placing agents behind enemy lines and of retrieving them by air was not an entirely new one. The flamboyant French aviator, Jules Védrines, winner of many early international air races, is renowned for his daring flights in a small monoplane across the German defences during the First World War, to land and pick up intelligence agents. The first such operation by the British was attempted by a Captain Thomas Mulcahy Morgan in September 1915, but both he and his clandestine passenger were badly injured after their plane crashed on landing and they were both captured. Other more successful missions were completed in the ensuing weeks and months.

From its Royal Flying Corps roots, the RAF therefore had some idea of what was required and, in September 1940, established No. 419 Flight, which comprised three Lysanders and two Whitley twin-engine bombers adapted for parachuting purposes. Originally based at North Weald near Epping in Essex, the flight was moved following a damaging German bombing raid to Stradishall in Suffolk only a month after its formation. One of its first 'customers' was the SIS agent Philip Schneidau, a man raised in Paris of two British parents, who played international hockey for France before choosing British nationality at the age of 21. His mission in France was to last ten days. The plan was for him to be dropped by parachute from a Whitley and recovered at the end by the squadron's commander, Flight Lt Wally Farley, who would land a Lysander on a pre-arranged field to the south of Fontainebleau. The two men had designed the inverted 'L' shaped pattern of lights on a table cloth at Oddenino's restaurant in Regent Street — a device that never needed improvement throughout the war.

Thick cloud and heavy rain prevented Farley from setting off from Tangmere on the predetermined night of the pick-up, but the following evening, 19 October 1940, he left in equally poor weather as he was concerned that Schneidau would believe he had been forgotten. Fortunately, the skies cleared over France, but not before the radio in the rear cockpit had been put out of action by the rain — Farley had left the sliding roof open to make it easier for Schneidau to clamber in. The pick-up went without a hitch, Schneidau using the fixed ladder he had invented for rapid embarkation. Someone on the ground had spotted them, however, because, shortly after take-off, a bullet shot through the bottom of the fuselage, passed between the pilot's legs and hammered into the compass.

Back over the French coast, the weather worsened and almost immediately, with no view of the ground, no compass and no radio, they became utterly lost. Although he realized his passenger was freezing in the open cockpit behind him, Farley felt his only option was to fly on until they could see something. They flew on for several hours, all the time fearing that the strong south-westerly wind had carried them over Belgium, Holland or even Germany. With all fuel spent and dawn breaking, they finally saw a coastline and Farley, gliding now, brought the Lysander down at the top of some high cliffs. The aircraft lost both wings on touching down thanks to poles which had been erected to prevent such landings, but both occupants were unhurt. Still not knowing whether they were on home or enemy territory, Farley decided he would go to find help and told Schneidau to strip naked and be ready to throw his incriminating civilian clothes over the cliff if he returned with a German escort. When he did eventually come back, accompanied by two armed and uniformed men, he greeted his shivering friend: 'I can't understand a word they are saying, but it appears we are in Scotland — somewhere near Oban.'

No further calls for clandestine night landings were made on the Lysanders of the re-numbered 1419 Flight for the next six months. Then, in April 1941, Flying Officer Gordon Scotter successfully retrieved an agent from a field north of Châteauroux, in spite of an encounter with night-fighters fitted with searchlights and a narrow escape from Vichy police on the ground. The following month, he flew to Fontainebleau to collect Philip Schneidau who had returned to France to set up an intelligence ring in Paris. The operation proved a far smoother affair than Schneidau's first return to Britain.

Demand now began to grow for special duties air operations, and the RAF expanded its facility accordingly. First, in August, the flight took on squadron status, No. 138, and moved to Newmarket, using the heath beside the racecourse as its runway. By December 1941, after four more Lysander operations, including John Nesbitt-Dufort's close encounter with a power cable, the squadron comprised eighteen aircraft. In February of the following year, a second special duties squadron was formed, No. 161, which, from its eventual home of RAF Tempsford near Sandy in Bedfordshire, it would bear responsibility for all the Lysander pick-ups in France until the end of the war.

By the end of 1941, the Lysander pilots had begun to perfect their routines both in solo navigation by moonlight and in reducing the time spent on enemy soil to a minimum. All the Lysanders in the squadron had been specially adapted for the purpose which, as well as Schneidau's ladder, included an additional torpedo-shaped 150-gallon fuel tank slung beneath the fuselage to give them the range required to get deep into France and back. The Mk III SCW, as it was known, carried no armaments and sported an all-black colour scheme for night-time camouflage. The paint pattern was later modified with the underside remaining matt black but with the top of the wings and fuselage reverting to dark green and pale grey, a better camouflage against night-fighters approaching from above in moonlight.

The pilots chosen to fly the Lysander missions had to be utterly self-reliant by nature. Even the training for the job was a do-it-yourself process. The minimum qualification was 250 hours of night-flying experience, and an ability to speak French was desirable if not essential. So too, albeit unstated, was an acceptance of very adverse odds on surviving any operation. One man, Hugh Verity, recruited into 161 Squadron in November 1942, described his training in his definitive post-war account of the Lysanders' special duties, *We Landed by Moonlight*.

The training — which I was largely left to work out for myself — had to turn me into a competent special duties Lysander pilot in about a month. I had to be able to fly the aeroplane, to fly it by night, to land it on a ridiculous little flare path and to navigate it by moonlight to any field in France.

I took stock of the situation. I had done about 850 hours, of which about 250 were by night. I had been trained as a navigator as well as a pilot, but I had not done very much pilot-navigation, and none of that had been at night. The others showed me how they prepared their route maps and worked out their flight plans, but I knew I needed a lot of practice.

Before his first flight, Verity sat in a Lysander cockpit with the twenty-page pilot's notes and taught himself how to locate all the controls by touch alone. He also learnt all the drills, checks and limits by heart. After that, he was ready to take the plane up. Strapping himself into his seat and sliding the cockpit canopy shut, he primed the engine and started up. Waiting for the oil temperature to rise to 5°C, he tested the flying controls and brake pressure. Then, against the brakes and the chocks, he opened up to 1,800 rpm and changed the pitch of the propeller to coarse. Noting the large drop in revs, he returned to the fine pitch position and throttled back. Now, almost ready to go, he checked that the tail plane trim wheel was set for take-off, that the fuel mixture control was at 'normal' and that the gills were open to increase air-flow over the engine. Finally, with chocks removed, he taxied onto the runway, eased the throttle fully open and, travelling at a speed of 80 mph, pulled the stick back and climbed away.

The pilot's view of the Lysander instrument panel. (*Edward Wake-Walker*)

The next stage of his training was to practise the landing and take-off routines repeatedly in daylight on a grassy field at Somersham, not far from his Tempsford base, using yellow flags in place of torches. Then he tested himself landing at night and on one occasion accomplished eight landings in a space of forty minutes. In barely a week, he had become completely at ease with bringing a Lysander down in darkness with the aid of three pocket torches marking a landing site just 150 yards long.

Much of his earlier flying with the RAF had been done with the luxury of a navigator so, as part of his training, he took himself on extended flights over England by both day and night to improve his path-finding ability. Apart from one panic-inducing moment during a night-flight when he thought for a while that he had become completely lost and would have to face the ignominy of radioing for his position, he generally kept his bearings, including during a three-hour, non-stop round trip between Tempsford and Exeter.

The last part of Verity's initiation came when he went to join the other Lysander pilots of the squadron who had moved to their advance base at Tangmere for the moon period operations. To prove his ability in finding an exact position over enemy territory, he was given a pin-point to fly to, south of Saumur, on the Loire. He was shown how to make his way through a corridor free of flak and how to cut strips out of 1:500,000 maps, showing the track he was to follow with about fifty miles on either side for easy reckoning. The corridor did not prove to be flak-free, but he watched the tracers just miss him as he carried on, following his course with little difficulty. When he reached the given position, he was astonished to see a brilliantly lit rectangle which he took to be some kind of prison camp. On his safe return to Tangmere, he reported this strange sight amid all the blacked out darkness and was immediately told he had passed the final test as it proved he had actually been to where he was meant to go. The camp was the same gipsy prison which had so disconcerted Guy Lockhart on his flight out with Renault the previous March.

If the success of the Lysander missions depended on the exceptional skills of the pilots, they could have accomplished little without a practised reception party in France. This was achieved by getting prospective agents and pilots together for training both at Tempsford and at nearby Somersham for practical work. The agents, all dressed as British Army officers, were taught how to set up a flare path into the wind with the man in charge and the waiting passengers posted nearest to lamp 'A', the touchdown point. Lamp 'B' should be positioned 150 metres further upwind with lamp 'C' fifty metres to the right of it, completing the shorter length of the inverted 'L'.

The flare path needed to begin at least 100 metres from the nearest hedge on a clear, firm, level strip of ground, a good 600 metres from hedge to hedge. There could be no trees of any height in the way of the approach or take-off zones and any cart tracks needed to be well away from the landing area. Short-grazed grass was the ideal surface but a firm field of stubble would do. Mud had to be avoided at all costs. During part of the week-long course, agents would be driven around the local countryside and asked to point out to the pilots fields which they believed fitted their specifications. Back in the classroom, they would learn how to draft descriptions of their chosen landing sites for the wireless messages sent back from France. This was important, not only for the Lysander pilots themselves, but for the daytime missions that would be sent in advance to take high-altitude photographs of the proposed sites for approval by the RAF.

The landing routine itself began with the agent in charge flashing the predetermined signal letter on lamp 'A'. Once the Lysander had acknowledged this, the agent or his assistant, if he had one, would light the other two lamps. They were taught how to lash these three torches to sticks, pointing downwind and slightly upwards. They would then rehearse a three-minute turnaround on the ground whereby the last outbound passenger would pass down his own luggage and load that of those leaving France before he left the aircraft, then the new passengers would clamber aboard and, with the canopy slid shut, the pilot, receiving a thumbs up from the man in charge on the ground, would open up the throttle and pull away.

The Lysander was used in 204 separate operations over France between October 1940 and August 1944 and was unarguably the principal instrument in the task of ferrying men and women in and out of occupied France. There was, however, another aircraft flown by 161 Squadron for the same purpose which should not be overlooked. This was the American-built Lockheed Hudson, a military conversion of the commercial airliner, the Lockheed 14 Super Electra, perhaps most famous for conveying Neville Chamberlain to and from Germany during his ill-fated pre-war shuttle diplomacy with Hitler. The main reason the squadron had a Hudson at its disposal appears to be that its first commanding officer, Wing Commander E.H. (Mouse) Fielden, who had just come from the job of pilot to the King, had brought the plane with him from the King's Flight.

A low-wing monoplane with twin Cyclone radial engines, the Hudson was recognizable particularly by its long tail-plane with twin pear-shaped fins and rudders near the rounded ends. The nose of the plane was fitted with Perspex windows for the bomb aimer and a gunner's turret projected from the top of the rear fuselage. Most of this reconnaissance bomber's wartime service was spent over the Atlantic, giving protection to convoys against submarines.

For the clandestine purposes of 161 Squadron, the Hudson was a far less subtle instrument than the Lysander. It was about three times heavier and came in to land a good ten knots faster, needing a flare path of 350 metres in a field no shorter than 1,000 metres. It was therefore a considerable headache for agents in France to find suitable landing sites and required many helpers, including armed guards at the perimeters as the larger planes attracted far more attention than the agile Lysander. The advantage was the plane's greater range and, above all, its capacity as it could take up to ten passengers and their luggage. As the war progressed and the intelligence and SOE networks grew, increasing numbers had to be flown in and out of France and it was therefore preferable to use one Hudson rather than three or even four Lysanders on a single operation. Another considerable advantage to the pilot of a Hudson was that there was space for a navigator on board. In all, the Hudson was used in thirty-nine missions to deliver and collect agents.

In one of these operations, the greater range of the Hudson led to an unexpected and, in political circles, unwelcome outcome. In May 1943, Winston Churchill was very keen for the SIS to organize the retrieval from France of General Georges, an anti-Vichy ex-five-star Army Chief of Staff. Churchill felt, if he could speak to the general before he saw de Gaulle, he could persuade him to act as an influential go-between who, by his military seniority to de Gaulle, might even persuade him to take some orders.

Hearing that such an important passenger and his entourage needed bringing out of France, 161 Squadron's commander, Group Captain 'Mouse' Fielden, insisted that he should carry out the task himself in a Hudson. It was, he felt, the sort of job tailor-made for the pilot to the King. However much the others in the squadron admired him, they wished that he had given the job to a younger pilot and one more experienced at landing by moonlight. Although Fielden had been in charge of the squadron for more than a year, he had only attempted three previous landings in France, all in a Hudson and all aborted for one reason or another.

The target was a long way south in France, an aerodrome near Florac among the mountains of the Cevennes and not far from the Mediterranean coast. The group captain found the airfield, duly marked out by the resistance reception party, and landed with no difficulty just after 2 o'clock in the morning. There was a ten-minute wait for the General's car convoy to arrive, by which time Fielden had made the cautious decision to take the long route home via Algiers and Gibraltar rather than risk flying back over northern France as daylight broke. The decision was justified in as far as he got home safely, but not as far as Churchill was concerned. The prime minister's precious General Georges was not on board; he had disembarked in Algiers to ally himself with General Henri Giraud, who had taken on the leadership of the liberation movement in French North and West Africa.

As quite often happened to the special duties pilots, Fielden was presented with gifts by his grateful passengers during this trip. Among them was a bottle of good wine which Fielden decided he should present to the King on his return. The King apparently shared the bottle with Churchill who was in turn mystified as to how his monarch had come by a 1941 vintage French wine and infuriated by the King's refusal to reveal its provenance. He might have been even more infuriated had he known.

CHAPTER 5: THE PILOTS OF 161 SQUADRON

The men who flew the Lysanders ('A' Flight) of 161 Squadron were a select few. At any given time, they would number no more than five and, throughout the years between October 1940 and August 1944, when the moonlit operations were run from Tangmere, only thirty-five pilots were involved in total. It meant, of course, that they were a close-knit team, living at close quarters, particularly during the moon periods at Tangmere and learning off one another's experiences, both good and bad. Each must have felt a sense of utter loneliness every time they set off into the night to pick their way across a dark and hostile terrain towards their unmarked target. Even when an operation involved two or three Lysanders at a time, they could not follow a leader but had to find their way on their own.

Hugh Verity, who commanded the Lysander flight for the whole of 1943, its busiest year, had flown thirty-six missions in that time. He later wrote,

> The end of my tour of operations released the tension on the spring which I had kept more tightly wound up than I had realized. I suddenly collapsed and was good for nothing but staying in bed for the best part of a week. A medical check-up revealed that I was totally exhausted. From 6 to 16 November we laid on operations on eight nights out of eleven. I had myself flown on five of these nights and been responsible until pilots were safely landed and debriefed on all eight. Apart from the nervous tension — which one did not notice

at the time — this routine left us all very short of ordinary sleep.

It was a strange way to fight a war. Apart from the pistol each pilot carried for self-defence, there was no means of combat. Half of every month was spent completely free from danger in rural Bedfordshire, training agents and visiting home and loved ones while waiting for the next moon period. The other half, by contrast, was a fortnight of intense anticipation by day followed by a night of either high adventure or frustrating anti-climax when bad weather intervened.

Life on the ground at Tangmere was spent mainly at what was known as 'The Cottage'. Standing opposite the main gates of the RAF station behind a tall hedge, it was a seventeenth-century dwelling which had been extended considerably over the years. Apart from its kitchen where the establishment's two flight sergeant security minders doubled as cooks, preparing mixed grills and sumptuous breakfasts for returning pilots and agents, there were two other rooms downstairs. One was for dining and the other was the operations and crew room. In it was a large map of France with the areas defended by flak marked in red. As well as a table and a map chest, an assortment of armchairs was arranged around the coal fire. The only real clue to the clandestine role of the cottage's inhabitants was a green 'scrambler' phone positioned next to the standard black one.

Upstairs, there were some six bedrooms, all with as many beds as there was space for. It was not only the pilots these had to accommodate before and after operations, but SOE agents and all other passengers except those chaperoned by the SIS, who were lodged at Bignor Manor. There was generally a happy, casual atmosphere about the place and, when operations were cancelled, impromptu parties involving the

Lysander ground crew members and anyone else in the know were often arranged.

The exuberance of these young pilots, most in their early twenties, occasionally bubbled over beyond the confines of the cottage. They would sometimes take their planes up on days of cancelled operations and swoop low over Bignor Manor, terrifying both Barbara Bertram and her goat, Caroline. At one stage, an order appeared in the flight headquarters forbidding any low flying over Bignor until Caroline was delivered of the kid she was expecting. Caroline, a celebrity among both agents and pilots, was later immortalized when her name was used for one of the pick-up operations. All week prior to the operation, the BBC had solemnly announced news of Caroline: 'Caroline has a new hat'. 'Caroline is well'. 'Caroline went for a walk'. Finally there came: 'Caroline has a blue dress' — blue being the associated word telling the French landing party that the mission was on for that night.

Nicky and Tim Bertram with Caroline the goat. (*The Bertram Family*)

The pilots who flew the Lysander missions later in the war owed much to two of the pioneers of special duties pick-ups, John (Whippy) Nesbitt-Dufort DSO, Croix de Guerre, and Alan (Sticky) Murphy, DSO, DFC, Croix de Guerre. These two skilful aviators and impressive individuals were anything but the run-of-the-mill caricatures of wartime RAF pilot officers suggested by their schoolboy nicknames and moustachioed looks. Both brought back valuable lessons to the squadron after narrow escapes on enemy soil and one ultimately owed his deliverance from a Gestapo manhunt to the other.

John Nesbitt-Dufort, born in 1912, was brought up in the Home Counties by his grandmother and uncles and aunts after his French father was killed on the Western Front in 1914 and his English mother died a few years later. Passionate about aeroplanes and engines from a very early age, he was accepted as an RAF trainee pilot officer at the earliest permissible age of 17½. Showing above-average aptitude on gaining his wings, he spent his short commission with a fighter squadron, then as an instructor. When war broke out, he had left the RAF and was working with de Havilland, teaching young men destined for military duty to fly Tiger Moths. He soon joined up again and, after a spell of training bomber pilots, then piloting a night-fighter, he was recruited for special duties with 138 Squadron.

He flew five missions during his tour of duty with them between September 1941 and March 1942. The first, the nearly disastrous encounter with a French power cable, convinced his superiors to step up the training for agents in charge of pick-ups in the selection of appropriate landing sites. The second, to a field west of Soissons, near Reims, went without a serious hitch, while the third, to around the same region of France, had to be abandoned when mist obscured the agents' landing lights. Nesbitt-Dufort returned the following night, however, and brought home one of the SIS's star Polish agents, Roman Garby-Czerniawski, who was head of the Paris-based network *Interallié*. The weather, especially in winter, presented as much danger to the Lysander operations as any German fire power and, when Nesbitt-Dufort set off on his fifth mission in January 1942, it all but got the better of him and his passengers.

Apart from some mercifully inaccurate flak over the French coast, the outward journey and landing in a field near Issoudun went according to plan thanks to clear moonlight over central France. Roger Mitchell, a French agent recruited by Passy to organize pick-ups in France and now on his way back to England with important courier, had done his job of field selection well. In a matter of minutes, he and his companion, Maurice Duclos, alias Saint-Jacques, were crammed into the Lysander's rear cockpit and watching the dark French countryside shrinking beneath them. Duclos, Passy's very first agent, had been on the run in France since the previous August when his Paris-based network had been betrayed by the Luxemburg double agent, André Folmer. Although he had narrowly avoided capture, many of his network were caught and eventually shot while his doting older sister and her niece, with whom he lived, were tortured by the Gestapo and sent to a concentration camp. Duclos had lost all the geniality of the man volunteering for the Free French just eighteen months previously and, as Nesbitt-Dufort was shortly to observe, now 'displayed a hardness that would have made high-tensile tungsten steel appear like putty.'

The flight back over France at about 7,000 feet was uneventful until, eighty miles south of the French coast, the air started to become turbulent. 'Suddenly I saw it.' John Nesbitt-Dufort recalls in his book, *Black Lysander*:

> It must have formed up rapidly along the north French coast during the last three hours. 'It' was the most wicked-looking and well-defined active cold front I had ever seen. It extended right across my track to the east and west as far as the eye could see and the top of that boiling mass of cumulonimbus clouds, seething upwards like the heavy smoke of some gigantic oil fire, must have risen to well over 30,000 feet — way above the maximum altitude of the Lizzie. From the base of that horror, which was only about 600 feet above the ground, torrential rain fell, while lightning played continually in its black depths.

Seeing that there was no way round either to the west or to the east, Nesbitt-Dufort first opted to descend to 1,000 feet and attempt to fly under the mass of cloud. He soon realized this was a mistake; in the pitch darkness, the rain was forcing his plane ever lower to the ground and his windscreen was white with ice. He made an about turn and emerged again in the clear air, thoroughly shaken up. His next attempt was to fly through the middle of the cloud at about 10,000 feet, relying entirely on his instruments to see him through. Almost immediately, the Lysander began to be tossed around, as he put it, 'like a leaf in a whirlwind'. Blinded by the continual lightning, his compass unreliable from the amount of static and his air speed indicator iced up and useless, Nesbitt-Dufort fought on at his controls using all the power he could squeeze out of the engine. But the aircraft was losing height. Opening the cockpit window, he thrust his gloved hand into the slipstream and when he brought it back found it petrified in a clear coating of ice. The same would be happening on all the exterior surfaces of the Lysander, the wings unable to provide the lift needed for the extra weight.

Then the engine, its carburettor choking with ice, began to splutter and, down to 7,000 feet, the aircraft was tumbling, virtually out of control. Nesbitt-Dufort got on the intercom to his two passengers — whom he had tried unsuccessfully to rouse earlier in the flight — and told them, in no uncertain terms, that they should prepare to bail out. There was no reply from them and he soon realized to his horror that they had failed to don their helmets for the flight so were unable to receive the command. They had, in fact, also failed to fit their parachutes but with no visual communication between a Lysander pilot and his passengers, Nesbitt-Dufort would not have known this. All he did know was that if his 'Joes' were sitting tight, he would have to do the same. At 5,000 feet, he pointed the nose downwards in an attempt to gain speed to have enough control to turn the plane through 180 degrees in a desperate attempt to retreat from the storm. At any moment, he expected the wings to come off in the turbulence but, to his astonished relief, with the altimeter reading 900 feet, he broke cloud. The engine, although still extremely weak at first, picked up enough for him to fly on for an hour until, very short of fuel, he put down in a field. The field, unfortunately, had an unseen ditch running across it which caught the Lysander's undercarriage, tipping it onto the propeller and throwing pilot and passengers violently forward. Much later in his life, an x-ray revealed scars from a triple whiplash fracture, but at the time he assumed that he had simply cricked his neck.

Although he knew he must have landed somewhere in central France, Nesbitt-Dufort had no idea where. As for his passengers, they were asking where the car was to take them to London and expressed exasperated disappointment when told where they had fetched up. It took some explaining by their pilot to convince them how fortunate they were to still be breathing. They would later learn just how fortunate; that same night, thirty-six British bombers failed to return from a mission, nearly all their losses due to the effect of icing in the storm.

John Nesbitt-Dufort's abandoned Lysander is inspected by officials after he was forced to land in central France after encountering nearly fatal weather conditions on a return trip to England with two agents aboard in January 1942. The plane hit a ditch on landing but the pilot and passengers escaped capture and made it back to Britain a few weeks later. (*The Bertram Family*)

Orders were to destroy an abandoned plane in France but, despite three attempts, it would not catch fire, mainly because all the fuel had been used up. The next priority was to put distance between them and the Lysander and discover where they were. They made off across muddy fields and through undergrowth in the darkness and freezing rain which had now reached them, until they came upon a road and a signpost on which they could just make out the words St Florent. The three men crouched in a hedge while Nesbitt-Dufort pulled his RAF-issue survival kit from his hip pocket. Amongst its contents of Benzedrine, a compass, matches, a water purifying kit, chocolate and Horlicks tablets, he was looking for a tissue-paper map of France. By the light of Mitchell's torch, he fumbled with its folds until, spread out before them, they found themselves peering at a detailed map of Germany. There was also some German currency enclosed. After a moment's silence, Mitchell and Nesbitt-Dufort could only laugh at this administrative howler. Duclos, however, was far from amused and eyed the Englishman with profound suspicion.

However, Duclos believed he now knew roughly where they were, about a twenty-mile walk from Issoudun, the town close to which they had taken off several hours earlier. They continued their long cross-country trudge towards the town until, still five miles from their destination, Nesbitt-Dufort, close to collapse following his seven-hour ordeal at the controls of the Lysander, insisted on getting some sleep in an empty shepherd's shed. While Mitchell kept watch, Duclos went on to find help. At Issoudun, he had brazenly walked into the station bar and shaken hands with everyone present, using the secret *cagoulard* means of identification. A number of the railwaymen there were Freemasons and, mistaking his sign as a Masonic one, immediately offered to help him. Duclos returned to the shepherd's hut with a man and his motor car and three sets of railway track workers' overalls as disguises. The fugitives were deposited at a level crossing on the outskirts of Issoudun and shambled, in character, along the track towards the station. It had been the station master, M. Combeau, who had organized their cover and it was into his small trackside house into which they now disappeared where, for the next five weeks, the three men would be kept in hiding.

The station master, his wife and fourteen-year-old daughter shared their house and meagre rations with extraordinary hospitality and goodwill, considering the risk they were running. They received news that the Gestapo had arrested the newly arrived priest at the village close to where the Lysander had crash-landed, believing that he was actually the English pilot in disguise. Nesbitt-Dufort, who could not follow the French conversation of his fellow fugitives and their hosts, was not told of this development until news came that the *curé* had convinced his captors of his innocence. They had been concerned that their English friend would have given himself up to save the priest and exposed them all under torture. The release of the priest meant a renewed effort to find the real pilot and passengers and the station master's house was thoroughly searched with the fortunate exception of a tiny basement where the three men hid behind some plate-layers' tools. German hackles must have been further raised when the man they hired to salvage the abandoned Lysander contrived to get its tail wheel caught in the tracks as it was hauled across a level crossing, suspiciously close to the pulverizing arrival of an express train.

While Duclos and Mitchell had identification papers and could therefore venture out into the town, Nesbitt-Dufort could never leave the house until, with typical nerve and resourcefulness, Duclos succeeded in stealing a blank *carte d'identité* from the town hall and, by cutting a stamp from a rubber heel, supplied instant fake French citizenship to the Englishman. Meanwhile, Mitchell had taken the considerable risk of a trip to Paris where he hoped, via his Franco-Polish network, to make radio contact with London to let them know that they were still alive and that they needed a plane out. He returned several days later with the news that the RAF would make the unprecedented move of sending a twin-engine plane, powerful enough to carry the three men plus a Polish General, also on the run, who would join them on the night they were due to go.

A disused airfield close to Issoudun had been identified by Mitchell, photographed by RAF air reconnaissance and okayed by 619 Squadron as suitable for a night landing by an Avro Anson. Finally, on the evening of 1 March, the eagerly anticipated coded BBC message came through and the four men made the arduous journey on foot to the airfield. Nesbitt-Dufort was very concerned, when they got there, that the grass field was barely firm enough to take the weight of this 3½ ton aircraft. The plane eventually came in at 12.30 a.m. and made a good landing but, with all men and luggage on board, the wheels stuck in the mud when the pilot opened the throttles for take-off. Nesbitt-Dufort knew what to do, however, and shouted to his fellow passengers to copy him and bounce up and down. The ploy worked and the Anson began to roll forward and then accelerate.

Once in the air, Nesbitt-Dufort went forward to find out which pilot had pioneered this daring landing in such an unconventional aircraft and was delighted to find his close colleague Sticky Murphy at the controls. He was greeted with the words: 'John, you old bastard! You stink like the Paris Metro. Get the ruddy undercart up, will you?'

On hearing that Nesbitt-Dufort had survived the dreaded report of 'missing, believed killed on operations', Murphy had volunteered to fly the mission. The flight touched down at Tangmere three hours later without further incident, blazing a trail of encouragement for the later twin-engine pick-ups using

Hudsons. Four very happy and relieved passengers disembarked from the plane and were quickly immersed in the customary celebratory hospitality at the cottage.

They could have been forgiven for not thinking of it at the time, but they would later ruefully reflect that, contained in the courier that they would have delivered five weeks earlier without their mishap, was intelligence that the battle cruisers *Scharnhorst* and *Gneisenau* were about to leave Brest for a dash up the Channel. By the time the packages were finally opened and deciphered, the two ships, between 11 and 13 February, had already famously slipped through the Royal Navy's hands and were moored safely in German waters.

After his safe return to Tangmere, the authorities decided that John Nesbitt-Dufort should be moved from special duties flying. This was no reflection of his conduct, for which he had already been awarded the Distinguished Service Order, but because they felt that he knew too much about both the SIS and SOE circuits and their agents' identities in France to risk his capture and torture if things went wrong again over France. The mantle of most experienced pick-up pilot was therefore passed to his friend and saviour, Squadron Leader 'Sticky' Murphy.

Murphy, from all accounts, was a cheerful, athletic extrovert whose limpid drawl reminded his fellow officers of the film actor, Leslie Howard. His very first Lysander mission, on the night of 8 December 1941, could easily have been his last. He was to pick up an SOE agent from a disused airfield near the southern Belgian town of Neufchâteau but, when he arrived over the airfield, the familiar 'L' of lights was visible but the signal being flashed was not the agreed Morse code letter. Wanting to believe that the agent had simply made a mistake or was even in some kind of distress, Murphy decided to go ahead with the landing. Seconds before touching down, his landing light showed a deep depression in the ground ahead so he opened the throttle and flew round again. This time he chose to land a considerable distance from the flare path and sat waiting with his engine running and his pistol at the ready.

Suddenly out of the darkness came what seemed to be an explosion accompanied by a series of bright flashes. He was being fired at by an advancing company of German soldiers. Instinctively, he thrust the throttle lever forward and the Lysander, apparently in working order, was airborne again after a run-up of less than forty yards. Murphy had been hit by a bullet in the neck and, after he had gained some height and set a course for Tangmere, he pulled out a silk stocking which belonged to his wife and which he always carried as a talisman and wound it round his neck to reduce the bleeding. By the time he could call the tower at Tangmere, his voice had become drowsy from loss of blood. His course had also become erratic but thanks to the control tower's arduous efforts to keep him awake by reciting the most obscene limericks they could remember, he made it home. The Lysander was found to be peppered with some thirty bullet holes.

Back in Belgium, the agent Captain Jean Cassart was also nursing a bullet wound in the arm. He, his radio operator and another helper had been surprised by the German soldiers just as they were about to switch on the flare path lights. All three had managed to escape into the darkness amid a volley of German bullets. Cassart, hidden beneath the wall of Neufchâteau cemetery, willed the Lysander pilot not to land as he watched the Germans light the three torches.

In spite of his eventual capture and incarceration in Germany, Cassart made a miraculous escape while being tried in a Berlin courtroom and eventually made it back to England and survived the war. Sticky Murphy was sadly not so fortunate. He recovered from his neck wound and went on to fly five more wholly successful special duties missions. These included one that airlifted Gilbert Renault from a snow-covered field near St Saëns, between Dieppe and Rouen in the occupied zone, and the Anson pick-up of the following March. He was posted elsewhere in June 1942 and, having reached the rank of wing commander at the age of 27, his luck finally failed him when piloting a Mosquito on bomber support in December 1944. His plane was hit by flak over the Netherlands and crashed near Zwolle, killing himself and his navigator.

Guy Lockhart, having risen meteorically from the rank of flight sergeant to that of squadron leader in less than three years, succeeded Sticky Murphy as commander of the Lysander special duties flight in June 1942. By then, he had already completed four pick-up missions from Tangmere (including the successful Operation Baccarat II described in Chapter 1), and had previously served with distinction as a Spitfire pilot. He had had more than the fleeting acquaintance with occupied France enjoyed by most Lysander pilots, having been shot down in his Spitfire the previous July, some twenty miles inland from Boulogne. Like Nesbitt-Dufort, he experienced the hospitality and bravery of those working under cover for the allied cause, being spirited first to Marseilles in the free zone, then on to the Pyrenean border where he was led across the mountains into Spain with a party of other fugitive British airmen. Lockhart was arrested in Spain and spent some weeks in the nationalist concentration camp at Miranda del Ebro before his release and repatriation in October 1941.

As flight commander, Lockhart continued to do his share of the work, successfully navigating his Lysander to an old airfield in the Auvergne, east of the town of Ussel and close to the limit of the aircraft's range. Here, he collected Léon Faye of Fourcade's *Alliance* network. A few days later, on 31 August 1942, he set off again, this time for a field among the vineyards of Burgundy. Christian Pineau's story, later in this book, will reveal the near disastrous touchdown.

By this time, 161 Squadron had six Lysanders at its disposal, plus one in reserve, to meet the increasing demand for pick-ups in France. The web of intelligence agents and resistance cells was continually growing along with the need to ferry key individuals in and out of Britain for high-level briefings, for training or simply to provide sanctuary from the Gestapo. Whereas in the early days there may have been one or two operations during every moon period, by the end of 1942, this had increased to as many as twenty if the weather was favourable. A string of individuals of appropriate skill and character were now drafted in to fly the missions.

They ranged widely in age and experience. The tall, laconic, jazz-loving 19-year-old Peter Vaughan-Fowler had applied and been selected after the signal asking for volunteers had omitted the word 'night' in its intended specification of 'at least 250 hours of night flying experience'. He had less than 250 hours in total under his belt but proved to be a very fast learner, completing twenty-six missions without mishap before his eventual re-deployment as a Mosquito pilot.

Pilots of 161 Squadron in summer 1943, (l to r), Robin Hooper, Jimmy McCairns, Peter Vaughan-Fowler, Hugh Verity, Frank (Bunny) Rymills and Stephen Hankey. (*The Bertram Family*)

On the other hand, John Bridger, older than the other pilots and a man of few words, was a highly seasoned recruit with 4,000 hours of flying already behind him. He, too, ended his time with the squadron unscathed after a dozen sorties, although only his handling skill saved him on one occasion in April 1943. His Lysander overran the plateau designated for his landing south of Clermont-Ferrand and, in his desperate attempt to become airborne again, he hit the crest of the ridge beyond, destroying one of the tyres of his undercarriage and flying through high tension cables between two pylons. Recovering his vision from the blinding flash this had caused, he brought his plane round again and made a successful landing. In order to take off from the field on an even keel, he punctured his one good tyre with several shots from his pistol. His eventual landing back at Tangmere was uneventful in spite of the punctured tyres, except that seven metres of thick copper wire could be seen trailing behind him as he touched down on the tarmac.

Frank 'Bunny' Rymills, a veteran of twenty-six bombing raids and twenty-four clandestine parachute drops, was still only 21 when he joined the Lysander flight. On the ground, he was inseparable from his cocker spaniel, Henry. A former student of architecture and an avid beekeeper, Rymills was also a skilled poacher, the mentality for which must have suited the nocturnal stealth and daring required of a Lysander pick-up pilot. He only spent six months with the squadron, but still carried out twelve operations, ferrying some thirty agents in or out of France.

On one occasion, in June 1943, Rymills forgot to switch off his radio transmitter while communicating with his two female passengers, Cecily Lefort and Noor Inayat Khan, as they flew over the French coast on their way to a landing site near Angers. Possibly to calm their nerves, he was pointing out how beautiful it looked in the summer moonlight and identifying towns and other landmarks to them. This was a double Lysander operation and it was with considerable horror that James McCairns, his fellow pilot, endured more than thirty minutes of this running commentary over his headphones, knowing that the Germans would be listening to every word. Rymills' indiscretion would not affect the safe completion of the mission, and all four outward bound agents (McCairns was carrying Charles Skepper and Diana Rowden) were successfully spirited away to take up the various assignments they had been given by the Special Operations Executive. Tragically, not one of this quartet would make it back to Britain. All were eventually caught and tortured by the Gestapo; Cecily Lefort never returned from Ravensbrück concentration camp, Noor

Inayat Khan was executed at Dachau, Diana Rowden at Natzweiler and Charles Skepper also died in Germany from the injuries inflicted by his captors.

James McCairns, or 'Mac' as he was known, had joined the Lysander flight in the autumn of 1942. Still only 23, he had flown a Spitfire as a sergeant-pilot in Douglas Bader's renowned 616 Squadron. McCairns' service alongside the legendary pilot that he so greatly admired was cut short in July 1941 when he was shot down, wounded and captured by the Germans. By the following January, he had recovered sufficiently to make a successful escape from his prisoner-of-war camp in Germany and had reached Belgium. Thanks to the Belgian underground and MI9's escape organization in Europe, McCairns was smuggled to Gibraltar and returned to the UK. During his concealment in Belgium, he had heard about the black Lysander operations and at one point was expecting this to be his way out of occupied Europe. Back in service with the RAF, he became determined to repay those who had helped him escape by volunteering as a pick-up pilot.

As a non-commissioned pilot with limited flying hours due to his incarceration, his application was scrutinized closely by the Tempsford commander, Mouse Fielden. However, the understanding he had gained of how the Resistance worked while he was on the run stood him in good stead and he was taken on. The decision was undoubtedly vindicated as McCairns went on to complete twenty-five successful pick-ups and earned the Distinguished Flying Cross and Military Medal, even though his second operation on 22 November 1942 led to his being temporarily suspended. It was a double Lysander mission with Peter Vaughan-Fowler and, as with all double missions, there was a strict rule that either both planes should land at the target or neither. Furthermore, Vaughan-Fowler, as the senior pilot, should land and take off first.

It was quite a short trip to the east of the Seine, between Rouen and Paris, but there was low cloud and patchy fog over France and the landing site was difficult to locate. The two pilots lost sight of each other as they searched for the agent's signal and radio contact was fitful. McCairns mistakenly thought that Vaughan-Fowler's brief and indistinct message that he was setting course for home meant that he had landed successfully and exchanged his passengers. Therefore, when he spotted the correct signal, he brought his plane down and was disconcerted to hear from the reception party that the other Lysander had never put down. Five people were waiting on the ground for their flight to England and the decision was taken to cram four of them into the Lysander cockpit — the first time such a number had been carried. Amid all the recriminations McCairns encountered on his return to Tangmere for having unintentionally disobeyed orders, he was able to take some comfort in the fact that the four he had rescued were Max Petit, an important operator in Gilbert Renault's network whose cover had just been blown, his wife and their two young sons. In fact, although he did not know it at the time, the Gestapo arrived to arrest the family only one day after their airlift to safety.

The man responsible for disciplining McCairns was the newly appointed commander of 619 Squadron, Wing Commander Percy Pickard. 'Pick', as he was universally known, was 27 and already a highly distinguished figure in the RAF and seemed a good ten years older to his contemporaries. He had earned the DFC, the DSO and a bar flying bombers and had led the famous parachute raid on the German radar station at Bruneval on the French coast near Le Havre in

February 1942 (about which more will be told in Gilbert Renault's story in the next chapter). He went on to become the first RAF officer to win a second bar to the DSO in 1943 as a result of his work as a Lysander and Hudson special duties pilot. Pickard's face was also well known outside the RAF because he had appeared as the pilot of 'F' for Freddie, a Wellington bomber featured in an Oscar-winning 1941 documentary, *Target for Tonight*. He was a tall, heavily-built man with very fair hair and a pointed nose. He was seldom seen out of his cockpit without his pipe and his Old English sheepdog, Ming.

He clearly also believed in taking some home comforts with him on operations. In January 1943, he was returning from a field near Issoudun with the former French ambassador to Turkey, René Massigli, and André Manuel, Passy's right-hand-man in the Free French intelligence service, on board. To his great concern, he could not recognize where he was as he crossed the French coastline. Trusting his compass, he carried on across the Channel but as his fuel gauge continued to fall, there was no sign of land ahead. At last, with the needle on empty, a rugged coastline appeared: it was the southernmost tip of Cornwall. Fortunately, there was fortunately an RAF airfield at Predannack, near Lizard Point, and he made it down without a drop of fuel left in the reserve tank. It transpired that the Lysander's compass had been affected by a metallic object in one of Pickard's flying boots. It might have been the bayonet he carried there or it could have been the stainless steel whisky flask he had shoved into the top of his boot after a fortifying swig.

As well as doing his fair share of Lysander pick-ups, Pickard was the man to demonstrate the suitability of the larger Hudson for moonlit landings in France. He developed the technique of bringing the aircraft in to land at a speed much slower than the 75 knots recommended in the pilot's handbook and needing only 350 yards to pull up on landing. He then flew 619 Squadron's first successful Hudson mission in February 1943, bringing seven agents back from a field south-east of Arles in the Midi. It was only a year later when, as the leader of a Mosquito squadron, he was part of the daring Operation Jericho, a bombing raid on Amiens prison to free resistance fighters condemned to death by the Gestapo. Although the raid succeeded, Pickard was caught from behind by a German fighter plane as he left the scene, his tail was severed and he and his navigator died as the plane turned turtle and crashed to the ground. He left a wife, Dorothy, and a one-year-old son.

Pickard's new Mosquito command and the posting of Peter Vaughan-Fowler to fly in the same squadron, together with other impending departures, meant that replacements were required for Lysander special duties in the later months of 1943. They came in the shape of four men, Jim McBride, Robin Hooper, Jimmy Bathgate and Stephen Hankey. Jim McBride, a tall, muscular but shy man was a product of Strathallan School in Scotland and St Catherine's College, Cambridge, who left university to join the RAF in 1940. His flying experience had been with Wellington bombers over much of Europe. Robin Hooper, an Oxford graduate, who had learnt to fly with the university air squadron, had entered the Foreign Office before the war but had persuaded his masters to let him pursue active service with the RAF when hostilities began. He had already been carrying out special duties with 138 Squadron, parachuting agents and supplies as a Halifax pilot.

Jimmy Bathgate was a small, fair-haired New Zealander, an accomplished pilot and a scrupulously careful navigator. In ten missions between September and December 1943, he carried twenty-seven passengers in and out of France. On the night of 10 December, he set out from Tangmere on a double Lysander operation with Capitaine Claudius Four on board, an important co-ordinator of the Resistance in central France. Jim McBride was flying the other aircraft and their target was a field near Laon, to the north of Reims. The weather was very poor and it was no surprise to the ground crew at Tangmere when McBride reported a failed mission on his return. To their mounting concern and ultimate dismay, there was no second Lysander home that night. No one knew what had happened and it was only six months later that news came out of France that Bathgate's plane had been shot down near a German night-fighter base at Juvincourt on the Laon to Reims road. Both he and his outward bound passenger had been killed.

It was after sombre events such as Bathgate's failure to get home that pilots of the squadron looked to the most flamboyant of their number, Stephen Hankey, to lift them from their gloom. If his patrician demeanour gave the brief impression of a Bertie Wooster, it was soon dispelled by his sharp and outrageous wit and a resourcefulness which would not allow the strictures of his and his fellow pilots' military life get in the way of their well-being. 'Any bloody fool can be uncomfortable', he would say as he organized, against all regulations, to install his wife and two young daughters in a cottage close to Tangmere. He had made a similar arrangement at the beginning of the war, finding a flat in Paris for his wife so that he could make frequent visits from his posting with one of the army co-operation Lysander squadrons which took such a battering over northern France prior to Dunkirk.

Hankey felt very much at home at Tangmere, having been brought up as the youngest son of a distinguished Sussex family in a large country house, Binderton, on the other side of Chichester from the aerodrome. Barbara Bertram, a long-standing friend of the family and nine years Stephen's senior, had watched him growing up and was delighted to welcome him, along with the other Lysander pilots, to her impromptu parties at Bignor Manor. The Hankey family had, in fact, vacated Binderton House during the war and loaned it to their friends Anthony Eden and his wife Beatrice, who used it as a retreat from the exigencies of a wartime Foreign Office. On one occasion, Hankey invited the Edens over to tea at the Cottage in Tangmere. After he had given him a guided tour of their establishment and introduced the pilots, Eden confessed that he had no idea that 'all this' was going on. As he was Foreign Secretary, everyone roared with laughter.

Hankey's flying career had only begun after a short spell in the army which had marked him with a broken nose sustained while boxing at Sandhurst and which sometimes gave him agonizing sinus pain when at the controls of a plane. After trying his hand as a salesman of Delahaye sports cars in London, he joined the RAF and, following his traumatic tour of duty in France, was sent to the Middle East to train allied aircrew cadets. Each button on his RAF tunic was from a different air force as a memento of this work. At 28, he came to 619 Squadron older than most newcomers and with very little night flying experience. He trained hard, however, to come up to the standard of his fellow pilots and flew his first mission, a successful pick-up to the west of Paris, on September 14, 1943.

The man whose memoirs we have to thank for so much of this information about the Lysander moonlight flight is Hugh Verity who, having qualified as one of its pilots in November 1942, simultaneously became its commanding officer at the tender age of 24. The son of an Anglican clergyman, educated at Cheltenham and Queen's College, Oxford, where he read French and Spanish and learned to fly with the university air squadron, he joined the RAF when war was declared in 1939. By the time he volunteered for the special duties squadron, he had flown bombers with coastal command and spent a year as a night-fighter pilot. These postings had not been enough to convince him he had yet quelled the demons of physical cowardice that had beset him on the rugby fields of Cheltenham and he was determined to prove his courage in the lonely night skies over enemy territory.

Although his book, *We Landed by Moonlight*, never makes it obvious, it is easy to deduce that this calm, courteous and competent airman commanded great respect from the unconventional group of pilots for whom he was responsible. He flew more missions than any of them during his time in charge and made as many life-long admirers among the French Resistance men and women as he did among his RAF peers. His book makes it very clear how important the bond was between the Lysander and Hudson pilots and the agents responsible for their reception on French soil. The chances were that the pilot and agent in charge of a landing would know each other well because they had trained together in England. Warm greetings took place up at the pilot's cockpit in the brief minutes of a passenger exchange and generous black market gifts of wine and perfume were thrust into the pilot's hand.

Hugh Verity had established a particularly strong relationship with one of the SOE's most trusted and frequently called-upon agents, Henri Déricourt. Déricourt, himself a skilled aviator, had come to Britain in 1942 via Spain and Gibraltar thanks to the MI9 escape network and hoped to secure a job flying for

BOAC. The MI5 vetting process for newly arrived foreigners channelled him towards the SOE, however, who took him on in spite of a somewhat equivocal report on his credentials. The Frenchman clearly had great charm and easily convinced Maurice Buckmaster, head of the SOE's F Section, to give him responsibility for organizing their agents' arrivals and departures in France. Déricourt's beguiling nature was such that Hugh Verity was moved to write to his wife at the end of their pick-up training together to say, 'I have a very good friend called Henri. I have given him your telephone number and told him that you would do whatever you could to help him, no matter when. Don't forget, Darling, even if he rings up after several years, to think of him as an old friend of mine. You will find him very nice.'

It is now widely believed that Déricourt was a traitor. His trial in Paris in 1948 failed to convict him and this was partly because his SOE masters seemed so reluctant either to believe in or admit to his duplicity. None of them gave evidence against him and one, Nicholas Bodington, appeared in his defence. German records have nevertheless shown him to be in the pay of the *Sicherheitsdienst*, the SS security service, and one of its officers had borne witness to his dealings with them. An even darker theory that Déricourt was a triple agent, secretly working for the SIS who were happy to sacrifice agents of the SOE to the Gestapo as they had been fed false information about where and when the allied invasion was planned, has yet to be convincingly proved.

The sense of betrayal must have been doubly bitter for Hugh Verity; not only because of his fondness for the man but also because he discovered that, on each of the eighteen occasions that Déricourt had led the reception committee for Lysander pick-ups, he and the other pilots had been delivering brave men and women to their near-certain capture, torture and death. The lucrative deal that Déricourt struck with the Germans meant that, while the planes were allowed to land and take off unscathed, he would supply details of every incoming and outgoing flight and individual on board. (The quartet flown out by Rymills and McCairns in June 1943 were probably victims of his treachery). He also made copies of all the messages due to be flown back to London and passed them on to the Germans.

The safe passage granted the unwitting Lysander pilots on some of their flights made them no less courageous. They understood very well the kind of fate that might await them if they were caught on enemy soil, especially as the war lengthened and stories got back about the Gestapo's methods of extracting information. It was only by sheer good fortune and by the bravery of those who sheltered them that every pick-up pilot stranded in France evaded capture and eventually made it home. By the end of the Lysander special duties into France in 1944, five more pilots besides Jimmy Bathgate would lose their lives, however — victims either of bad weather or enemy fire. Compared with other RAF wartime operations, the ratio of such losses to successful missions was remarkably favourable and testament to the skill and daring of the men who flew them.

CHAPTER 6: THE BIRTH OF AN INTELLIGENCE NETWORK

Gilbert Renault's Story — Part 1

Barbara Bertram might have found it difficult to believe that the determined and highly prized agent of the Free French and British intelligence services, who had bid her a tense farewell on the doorstep of Bignor Manor in the early spring of 1942, was the same man who, twenty-one months earlier, had found himself so paralysed by indecision at his home in Vannes, Brittany.

Gilbert Renault, alias Rémy, creator of the intelligence network, *Confrérie de Notre-Dame*. (*Musée de l'Ordre de la Libération*)

Gilbert Renault had faced an excruciating dilemma as the German army forced its way westward towards its coveted prize of the French Atlantic coast in the days leading up to Pétain's armistice of 22 June 1940. Every ship of the French Navy had been ordered to leave their west coast home port before the invaders reached them and sail either to British or North African waters. Renault had heard rumours that they were taking on board able-bodied civilians prepared to offer themselves for the fight against Germany and the squadron based at nearby Lorient was due to set sail at any moment.

At the outbreak of war the year before, Renault had immediately volunteered for the army but his age had counted against him and he had remained a civilian, pursuing his career as a film producer, having previously worked for a bank and an insurance company. He was a devout catholic and an ardent nationalist, subscribing to *Action Française*, an extremely right-wing daily newspaper that advocated the return of the monarchy and the reinstatement of Roman Catholicism as the state religion. Now, his sense of outrage at France's humiliation kindled a fierce desire to flee the French mainland and help perpetuate the fight from an unoccupied shore.

But to do so, this quintessential family man would be abandoning a pregnant wife and four young children to an unknown fate at the hands of the Nazi occupiers. They were not his only responsibility; he was the oldest of nine children and his widowed mother and five of his sisters (the sixth was married and living in England) would be left without his protection. Of his two brothers, one was serving locally as a marine and the younger, Claude, who was not yet twenty, had resolved to accompany Gilbert should he decide to make an escape.

It was his wife, Edith, who, in spite of her tears, helped Renault to make up his mind by telling him he should go. With two young friends of Claude, also keen to carry on the fight from abroad, the four men set off westward to Lorient in an ancient and temperamental Citroën. German tanks had already reached the outskirts of Vannes, but the Frenchmen's local knowledge allowed them to circumnavigate the blockade and eventually reach the harbour at Lorient, which was shrouded in black smoke after the fuel depots had been set ablaze by German bombers.

But the Navy squadron had already sailed and it was only by chance that they came upon a trawler, *La Barbue*, which was being loaded with 500 million francs' worth of bank notes and ledgers, salvaged by the Banque de France ahead of the advancing Germans and destined for Casablanca. The trawler was to provide the first leg of the shipment as far as Le Verdon at the mouth of the Gironde estuary. A sympathetic naval officer they had met on the quay helped them persuade the trawler's skipper to take the four men with him. There would be a better chance at Le Verdon for them to find a ship bound for England or North Africa.

Although their slow journey down the west coast of France was without incident, they were fortunate. Only a few hours after they had sailed, another trawler, *La Tanche*, weighed down with a crowd of young naval trainees, had attempted to leave Lorient. Twenty minutes out of the harbour she struck a mine, recently laid by the Luftwaffe, and quickly sank. There were only twelve survivors. On the quay at Le Verdon, Renault and his companions witnessed the hasty embarkation of a number of French politicians fleeing to Morocco as well as the British Ambassador and his wife boarding the captain's barge of a Royal Navy ship, waiting in the estuary to take him home.

They were still just one step ahead of the German ground troops although they only narrowly escaped a salvo of bombs dropped on the harbour by the Luftwaffe.

By pure chance, the four men, despairing of finding anyone willing to help them gain a passage to England in spite of the hundreds of ships moored in the mouth of the Gironde, came upon a man digging the flowerbed in his garden as they wandered aimlessly through the small town. He turned out to be the captain of the port, Henri Guégant, and became determined to help the quartet make their escape. He had been inspired by General Charles de Gaulle's first BBC broadcast from London two nights previously, on 18 June, and with sadness showed Renault his local paper which had reproduced a vehement disavowal of the general's words by the French government from their temporary Bordeaux headquarters.

Through the offices of the port captain, the skipper of a Norwegian freighter, the *Lista*, was found to be willing to take Renault and the others aboard his ship. That same evening, the fugitives were heading north-west, bound for Falmouth and on a route that would take Renault back past the Gulf of Morbihan, painfully near yet so far from the family he had left only a few days earlier.

At Falmouth, Renault and his companions were corralled with hundreds of other newly arrived refugees from France in a theatre building with scarcely enough space to sit on the floor. While they were waiting to be interviewed by immigration officials, someone passed them a copy of the *Sunday Times* which carried the shocking news that Pétain had accepted Hitler's armistice terms. Another semi-prison awaited the four men in London where they had been sent, having told the officials they wanted to fight. This was a makeshift recruiting centre for foreigners set up at the Camberwell

Institute in Peckham and from which they were forbidden to stray. Days went by with no sign of any call-up for them until Renault discovered a telephone booth and made a forbidden call to Kay Harrison, the London director of Technicolor and a man he knew well through his film production work.

Harrison was able to persuade the authorities that the Renault brothers were no threat to security and arranged for them to be put up in a colleague's house in Gerrards Cross. From there, they were free to pay a visit to General de Gaulle's headquarters at St Stephen's House in Whitehall. This was a day or two after the harrowing news had reached them of the Royal Navy's 3 July attack on the French fleet in the Algerian harbour of Mers-el-Kebir, in which 1,300 Frenchmen had lost their lives. While the French admiralty had considered their navy still to be an independent fighting force, the British, fearing that its ships would fall into German hands, opened fire when they refused either to hand over or scuttle the fleet.

Both Gilbert and Claude had taken great comfort in de Gaulle's angry but measured reaction to the news and were all the more determined to swear their allegiance to his cause — and, if at all possible, to the general himself. In the event, they had to content themselves with a meeting with a recruiting officer, but they were assured that their names were now on the list and the call would come for them in due course.

Waiting for that call was a painful time for Gilbert Renault. He spent long, hot summer days with little to do but lounge on the lawn of his Gerrards Cross hosts and read what he hoped were exaggerated newspaper reports of Nazi brutality in occupied France. Sometimes he would watch clouds drift overhead and imagine the same clouds carried across the Channel to France, soon to pass over his loved ones in

Brittany. He began bitterly to regret leaving them to an unknown fate.

A yearning to return home was what led him to pay a second visit to St Stephen's House and to put an idea to the recruitment officer he had seen a few weeks earlier. His passport contained visas showing that he had been given permission to enter both Spain and Portugal on several recent occasions while making a film about Christopher Columbus. He was sure he could get further permission to enter these two countries again from their UK consulates. Might that not be a means for him to regain French soil and to carry out some kind of secret mission against the occupation?

Renault was immediately referred to the *Deuxième Bureau*, de Gaulle's intelligence service, and found himself sitting opposite its chief, André Dewavrin, alias Captain Passy. This youthful but prematurely balding man, often nervously biting at his nails, showed little enthusiasm, it seemed to Renault, at his impromptu explanation as to why he was so well served with his business connections throughout France to carry out clandestine work. Passy, who excelled at succinct summations of his first impressions, recalls '... a chap of about 35, solidly built with a strong, rounded, slightly balding head. Full of go and dynamism, he spoke in a measured, precise way and showed an almost uncanny sensitivity to nuances.'

During the interview, a man in a lieutenant's artillery uniform had entered the room and shown a more demonstrative interest than Passy in Renault's proposition. This was Maurice Duclos, alias Saint Jacques, an early recruit into the *Deuxième Bureau*, who would play an important part in intelligence-gathering in France in the ensuing months and years.

Renault was again summoned to St Stephen's House where a less reserved Passy told him that he had spoken to his British counterparts who also thought his access via Spain and Portugal was valuable. He was instructed to apply immediately to the two embassies for an entry visa and to await further instructions. He should not set foot again in St Stephen's House and no one should know about their meetings.

Meanwhile, Renault's brother, Claude, had received his military call-up and was already at a training camp. His perplexity as to why his brother's application was taking so long turned to bitter astonishment when Renault eventually had to tell him that he had had second thoughts about abandoning Edith and the children and would return home via Spain in the next few days. It would be four years before the two brothers saw each other again and Claude could know the truth. If his brother's disillusionment was hard to bear, it was still less burdensome to Renault than sensing the distress of his wife, who would have no idea where he was or what had become of him. Any attempt to send a letter by post would have risked reprisals against them. However, an idea he had of sending a message via the BBC French service to his wife, containing nothing that could identify sender or recipient, bore spectacular fruit. He was invited by the BBC to their studios to read the letter over the air himself. Although the letter contained personal references which would leave Edith in no doubt who it was from, it also expressed sentiments of defiance against the Pétain/Germany pact and of extreme anguish at abandoning one's family to the invaders which would be felt by thousands of French exiles in Britain.

Renault knew that he had definitely been accepted into the world of clandestine intelligence when Passy told him to report to the British Secret Intelligence Service with a memorandum outlining the methods by which he intended to gather information about the enemy in France. It soon became very clear to Kenneth Cohen, the Royal Navy officer who received him, that this new recruit knew nothing about working under cover. Renault deduced, however, that it was his honest confession to that effect that convinced his interviewer that he was, at least, trustworthy and that they had better make the most of what they had.

The most crucial practical tool of all in his new role would be to be able to operate the system of encoding and deciphering messages between London and France once he was in the field. Renault's instruction in this was delivered in one brief session by a large, moustachioed, Scots officer in tartan trousers. The system was based on a random five-letter key that would change each time a message was sent. This was done by selecting a five-letter word from a book, an identical edition of which would be held by both agent and London. The sender would identify the key word by a number made up of the page, paragraph and word number in that paragraph. For instance, the code 161 4 23 would indicate page 161, paragraph 4, word 23.

Say this gave the key word 'under', it would be entered in a grid as shown below. Beneath each letter would be shown a number corresponding to its position in the alphabet. Then the message itself, for instance, *details required on U-boats in Brest*, would be entered into the grid. Then a second grid would be filled in by taking the vertical column under the lowest numbered letter, in this instance, D, and writing it horizontally into the grid. Then the next lowest numbered column (E) would follow on as shown below. This provided the jumbled message for transmission. To decode the message, the five-letter key would be used to reverse the sequence.

U	N	D	E	R
21	14	4	5	18
D	E	T	A	I
L	S	R	E	Q
U	I	R	E	D
O	N	U	B	O
A	T	S	I	N
B	R	E	S	T
T	R	R	U	S
E	A	E	E	B
I	S	E	S	I
N	T	R	I	Q
D	O	N	T	D
L	U	O	A	B

Learning how to work this code, along with instructions on the use of invisible ink, was the only training Renault was to receive before he was summoned to the Free French headquarters, now at Carlton Gardens. Here, Passy handed him his air ticket to Lisbon, a few dollars for his time in Portugal and Spain and some 20,000 francs for when he arrived in France. He stressed to Renault how he was primarily an agent of Free France and should only follow directives signed by him and that all messages to do with the administration of his network should be sent in a code only decipherable by the *Deuxième* Bureau. The fact he gave no indication of precisely how he was to establish an intelligence network seemed not to concern either man unduly. By chance, Renault encountered General de Gaulle himself on the staircase as he was leaving Passy's office and introduced himself proudly as one of his soldiers about to leave on a mission to France. The general, after a few brief questions about how he had come to England, shook Renault's hand and assured him he was counting on him.

Renault left the UK in considerable luxury aboard a Sunderland flying boat, which took off at breakfast time from Poole Harbour and landed him in the Tagus estuary at 5 o'clock in the evening. From there, he made his way to Madrid, a city he knew well and where he had several valuable friends and contacts from his preliminary work the previous winter on the Christopher Columbus film. To some, such as Mme O, a German woman who worked as an embassy official in the Spanish capital but whom he still counted as a great friend, he professed a view that the war would soon be over, with Britain going the same way as France, and explained that he had come to Madrid to continue work on the film. She was able to use her contacts to extend Renault's permission to stay in Spain from forty-eight hours to a month.

But to an even greater friend, Jacques Pigeonneau, the French consul in Madrid, Renault revealed his real reason for returning to Spain. For his part, Pigeonneau showed Renault secret correspondence he had entered into with de Gaulle, telling him of his intention to resign his position under the Vichy government and put himself at the general's disposal. De Gaulle had replied that he would be of more value to him if he remained in post. Renault's arrival on the scene persuaded Pigeonneau to do as de Gaulle suggested and he immediately agreed to receive reports sent by Renault from France and to deliver them to Passy's letter box in Madrid.

From Madrid, Renault had also been able to get a letter home. His hotel doorman knew an employee of the German embassy who travelled regularly to Paris and who, for 100 pesetas, would post Renault's letter in occupied France. For the benefit of German eyes, and hoping his wife would read between the lines, he repeated his sentiments about the war being nearly over and told her to bring the children to Madrid while he began work on the film. The letter got through and Edith was even able to send an answer confirming that she would make her way to the Spanish border. Meanwhile, Renault made a trip back to Lisbon, where he delivered messages and blank French passports (taken from the French consulate's safe and invaluable to Passy) via a British-run letter box. On his flight back to Madrid, Renault found himself seated next to a senior officer in the Gestapo, whom he entertained with some of the ribald stories about Hitler, Churchill, Mussolini and Goering that had been circulating in France before the invasion. When he landed, the news awaited him that, thanks to his embassy contacts, his family had made it safely to San Sebastian on the north Spanish coast. He was with them the very next day.

Scarcely had Renault installed his family in a Madrid apartment than he received an urgent message from London to return once more to Lisbon. He thought Passy himself had flown out to meet him, but he was confronted instead by an Englishman who identified himself as Major 'J' of the British SIS. He told Renault, somewhat boorishly, that he was his boss (at which Renault had to suppress a sharp objection — the French secret service worked in co-operation with the British, not in subordination to them), and gave him a rendezvous for later that day on the ferry across the Tagus.

As the two men strolled in the open air on the opposite bank of the estuary, the Englishman passed Renault a piece of folded paper and told him not to look at it until he was back in his hotel room that evening, where he should memorize its contents and then burn it. Mildly irritated and amused at such typically obsessive British secrecy, Renault nonetheless obeyed the instructions. The note consisted of twenty questions about the German submarine base that was being built in the Bacalan basins at Bordeaux. His first mission in France would be to find the answers to these questions and to find a means of conveying them back to London with the minimum delay. At that time, November 1940, sufficiently portable and user-friendly radio transmitters were thin on the ground, although Renault had been told that the British were working on procuring one for his purposes.

Having been able only to secure a one-way visa from the Spanish authorities to enter France, Renault nonetheless promised his wife that he would be back in Madrid for Christmas. His train journey across the border took him to Pau at the foot of the French Pyrenees where every shop window displayed re-touched photographs of the beloved Marshal Pétain. At his first port of call, Renault was shocked by the attitude of a friend and former colleague, Jean Ribes, whose country house lay near the neighbouring town of Tarbes. He had had no qualms about telling this man of his mission in France, hoping that he would become a key contact, lending Renault facilities at his Paris office as and when they were required. Ribes made it very clear that he believed Renault's enterprise to be hopeless, even though he said he could be counted on as a last resort. This defeatism, from a man he knew to be an enterprising, risk-taking businessman, was echoed in all the newspapers Renault found on sale at Tarbes railway station. Their sermonizing tone, implying that France had somehow deserved her defeat and needed now to earn her redemption under the strictures imposed by Pétain and the Germans, depressed and repelled Renault.

Although it was still by no means certain that London would be able to make a radio available, Renault nevertheless set about first in search of an operator in the hope that they would. Passy's office had given him the name of a café owner in Marseilles, apparently a patriot who could identify an operator. But to Renault's horror, although the restaurateur said he knew the man who had given his name, he had absolutely no contacts with radio operators and, anyway, would not support such an activity.

Renault made a hasty retreat, wondering how often and to whom the man would repeat the story of his meeting with one of de Gaulle's undercover agents. He took a train to Grenoble, hoping to find a more sympathetic reception and some leads from Passy's wife, who lived there in a small apartment with their two children. However, he was concerned to discover when he met her that there were a number of French servicemen in her circle who knew precisely what her husband's role was in London. Renault told her that inevitable gossip would eventually reach the police and she must prepare to take her leave with her children and that he would arrange for their safe passage across the Spanish border in due course.

Failing to find any potential recruits or radio operators in Grenoble, Renault headed west again to the Dordogne, where London had told him there was a man named Paul Armbruster, sympathetic to the Gaullist cause, who had fled the occupation of his native Alsace and was living close to the demarcation line outside Sainte-Foy-la-Grande. He should be able to help Renault find a way to cross the line undetected for his mission in Bordeaux. Agreeing to join Renault's embryonic network, Armbruster told him to find his way to the somewhat dilapidated château of La Roque near Saint-Antoine-de-Breuilh, on the river to the west of Sainte-Foy. This was the ancestral home of Louis de la Bardonnie, his wife and eight children. This local wine grower had already established a small local intelligence organization of his own in support of the Free French and had set up a method for crossing into occupied France, the demarcation line running close to his house. He had made his outfit known to London and was hoping to be sent a radio transmitter and someone to direct their efforts. Renault, arriving panting from the steep climb to the château on his recently acquired bicycle, was, whether he knew it or not, about to fulfil the second of these requirements.

Louis de La Bardonnie's château La Roque, close to Sainte Foy-la-Grande on the Dordogne where Renault began to build his network and where the first radio link with London was established. (*Edward Wake-Walker*)

After a convivial dinner at the château, Renault realized that the time had finally come to place himself in genuine danger. The next evening, he was to make the crossing into enemy territory and, for the first time since he had left Vannes, he felt fear. The demarcation line crossed the main road between Bergerac and Bordeaux and ran along a small tributary to the Dordogne called the Lidoire. De la Bardonnie, who had a pass to cross the line, cycled with Renault as darkness fell to a farm which lay just beside the main road and about 500 metres short of the German control point. The farmer and his family then took welcoming charge of Renault, while de la Bardonnie set off on his bike to cross the frontier, ready to receive Renault on the other side.

Meanwhile, Renault was escorted in darkness and in silence across a large field which ran beside the main road. At one point, his escort whispered to him that next time he should not wear his raincoat. Its colour was too light and potentially visible from the road. They were only about 100 metres from the checkpoint when they reached the stream. It was not too full of water and Renault was instructed to take off his shoes and socks and roll his trousers up to his knees. He slipped on the steep and muddy bank and landed in the water with a loud splash. After an anxious pause, he heard a faint whistle from the opposite bank giving him the all clear and he waded the five-metre width of the stream to the opposite bank. De la Bardonnie was there ready to haul him up the slope and lead him to a small farmhouse tucked beneath the embankment of the main road. Here, another farming family, the Rambauds, greeted him warmly, gave him a glass of blackcurrant brandy and a bowl of steaming water into which to plunge his frozen feet. Renault would get to know the Rambauds well on his future crossings of the line, on one occasion arriving naked at their door having had to remove all his clothes to cross the Lidoire in winter spate.

The river Lidoire, tributary to the Dordogne, at the point where Gilbert Renault would wade across at night to enter and leave the occupied zone. (*Edward Wake-Walker*)

After this brief interlude, de la Bardonnie checked the main road for border guards, beckoned Renault across it and led him to a car parked off the road on the other side. It was driven by a doctor friend of de la Bardonnie, who took them westward along the main road and then north to the doctor's house in the small town of Puisseguin. Here, Renault was reunited with his suitcase which de la Bardonnie had carried across the line on the back of his bicycle, and a sumptuous dinner was served up. The doctor had invited two friends from Bordeaux who offered to help Renault, one of whom, a postmaster, said he had details of all the anti-aircraft gun emplacements.

The next day, Renault set to work in earnest and with an astonishing energy which would characterize his entire mission during the war. In Bordeaux, he did not get any nearer the answers he needed about the U-boat pens, the area being closed off to French civilians. Through a Breton sea captain he knew who was working in Bordeaux, he did, however, make contact with a radio operator aboard a laid-up freighter who agreed to work for Renault if and when he obtained a transmitter. Wasting no time, he then caught a train to Nantes as he had been asked to include the entire French Atlantic coast in his intelligence-gathering and had much ground to cover. Jacques Pigeonneau had mentioned to Renault in Madrid, that the parents of a certain Marc de Saint-Denis, who lived in Nantes, had been enquiring through diplomatic channels about their son, of whom they had heard nothing since his attempt to get to England ahead of the German occupation. Renault was now about to pay these worried parents a visit and tell them their son had safely reached London because, by coincidence, he had also been aboard the Norwegian freighter, the *Lista*, on her passage to Falmouth back in June.

The delighted couple were eager to give Renault any assistance they could in Nantes and introduced him to their jovial and obliging wine merchant, Alphonse Lavédrine, whose calls on his German customers had given him close access to the construction site of a new submarine base at St Nazaire. Renault dictated to him the same list of questions he had been given for the Bordeaux base and then set off for his home town of Vannes, where he was able to surprise and delight his mother and sisters by arriving at daybreak at their front door. Learning, to his relief, that the Germans had not bothered his family and had not been concerned about Claude's and his absence from home, Renault set about further recruitment. Two young men who were friends of the family and whom Renault code-named Lavocat and Prince undertook to work for the network around Vannes, paying particular attention to the nearby airbase at Meucon, which the Germans had begun to develop.

Renault also went in search of his brother, Philippe who, demobilized, was living with his wife and parents-in-law on the Ile-aux-Moines in the Gulf of Morbihan, earning his keep as a lobster fisherman. Philippe was at sea when Renault got there, but he nevertheless elicited a promise from his father-in-law, a merchant navy captain, to track down a radio operator for the network. Returning to Nantes, Renault discovered that the wine merchant had already completed his questionnaire, which indicated a sizeable installation under construction at St Nazaire. Even if he had nothing yet on the Bordeaux pens, at least he had something of substance to include in his first despatch back to London.

For its delivery, he needed to return across the demarcation line and make his way to Perpignan, where Martha Pigeonneau, the Madrid consul's wife, had arranged to meet him and carry the documents back across the Spanish border. Renault crossed the line by daylight, this time, and at a different spot to the north of the main Bergerac to Bordeaux road. It meant crossing a road patrolled by German guards and then wading across the Lidoire a little nearer its source. Once again, in the capable hands of the doctor and de la Bardonnie, he made it across without mishap and reached the safety of the de la Bardonnie château.

It was with some pride that he handed a bulging package to Martha Pigeonneau two days later in Perpignan, his first despatch of carefully encoded intelligence reports from behind the enemy lines. Renault was astonished to discover, staying in the same Perpignan hotel as him, two men he had last seen in Passy's offices in London. One was Maurice Duclos, alias Saint Jacques, the man who had persuaded Passy that Renault was worth engaging; the other was Pierre Fourcaud. Both had been sent on similar network-building missions as Renault and both were now destined to return to London (via Algeria, Morocco and Portugal) to report on their progress to General de Gaulle.

Renault felt he needed to make one more foray into occupied France before returning to Pau on 20 December, in time, he hoped, to acquire a visa to allow him back as promised to his family in Madrid for Christmas. The trip across the line and back went smoothly, and he was pleased to find that his new recruits in Bordeaux, Nantes and Vannes were warming to their task. However, back at Pau, it soon became clear that the Spanish consulate could not obtain his visa until after Christmas. He telephoned Edith with the sorry news and then decided to pay a visit to Passy's wife in Grenoble to warn her that her escape into Spain could not be arranged until the end of January. He was back in Pau on New Year's Eve and found a message at the consulate asking him to ring home urgently. Edith could barely speak; their youngest child, Manuel, just eighteen months old, had contracted diphtheria and had died on Christmas night.

Renault did eventually obtain permission to return to Spain where he was able to witness the birth of his next son in January 1941. The event helped to distract the family from the hammer-blow of their loss and, meanwhile, other issues began to force themselves in on Renault's grief. First was the operation to smuggle the first radio, codenamed Romeo, into France and to bring Mme Dewavrin and her children back into Spain. This was successfully accomplished by Fourcaud, now back in France, and Pigeonneau, who drove his official car across the border to deliver the radio, hidden in a large leather suitcase and weighing some thirty kilos, and collect the fugitives. Second was the fact that the Spanish authorities were becoming suspicious of Renault. Through his diplomatic contacts, he learned that his arrest was imminent; he would receive one last visa to re-enter France, but could never expect to return.

For the next two months, Renault worked at a feverish pace. Knowing that the Germans had turned their attention away from an imminent invasion of Britain and were instead concentrating effort and resources on a massive U-boat offensive against transatlantic shipping, he was frustrated by how little he was able to pass on about *Kriegsmarine* activity on the Atlantic coast. What little information he was getting was losing its currency in the time taken to get reports back to London. The smuggled radio transmitter turned out be badly damaged and was under repair in Marseilles and therefore of no use.

This became particularly galling, as London had now parachuted in a trained operator for use by Fourcaud and Renault, who was kicking his heels at the de la Bardonnie château. Moreover, Renault had recently uncovered and enlisted two priceless new sources of information: one, the former harbour master at Bordeaux, Jean Fleuret; and the other, one of very few French navy officers being kept in employment at Brest. Not only were both able to supply all the answers to the SIS questionnaire, but they could give daily reports of comings and goings of every U-boat and surface vessel of the German navy in both these key ports. Lt Philippon, his Brest source, had even identified a radio operator for Renault, former shipmate Bernard Anquetil, who, in forced civilian life, was earning a living in a radio repair shop in Angers.

In spite of the risk, Renault was to make one more journey to Madrid. He had found that the Spanish visa office had erroneously given him a return pass and the excellent new intelligence from Bordeaux and Brest needed to be delivered as quickly as possible. When he returned to France, this time on a one-way visa, he had with him on the train not only his entire family but also a second radio transmitter hidden in a diplomatic postal sack provided by Pigeonneau. Thanks to the enthusiastic co-operation of a French customs official based at the Spanish border town of Canfranc, as well as a sympathetic engine driver on the border crossing line, on the same trip, Renault was able to establish a system of getting written despatches back to Madrid.

Edith Renault was delighted to be back in France, where she would at least have a chance of seeing her husband occasionally. They were temporarily accommodated in Pau, but later moved to Sainte-Foy to be near de la Bardonnie's house. It was here where, at last, the first successful radio contact was made with London; the first of the two transmitters had been repaired but would have to stay in the unoccupied zone and be shared by Fourcaud and Renault, as the second one had also been found to be inoperable and in need of repair in Marseilles. At this time, de la Bardonnie had not only the risk of housing this first radio link and its operator, but he had also just been entrusted with a suitcase containing 20 million Francs (equivalent then to about £100,000), which had been despatched across the border from Spain to sustain the three networks that had now been built up by Fourcaud, Duclos and Renault.

Renault's network continued to grow with new agents recruited in Bayonne and the Vendée. He had also found an 18-year-old volunteer in Nantes, Paul Mauger, who would prove a redoubtable assistant in the town where Renault had decided to set up his occupied zone headquarters. Meanwhile, Philippon, his navy source in Brest, had some important news to communicate. On 22 March, the two German battle cruisers, the *Scharnhorst* and the *Gneisenau*, had sailed into the port flying twenty-two flags on their halyards, which denoted the number of allied cargo ships they had sent to the bottom. He was able to give precise details of where they were docked, and these were passed back to London. On 6 April, there was more to report; the *Gneisenau*, out in the estuary on trials, was attacked by two British aircraft. One of the aircraft was shot down in a frenzy of flak, but not before a torpedo had struck the cruiser's stern and she had limped back into dry dock where repairs would take at least two months. Again, he was able to provide details of exactly where the RAF could find her during her enforced immobility.

For all such information to get back to London, Renault needed to cross the demarcation line again, but first he made a detour to Paris to organize distribution of the networks' money. His friend Ribes, having shed his earlier defeatism, was prepared to act as treasurer from his office in the capital. At the same time, Renault, who was staying with Duclos in Paris, agreed, against his better judgement, to take back a hefty envelope of courier from his network, in addition to his own. The result was almost a disaster. Renault was arrested by a

German border guard while sitting down to eat with the Rambaud family, prior to his crossing of the Lidoire. The guard had seen him further up the road in the doctor's car and had become suspicious.

Without time to offload the bulging packets of intelligence, he was marched to a nearby control point, where, by extraordinary self-possession, he was able to convince the officer in charge that, as stated on his *carte d'identité*, he was an insurance inspector carrying out his business at the Rambaud's farm. Renault was clearly so convincing that the Germans did not even search him, and they let him go. By the time they had had second thoughts and returned to the farm, he was already across the Lidoire and on his way to de la Bardonnie's château. Rambaud's story to the Germans was that Renault had been back to the farm and borrowed a bicycle to return to the station to resume his insurance business in the occupied zone.

Over the next few months, there followed a series of successes, narrow escapes and disasters which would characterize Renault's feverish existence as his influence spread. Always on the move between his contacts, he spent some forty hours every week on trains across the occupied zone and spent most of the rest of his waking hours preparing and encoding reports ready for the next London-bound package. Useful information was now flowing from all his west coast sources, but none more so than from Philippon. Fortunately, the second radio, codenamed Cyrano, had been repaired and Renault, with the help of his operator, Bernard Anquetil, had smuggled the hefty equipment across the demarcation line. Through a friend of his uncle, Jean Decker, in Saumur, he had also set up a transmitting base in a private house in the town. At last, with the help of his young assistant, Paul Mauger, Renault was able to get his regular reports from Bordeaux, St Nazaire and Brest encoded and passed to Saumur for transmission to London in less than twenty-four hours.

Thanks to these new lines of communication, the British Admiralty had information as early as 10 May 1941 that deep-water mooring piles had been laid in the estuary at Brest, ready to receive a large German battleship — almost certainly the *Bismarck* — before the end of the month. Then, on 25 May, Philippon was able to confirm the battleship's estimated arrival in Brest in three days' time. The Navy would later acknowledge the contribution this information made to ensuring that the *Bismarck* never reached her French destination — she was sunk by British ships and aircraft while making for Brest on 27 May.

The Royal Navy and the RAF had further reason to be grateful for Philippon's efforts two months later, when he was able to inform them that the *Scharnhorst* was putting to sea and heading south on a probable hunt for allied convoys. Renault and his assistant engaged in a frantic dash by train down the west coast to pick up news of any sightings from agents in the various ports. He soon learned that the RAF had found their prey moored at La Pallice, near La Rochelle, and had ensured her inaction for the next four months after she had limped back to Brest. Philippon was constantly disappointed, however, by the small amount of heed paid by London to his reports. He had supplied extensive details of the harbour defences, U-boat pens and berths for the *Scharnhorst, Gneisenau* and *Prinz Eugen*, and had once brazenly walked into the Germans' port control office during their lunch break and copied the plans of the submarine barrier. To his dismay, he could detect no greater discrimination in the attacks on Brest as a result of his work, and the town's inhabitants continued to suffer heavy casualties while the key targets remained untouched.

All the time, more people were now coming forward to offer Renault assistance. He had found someone in Paris with links to a German naval officer who was selling the position of U-boats in the Atlantic at 50,000 francs a time. Highly suspicious, Renault nonetheless played along with the source and was astonished to discover that both co-ordinates he had paid for had been correct and the U-boats sunk. Paris was not strictly in his field of operation, being part of Duclos' territory, but the two network heads worked closely together with Renault agreeing to allow Duclos to use his radio operator, Anquetil, for his messages to London.

Working for two networks and handling the plethora of reports now coming from the west coast of France, Anquetil found himself under extreme pressure in his upstairs room in Saumur. It was not in his nature to complain, however, and even after he reported to Renault that he had recently seen a German radio detector van in the area, he was determined to continue transmitting, especially as he had news of the *Scharnhorst's* damage to report. When Renault, back at his Nantes base, deciphered an urgent message from London that all transmissions should cease immediately as Anquetil had seriously exceeded the security limit, it was too late. The Gestapo had found him at his machine. Anquetil had tried to run from his captors, but was gunned down in the street. Still alive, he was taken into custody for his inevitable interrogation and torture. He gave nothing away, and he was eventually tried and executed three months later on 24 October 1941.

Anquetil's silence saved what would otherwise have been the obliteration of both Renault's and Duclos' networks. Until now, for both these men, their activities had felt like some rather intense game. The loss of their radio operator changed everything. Someone had died as a result of Renault's work and he was wracked with remorse. Although he had trusted Anquetil not to talk, he could not be certain of it. Too late, he realized how lax his security had been — Anquetil had been all over France with him and had met just about all of his key agents on both sides of the demarcation line. Renault did all that he could to warn his contacts to hide the evidence of their work, but they all knew their fate rested on one man alone.

As the threat receded, Renault set to work repairing his damaged lines of communication with London. From now on, he would rely on a pool of radio operators who would know only one messenger from the network. At least three much more portable radios were needed from London so that both transmitters and operators could move around, making their detection far less likely. He planned this in co-operation with Pierre Julitte, Passy's special envoy, who had parachuted into France in May 1941 and was tasked with facilitating the networks' radio traffic. In the process, Renault made a visit to Paris to pass on a letter to Duclos' second-in-command, Charles Deguy, giving instructions to their radio operator.

He had a rendezvous at Deguy's office on 9 August, but the doorman told him simply that he wasn't there, without giving a reason why. He decided to take the letter to a cousin of Duclos who worked in an office in the Place Vendôme with other members of the network. He walked in on a scene of devastation and was grabbed by one of the two Gestapo officers who were rifling through the papers. Once again, Renault's imaginative ad libbing saved him. He feigned utter bewilderment and explained that he knew no one in the office except the young telephonist whom, he confided, with suitable embarrassment, he had come to take out for an amorous lunchtime assignation. The Germans dismissed him without even searching him and Renault hurtled out of the building and into the comparative safety of some back streets.

Duclos' network had been infiltrated by a German double agent, a Luxembourger by the name of André Folmer. Charles Deguy had been arrested, as had Duclos' brother and sisters and all the others who worked in the Place Vendôme office, except the cousin who had been on holiday. Duclos himself had been in Le Havre and, as soon as word of the debacle reached him, he headed south to the free zone and laid low in the Midi until a safe route back to London could be organized.

Maurice Duclos, alias St Jacques, one of Passy's first recruits into the Free French intelligence service and the collapse of whose Paris network almost brought disaster to Gilbert Renault in August 1941. (*Musée de l'Ordre de la Libération*)

If Renault had not slipped through the Gestapo's fingers, two networks would have disappeared at a stroke. As it was, one of the trails they were able to follow led to Renault's uncle in Saumur, who had allowed his photographic shop to serve as Anquetil's letter box for both networks. Although his wife was eventually freed, he would never return from Buchenwald concentration camp. It had now become obvious to Renault that collusion between networks was highly dangerous.

A great void in intelligence-gathering from the occupied zone had now opened up and Renault acted swiftly to fill it. He moved his centre of operations from Nantes to Paris and installed his sister, Maisie, in an apartment there to relieve him of some of his work preparing courier which, now that he was responsible for the whole of occupied France, was growing by the day. And every day of that late summer and autumn, news — some good, some shocking — would assail him. Four new radios, three of which were highly portable, were successfully parachuted into a field near Thouars, ready for distribution. His family, long separated from him in Sainte-Foy, had been given permission to re-enter the occupied zone and arrived in Paris before returning to their home in Vannes. Fourcaud, whose free-zone network had begun to thrive, had been arrested by the Vichy police at Marseilles railway station and, worse still for Renault, de la Bardonnie, his vital link across the Lidoire, had been the victim of informers and was now languishing in a Périgueux police cell. So, too, was Maurice Perrin, Renault's messenger between Sainte-Foy and Pau, thereby removing any means of getting courier out of France.

The police swoop on de la Bardonnie and Perrin had also included a visit to the hotel in Sainte-Foy, recently vacated by Edith Renault and her children, and where they were asking for a 'Colonel Renault' and his family. News of another ominous visit, this time to Renault's mother in Vannes by a man with a poorly disguised German accent claiming to have shared a cell with his uncle in Saumur and asking how to find her son, showed Renault that a net was steadily closing round him. The growing danger to him and his family did not deter him from continuing to build the network from his Paris base during the autumn of 1941. His introduction to François Faure, a demobilized tank commander who soon became Renault's second-in-command, led to a rich vein of new recruits, thanks to a small band of former soldiers who Faure had brought together to act against the occupation in any way possible.

Until this point, the network had had no name, but Renault now christened it *La Confrérie de Notre Dame* — the Brotherhood of Our Lady. He firmly believed that providence had been responsible for his own recent narrow escapes and that, just as the old kings of France had placed their realm under the protection of Our Lady, he could do no better for all those risking their lives under him than to do the same.

The *CND*, as it became known, was now a hugely efficient and productive outfit. It could boast uninterrupted intelligence coverage on the coast from Bayonne to Cherbourg. It was also receiving information from the ports of Antwerp and Boulogne, as well as the area around Reims and the forbidden zone in the east. It was using standardized questionnaires for all the agents so that the information gathered could be collated and corroborated centrally in Paris before transmission. A team of radio operators played cat and mouse with the detector vans patrolling the streets of Paris, and priceless packages of detailed information were building up, waiting for a route back to London. This red-hot courier included the Germans' own plans of their U-boat bases in Lorient, Brest, Saint Nazaire, La Pallice and Bordeaux, all gathered in a single coup by Alphonse Tanguy, an engineer working for the Germans. There was also a suitcase of intelligence obtained from a certain Henri Gorce, the only remaining agent of the Paris-based Polish network *Interallié* without a price on his head, following its disastrous betrayal by the infamous double agent Mathilde Carré.

By mid-November, London not only wanted urgent sight of this material, they wanted to see Julitte back in their offices and, more importantly, Renault for a debriefing and to issue him with new instructions. Their first move was to send in Robert Delattre by parachute, a radio operator who had been training with Sticky Murphy of 161 Squadron and who was to serve as the network's expert on Lysander landing operations. He immediately approved a landing field, close to where he had been parachuted and which had been identified by the Thouars-based doctor, André Colas, who had organized Delattre's reception.

The operation to airlift Renault and Julitte from this field in the moon period just after Christmas 1941 had to be hastily cancelled following the arrest of the doctor who had also been helping the 'action' arm of the Resistance. Both Renault and Julitte had been hiding out with their families at a nearby country mansion over Christmas — Vannes was no longer a safe place for the Renault family — and returned to Paris to prepare for the next moon's attempt. Once again, François Faure's connections came up trumps. A couple who ran a café in the village of Saint-Saëns, north of Rouen, would provide the safe house for the operation, which would take place in a nearby field.

Faure was keen to introduce Renault to another of his Paris contacts while they waited for the next moon, a well-known left-wing journalist named Pierre Brossolette. Renault the royalist was very dubious about involving a man of such opposing opinions, but was won over by his sharp intelligence and his fierce repugnance at the occupation and asked him to prepare a report on press coverage for London. This link-up with the socialists would prove a significant development in de Gaulle's efforts to bring disparate factions of the resistance movement together under his Free French banner. Brossolette, in turn, allowed the trade unionist and anti-collaborationist Christian Pineau access to Renault, who agreed, when he got to London, to request a Lysander passage for Pineau so he could pledge his allegiance to de Gaulle.

The weather thwarted any attempt to land in the Saint-Saëns field during the late January moon period. Renault and Julitte, their relationship already somewhat frayed, had thus endured six nights sharing a single bed in an upstairs room of their hideout café for nothing. But at last, a month later on 27 February, a sufficiently clear night developed and, at around midnight, Sticky Murphy's Lysander lifted out of a snowy field with Renault, Julitte and their weighty cases of courier crammed into the rear cockpit.

As the plane climbed towards the coast, Renault's first thought was of Edith and the children, once again abandoned by him in a Paris apartment. Then, as he peered down over the Channel, he was reminded that only a fortnight earlier, the objects of so much preoccupation by the courageous Philippon in Brest, the *Scharnhorst*, the *Gneisenau* and the *Prinz Eugen*, had slipped through those same waters to safety, undetected by the British navy; and that despite Philippon's radioed warning on 7 February, of their imminent departure from Brest. What Renault could not know was that only fifty miles to the west of him, another small but telling event in the war was currently in progress.

Several weeks earlier, his network had been asked to supply detailed descriptions of the size and nature of the defences of a

German coastal radar station at Bruneval, on the Channel coast between Le Havre and Fécamp. The War Office was eager to discover how far German defensive radar had advanced and planned a paratrooper raid on the installation to capture telling components and to destroy the rest. The same weather window that had allowed Murphy's Lysander into France had given the raiders their opportunity to act. In a very slick combined services operation, led in the air by Wing Commander Percy Pickard (soon to lead the special Lysander flight), on land by Major Johnny Frost (of later Arnhem Bridge fame) and at sea by Commander F.N. Cook, they achieved their goal, parachuting the airborne forces exactly on target, surprising the German guards so that there was little resistance until the end, and evacuating the paratroopers from the beach below using landing craft.

Apart from anything else, the raid was a propaganda coup demonstrating that Britain was no longer purely in defensive mode against Germany, and that she could strike out effectively, as well. The War Office was first to acknowledge that Renault's intelligence had been indispensable and so his safe arrival at Tangmere could not have been at a more auspicious moment. Whisked away to London by the possessive Major 'J' of the SIS, he was put up in isolated splendour in the Waldorf Hotel, where he was told, to avoid unwanted attention, he should eat all his meals in his room, even when entertaining visitors. Such circumspection seemed ludicrous to Renault after the risks he had been running in Paris, but he conformed and was gratified to find himself wined and dined not only by the head of the SIS, Major-General Stewart Menzies and the notorious 'Uncle Claude' Dansey, but also by General de Gaulle and his intelligence chiefs.

During his month in London, Renault paid a visit to the little church, *Notre Dame de France*, off Leicester Square. He had worshipped there often on his previous stay in London and was upset to see that it had suffered considerable bomb damage. Inside, he was even more distraught to find that the much-venerated statue of *Notre Dame des Victoires* had been destroyed. Confiding to the priest in charge that he was about to return to France, Renault persuaded him to give him the head, which was all that was left of the statue, so that he could give it to a sculptor friend of his in Paris to reconstruct the remainder to the correct scale. Renault's precious package that he had jocularly held up before Barbara Bertram in the driveway of Bignor Manor on the night of 26 March 1942 was, of course, the head on its journey to France. But if Renault had appeared carefree to his hostess that night, it was only a gallant show of bravado. The day before his departure, he had learned of the arrest of his entire team of radio operators in Paris. One of them must have talked and he had no idea what awaited him on his return.

CHAPTER 7: THE MAN OF THE LEFT

Christian Pineau's Story — Part 1

In February 1942, when Gilbert Renault first met Christian Pineau in the basement of Pierre Brossolette's Paris bookshop in Rue de la Pompe, he seemed to be more fixated by the voluminous fur-lined boots Pineau was wearing than by any part of the earnest discussion he was holding with his socialist friends, Louis Vallon, Jean Cavaillès and André Philip. Pineau, he observed, was offering trite, acerbic remarks which he clearly intended to be taken as words of great wisdom. The four men were, he said, 'already in the process of reconstructing France to a socialist model'.

If Renault was metaphorically holding his nose in the company of people whose politics were far from his taste, Pineau, in his recollection of the meeting, was more charitable about the newcomer. 'Renault's preoccupations', he wrote in his memoirs, *La Simple Vérité*, 'were different from ours. Politics, propaganda, opposition to the Vichy regime, rebuilding the trade union movement were not his province. He saw himself simply as a soldier on an intelligence-gathering mission and had come to see us, after consultation with his bosses, with the sole purpose of organizing my departure'. And it was thanks entirely to Renault and his network that Pineau would find himself waking up to the smell of frying bacon and real coffee wafting from the kitchen of Bignor Manor on the morning of 27 March 1942.

Christian Pineau, a trade unionist appalled by collaborationist
attitudes in France. (*Gilbert Pineau*)

Christian Pineau was 35 years old when war was declared. The
son of an army colonel, he studied law and political sciences in
Paris before starting work at the Banque de France in 1931.
However, a career in banking would lead him in a very
different political direction to that of Renault. Pineau grew to
detest the inherent power of money and, by 1936, had become
the secretary of the federation of bank employees, an affiliate
to the national trade union movement, the *CGT* (*Confédération
Générale du Travail*). In 1937, he founded the banking journal

Banque et Bourse but, by 1938, he had lost his job at the Banque de Paris et des Pays Bas because he had organized a strike. Instead, he dedicated his time to trade unionism, becoming the full-time secretary of the economic council of the *CGT*.

In the chaos that followed the invasion of France in June 1940, Pineau had fled Paris, where he had also been running the private office of his stepfather, Jean Giraudoux, the famous novelist and playwright who was Minister of Information under the radical Prime Minister, Edouard Daladier. After days spent on the roads with hundreds of thousands of other refugees, he was reunited with his family in a small village in the occupied zone, not far from Royan at the mouth of the Gironde estuary. It was here that he and his wife Arlette had their first sight of their German invaders, a procession of motorcycles, machine-guns, tanks, lorries and troops lumbering along the single street. In the silence that followed its passing, they both felt instinctively that their survival lay in opposing this force rather than accepting it. In the house where he, his wife and children and some of his friends had taken refuge, discussions about their country's predicament lasted long into the night. To his despair, Pineau realized that the split between those who chose to follow Marshal Pétain and those who would resist the enemy and any collaboration would end lifelong friendships.

'Why shed any more French blood for the English and the City of London? It's my own country that I'm interested in — that's why I'm supporting the Marshal.' So argued one of Pineau's oldest friends and fellow strugglers against the might of the bourgeoisie. Meanwhile, there were other socialist allies of his who were more ardent even than he in their belief that the war was far from over but that it would not take much more than a year to oust the Germans. At a stroke, the line that divided France was no longer between the left and right but between those impassioned to resist and those who reasoned that appeasement was the way to save the country.

Ever the political animal, Pineau was determined to cross the other line that divided France, Hitler's demarcation line, to find out whether those not under direct Nazi rule had a different perspective. Lacking any other means of transport, he set off on a marathon bicycle ride to visit a friend from the union movement in the Dordogne. Crossing the line at that early stage of the occupation meant no more than making a detour via a farm track and, once in the free zone, he found himself an object of fascination to the French military and police, who would stop him on his route and question him about life in that sinister 'other world'.

At Périgueux, he made an impulsive decision to postpone his visit to the Dordogne and board a crowded train to Vichy to gauge for himself the true motivation of Pétain's government. The mood among his fellow passengers seemed almost triumphant. At last, France was free from the chaos that socialism had created and they had in Pétain a leader who would put things right. The fact that half of France was under enemy occupation seemed of little concern. One young couple were entertaining their two-year-old child in the congested compartment.

'Where's Maman?' one of them would ask. The toddler pointed to his mother. 'Where's Papa?' No mistake was made. 'And where is the Marshal?' This time, to the glee of his parents, the child placed a stubby finger on his heart.

The streets and cafés of Vichy itself seemed to be overflowing with civil servants, young women in neat make-up and countless uniformed police and servicemen. Pineau came across a number of his friends, all of whom talked about a resurrection or a new order and were busy seeking posts in one of the ministries. A professor among them was so bent on saving France that he had gladly accepted the position of floor sweeper in one of the government offices.

One of Pineau's former trade union colleagues had done considerably better than that. René Bélin had been appointed Minister of Works in Pétain's government, adding his signature, among other things, to a new law redefining the status of Jews. When Pineau called to see him and asked how he could reconcile his militant union beliefs with such a regime, he was accused of nostalgia and of failing to appreciate how the new order had prevented France from falling into anarchy and offering itself up to the communists.

Back on the Atlantic coast in the occupied zone, Pineau realized that he was almost as affronted by the attitudes of his own countrymen in Vichy as he was by those of the foreign invaders. Since he had been away, however, the latter had further alienated themselves. Someone had cut the telegraph line between Royan and Rochefort, and the Germans had compelled local farmers and other workers to mount a twenty-four-hour guard on the line during the crucial harvest season. At the same time as imposing such disciplinary measures, the Germans were striving vainly to maintain a charm offensive aimed at demonstrating the benefits of collaboration. They were at a loss to understand what the locals found so hilarious about the impeccably arranged line of soldiers queuing in the street day and night in solemn silence for their turn in Royan's only brothel and, when Pineau's wife refused to dance with a German soldier when out one evening in the town, his commanding officer came over to demand why. Reminded that there had been this war between them, the officer insisted that it was all over and that they were no longer enemies. The response came back that this still did not make them guests of the country, to which the officer stiffly remarked that the French had absolutely no sense of hospitality.

Christian Pineau with his wife, Arlette on a pre-war summer holiday with his children, (l to r), Bertrand, Claude, Gilbert, Daniele and Alain. (*Gilbert Pineau*)

More certain now of how he felt about his divided country, Pineau returned with his family to their home in Paris. His aim was to bring together as many senior figures as possible from the disbanded trade union movement who were opposed to the directives coming out of Vichy. He and the former secretary of the civil service union, Robert Lacoste, set to work writing a manifesto that made it clear that there were still people in France who believed in the freedom of the individual, in the principle of human rights and the condemnation of antisemitism and religious persecution of any kind. They succeeded in obtaining the signatures of twelve former secretaries of leading unions, who agreed to promulgate its contents as widely and openly as possible.

They were interested to discover that, while the Germans showed no concern over the manifesto, the Vichy government were greatly upset by it, and Bélin in particular took it as a personal attack, warning Pineau that he was to publish anything similar at his peril. The signatories were delighted by the Bélin outburst and put the Germans' lack of response down to a policy of divide and rule, nurturing any seeds of conflict between occupied and Vichy France. There was, however, a feeling amongst this group, who began to meet on a weekly basis under the cover name of the Committee for Economic and Union Studies, that if they were to build effective resistance to the Vichy regime and the German occupation, some undercover activity was required.

The question for all embryonic resistance movements at that time — and there were several — was the form of action they should take. So much depended on how long it would take Britain and her allies to launch a counter-assault on occupied France. Other than the French language broadcasts on the BBC, there was no communication between London and those disposed to work underground against the occupation, so all planning was based on guesswork. The optimists, who believed salvation would arrive within the year, thought in military terms, recruiting potential combatants ready to supplement the forces of liberation when they landed. The more cautious, which included Pineau's committee, were more politically inclined, keen to turn French hearts and minds against their German and collaborationist oppressors and create a mood of resistance which could readily be turned into action when the time was ripe.

And to this end, Pineau and his associates decided to produce a clandestine weekly newspaper aimed not so much at bald propaganda but at circulating real news and information about the state of the nation, wherever it could be gleaned. The only tool they had at their disposal was a portable typewriter, but this was enough for Pineau to put together the first issue of *Libération*, which came out on 1 December 1941. Six copies were produced and each was sent to a different contact who had access to a Roneo machine. It was then up to these people to distribute as many copies as they could to sympathetic colleagues and friends.

It soon became clear to Pineau that there was a considerable thirst for the information he was putting out with reports coming back to him of the news sheet reaching remote parts of the provinces as well as all areas of Paris. But it was a dangerous game he and his friends were playing. The very nature of the task meant that a widespread web of informants had to be recruited and it was virtually impossible to erase all traces leading back to the editor. The situation was helped by a stroke of good fortune when Pineau, realizing he needed to earn some money to sustain him and his family in Paris and thanks to an influential contact of his, landed a job with the Ministry of Supply, with the responsibility of setting up a statistics office. This was an ideal cover for him, not only because it provided him with countless new contacts and sources of information that he could legitimately claim to need for his job, it also gave him unrestrained access into the free zone.

As the influence of *Libération* grew, Pineau was somewhat unnerved to discover that other resistance groups were eager to contact him. The little he knew about undercover work told him of the need to keep contact between groups to a minimum to avoid a domino collapse should one be uncovered. However, he could not prevent a number of his acquaintances introducing him to people involved with other underground organizations. One such meeting was with a certain Captain Robert Guédon of Vichy army intelligence who was acting on behalf of Henri Frenay, the leader of a large action-oriented organization. Guédon saw it as his role to bring together all the resistance groups, and was busy forming an armed underground movement in Normandy. Pineau was appalled at his lack of security, pulling lists of people he wanted to meet and copies of his own group's clandestine newspaper from his pockets, oblivious to the risks of a random Gestapo search at the exit of any Metro station.

Pineau refused to open up to any of these approaches, but they did make him appreciate that the Resistance urgently needed centralized co-ordination, guidance and support but also that this should come from the untainted direction of de Gaulle's Free French movement in London. And, as time went on, Pineau realized that he should be of considerable value to de Gaulle, acquiring, as he was, a unique, all-round perspective of France under the occupation. His job made him a regular visitor to Vichy, where he heard every nuance of opinion. There were those who felt it was better to have the Germans than the communists in charge and who therefore wished Hitler God speed on his recently embarked offensive against Russia. Others sensed that the war on the eastern front was an unfavourable turning point for Germany and, with the entry of the USA into the conflict after the Japanese attack on Pearl Harbor on 7 December 1941, they began to find it easier to suppress their collaborative instincts.

One man who had demanded to see Pineau in Vichy was General Léon de la Laurencie, who, until recently, had served as Pétain's ambassador to the Germans in Paris. He knew, thanks to the leaky Robert Guédon, about Pineau's undercover newspaper, poured scorn on the Vichy regime and claimed that he was the natural head of the resistance movement which, come the liberation, would transform itself into the government of the new French republic. When Pineau suggested that General de Gaulle might have other ideas, de la Laurencie smiled indulgently and said that he planned for him to become the military governor in Strasbourg.

One thing that astonished Pineau was the almost total lack of concern in the free zone that the other half the country was under foreign occupation. In Lyons, he attended a meeting of resistance leaders, none of whom showed the least inclination to disguise their activities and all of whom saw their role as opposing Vichy rather than the Germans. Pineau made a point of seeking out an underground group in Clermont-Ferrand, who were also producing a newspaper called *Libération* for circulation in the free zone. Here, he was encouraged to find in the group's leader a sharply intelligent philosophy professor, Jean Cavaillès, who had a far more combatant attitude towards the occupation itself.

Soon after this meeting, Cavaillès moved to Paris to take up a post at the Sorbonne and he was thus able to join forces with Pineau's group, *Libération Nord*, as it had become known. And it was at their meeting with other resistance leaders in Pierre Brossolette's basement that Gilbert Renault promised to set up Pineau's trip to London. Pineau found that some members of his own committee did not share the same enthusiasm as he did for this opportunity to ally themselves to the Free French flag. Although they understood the need for co-ordination and resources, they were wary of handing over control to those who did not understand the risks they were running. The free-zone resistance leaders were altogether more supportive when Pineau travelled south again to tell them of his impending flight, and asked him to elicit messages from de Gaulle that made it clear that he was a democrat and opposed to all that Vichy stood for.

Returning once more to Paris, Pineau was in for a shock as he left the train at the Gare de Lyon. His father-in-law, Tristan Bonamour du Tartre, was waiting for him with the news that the Gestapo had called at his apartment in the Rue Verneuil that afternoon. René Parodi, a founder member of *Libération-Nord*, had already been arrested. No one else in the group had been approached and this convinced Pineau that he had Robert Guédon to thank for his and Parodi's exposure. He had heard that many in Guédon's action group in Normandy had recently been betrayed to the Gestapo and as it had been Parodi who had originally led Guédon to Pineau, it was likely that the Germans had obtained their two names through one of Guédon's many administrative indiscretions.

There was no question of Pineau staying in Paris at all now, let alone returning to his apartment. He gave himself just enough time to call an emergency meeting of his committee who, although realizing that their lives now hung on Parodi's silence under torture, promised that they would continue to produce *Libération* in Pineau's absence, come what may. (Parodi died in his prison cell, unbroken by his torturers; *Libération* never missed an issue up until Paris's liberation in 1944). Pineau also consulted Pierre Brossolette about his flight to London that he was now all the more determined to make. The earliest possible time for this, he was informed, was the March moon period, still some six weeks away. The important thing for the time being was to get Pineau undetected across the demarcation line and for his family to follow him as soon as possible.

Thanks to contacts of the *CND* network, Pineau made a night river crossing at Chalon-sur-Saône to reach the free zone and eventually arrived in the Vichy offices of the Ministry of Supply with a lot of explaining to do about why he was there. To his relief, he found in the ministry's secretary-general a man, if exasperated by Pineau's brush with the Gestapo, not entirely unsympathetic to his predicament and prepared to give him a job as a supply inspector. A few days later, his wife, children and parents-in-law arrived in Vichy having safely negotiated a line crossing in the Cher district, despite his father-in-law's sneezing fit in a wood close the German checkpoint. Arlette Pineau, who had been suffering considerably with the stress of her husband's double life in Paris, was hugely relieved they were all now safely installed in Vichy. Pineau could not tell her that, before long, he expected to be back in the occupied zone on an even more dangerous mission.

The plain envelope delivered to his Vichy hotel told Pineau simply: 'Tuesday morning, ten o'clock at the bookshop.' He decided that his wife should know about his escape to England only by a letter, which would reach her after his safe arrival. Instead, he told both her and his employer that he was visiting his son from his earlier marriage, who was living with his godmother not far from Châteauroux. From there, he wrote to the ministry claiming that illness had prevented him from returning to Vichy. He then travelled to Moulins, where he used his *Ausweis* (German identity card) to cross the line with a group of factory employees on their way to work. He left the train for Paris at the outskirts to avoid Gestapo surveillance at the Gare de Lyon and spent the night before his rendezvous with Brossolette in a hotel close to Fontainebleau. Two nights later, as recounted in Chapter 1, Pineau would find himself safe under the Sussex Downs.

> Hurtling from one rendezvous to the next that he was determined to keep with countless British and French individuals in spite of our constant reminders about the need for strict security, he nonetheless picked up what was required of him as a network head very quickly. Full of dynamism and courage, he absorbed the thousand essential details with astonishing ease and then sought to dispel his fatigue by abandoning himself with childlike joy to the rare distractions of English life.

Such was Passy's recollection of Christian Pineau when he arrived in London, and certainly Pineau was quick to appreciate the good things about being in a country where, he observed, 'you could tell there was no foreign occupation and no treachery just by the look in people's eyes'. If his star rating in the eyes of the SIS did not quite afford him the Waldorf Hotel luxury meted out to Gilbert Renault, a flat in Park Lane and a car at his disposal seemed flatteringly generous to Pineau. Armed with a wad of notes, ration cards, the pseudonym of 'Major Garnier' and strict instructions about concealing his real identity from anyone he met — Major 'J' of the SIS, or 'Crayfish', as Passy referred to him, had been sternly insistent upon this — Pineau joyously set out to buy clothes. He could not resist a little box of coloured soaps from a shop in Piccadilly but, wide-eyed at the choice and quality of clothing on offer, restrained himself from too outlandish a wardrobe as he had been instructed to dress as inconspicuously as possible.

Pineau realized, of course, that such lavish hospitality meant that his British and French hosts valued his presence considerably and were doubtless expecting to get more than a little in return. As Passy pointed out to him on his first visit to Duke Street (where the *Deuxième Bureau*'s offices had moved under the new name of *Bureau Central de Renseignements et d'Action*), he was the first Frenchman to come to London from the organized resistance movements. From Passy's point of view, Pineau was important in a military sense, first because he had links with the combat-oriented groups in France who, when the time came, could be called upon by de Gaulle to join forces with the allied invasion and ensure French participation in her own liberation. Pineau was shocked to hear from Passy that an invasion was still some eighteen months away and wondered how some of the 'action' groups in France would sustain themselves for that long.

Passy also had his eye on Pineau as an ideal intelligence network head and, although it was not until the end of his month's stay in England that he would explain precisely what he wanted from Pineau in this respect, he organized an intense course of training for him at the hands of the SIS, to include encryption, parachute and Lysander reception, movement of men and material, and the protection of radio equipment. When Pineau began to explain to Passy the need for the Free French to show the resistance movement that they understood their particular difficulties under the occupation and explain exactly what they stood for, he was told that it would be better to discuss such matters directly with de Gaulle.

His first of three meetings with the General took place on the evening of his arrival in London in the shape of a one-to-one dinner at the Connaught Hotel. Pineau found himself greatly intimidated by de Gaulle's cool and somewhat unresponsive demeanour. There were no personal questions about his risky flight out of France, life under German occupation or the safety of his family; he clearly saw anyone prepared to side with the Free French as one of his soldiers with no apparent sympathy for the additional dangers of operating inside France. He wanted to know from Pineau the mood of the nation and its readiness to support him. He understood very little about the resistance movement and found it difficult to be persuaded that only a minority of the population were actively involved in it and that there were plenty who still backed the Vichy government.

Although he was quite prepared to send Pineau back with a message for the resistance movement and the unions, he struggled to appreciate why they wanted to hear assurances that he opposed Vichy-type dictatorships and that France should return to a democratic republic in any post-liberation government. To him, the priority was the military one of freeing France of German occupation and all collaborators; post-war political solutions were for a later date. Pineau himself did not doubt de Gaulle's democratic credentials, even though the General clearly blamed France's defeat on the weakness of the last democratically elected government, Léon Blum's socialist regime. One Frenchman, the anti-Free French journalist Louis Lévy, whom Pineau met while in London, assured him that de Gaulle was tarred with the same fascist-leaning brush as a number of those working in the *BCRA* (*Bureau Central de Renseignements et d'Action*). Although Pineau did not accept this, he knew many of his socialist colleagues back in France would need contrary evidence in the General's message to scotch potential rumours.

One thing that disconcerted Pineau in his conversations with de Gaulle was the bitterness he expressed at the attitude of the British to his efforts and the obstacles they put in his way. From the BBC broadcasts Pineau and his friends had so avidly followed, it had seemed that de Gaulle, the British and the

Americans were shoulder to shoulder in the fight against Germany. The General's observation that the allies still viewed Vichy as more representative of French opinion than himself would, he knew, come as a severe blow to the resistance movement. When he was called to meet Major Sir Desmond Morton, head of Churchill's cabinet office, he found a man who clearly lacked confidence in the influence of the Resistance and who did not wish to believe that the movement would support de Gaulle in spite of Pineau's assurances to the contrary. He still thought that many in Pétain's government were playing a double game and would be the most able to rally support for the allies when the time came.

Pineau encountered similar doubts about the popularity of de Gaulle in France when he visited the BBC. The Free French were given only partial control of the French language broadcasts, as it was felt they did not necessarily speak for everyone in the country. While repeating his message that the resistance movement was keen to rally under the Free French banner, Pineau also impressed on de Gaulle's main broadcaster, Maurice Schumann, the need to express a better understanding than the General was inclined to show of life under occupation, together with much stronger condemnation of the collaborators at Vichy.

Pineau and François Faure were dined out in style by the SIS top brass. General Sir Stewart Menzies impressed upon Pineau that it was through intelligence-gathering that the Resistance could be of most value to the allies at this stage of the war. He urged Pineau to hold onto his position in the Ministry of Supply for as long as possible, as it was an excellent cover and a valuable source of information. To serve the allied cause best of all, he should forget his reputation among his political allies and proclaim his faith in Pétain. That way, he could get even closer to sensitive information; some of their best agents in France were notorious collaborators, he assured him. Pineau knew that he had a difficult enough task when he got home of rallying the resistance movement under the Free French flag, without also apparently having sided with the enemy.

Menzies and his team were also adamant that isolated terrorist tactics by resistance groups were currently doing more harm than good, bringing, as they did, cruel reprisals against innocent French citizens. Such actions should wait until the eve of the allied invasion, although they would not or could not say when this was planned. By contrast, the Soviet ambassador to London, Aleksandr Bogomolov, who was also keen to meet Pineau for lunch, believed that terrorism by resistance groups helped to destabilize the morale of German troops, and any reprisals only served to turn local populations more strongly against them.

As Passy had observed, Pineau's hectic sequence of appointments were punctuated by a sampling of London's entertainments, including a visit to Mirabelle's in Curzon Street. He was fascinated by the clientele, almost exclusively young uniformed officers with their partners, dining and dancing, apparently without a care in the world. The RAF pilots among them would be flying over Germany probably the very next day; some would never return. Although large volumes of wine, whisky, port and cognac disappeared during the evening, no one showed any signs of drunkenness and when, at midnight, the band struck up 'God Save the King', all stood stiffly to attention as though the King himself were present, and then began an orderly exit to the street.

The April moon period was now fast approaching and, once more, Pineau and Faure would soon be putting their lives in the hands of a phlegmatic officer at the controls of a Lysander.

It was only when Pineau's training was completed that Passy revealed precisely what he wanted from him on his return to France. He asked him to hand over his *Libération-Nord* responsibilities to someone else and give all his time to setting up and running an intelligence network from the free zone, reporting directly to him rather than via the SIS. He should keep his job at the ministry at all costs, as this would allow him unique access throughout France and enable him to set up a sister network in the occupied zone in due course.

Although Pineau had not bargained on agreeing to such an undertaking when he arrived in London, he realized that if he did not accept the mission he would not return to France with what he had come for, namely the money, the means of communication and the support to allow the resistance movement to co-operate and grow. The other object of his visit, a message signed by de Gaulle demonstrating his compatibility with the ambitions of the unions and resistance leaders in a liberated France, was in Pineau's pocket as he sat at Barbara Bertram's dining room table, struggling through nerves to eat what was in front of him.

Amid his anxieties about his impending flight and the perilous cloak-and-dagger existence he had agreed to take on for Passy was the concern that, in spite of his repeated representations, de Gaulle had refused to alter his message to underline the iniquities of the Vichy regime. When he arrived at the Tangmere Cottage and was about to board Sticky Murphy's Lysander, a motorbike rider from London delayed their departure. He handed Pineau an envelope with a revised draft of de Gaulle's message without any accompanying note of explanation. The changes were small, but each addressed the concerns Pineau had expressed and would make his task of convincing fellow resistance leaders to follow the General that much easier back in France.

When the Lysander touched down at the *CND* landing site just over a kilometre outside Saint-Saëns, the reception party was in a state of considerable agitation. A company of German soldiers had arrived that evening in the small town and there had not been time to warn London to cancel the operation. The Tangmere-bound passengers, Pierre Brossolette and his portly *CND* companion, Jacques Robert, were shoehorned with their voluminous courier into the rear cockpit in record time. The sound of the plane taking off was enough to wake everyone in the town but, after lying low close to the field for some four hours, Pineau and Faure were led to the café safe house in the town, where they spent the rest of the night undisturbed. The next morning, they caught a commuter bus to Rouen, the German soldiers showing no apparent interest in two passengers with an unusual amount of luggage.

Pineau ran the gauntlet of a short stay with some friends in Paris to give himself time for a secret meeting of *Libération-Nord*, where he proudly produced de Gaulle's message. Although his friends were pleased to see him back, the majority were less than enthusiastic about putting themselves under the orders of the General. They felt that he could lead them into harm through his ignorance of the delicate and dangerous nature of operating under German occupation. This reticence, however, did not stop them accepting a sum of money Pineau had decided to set aside from the amount he had been given by Passy to run his network. Pineau also found a replacement editor of *Libération* and, most important of all, secured the enthusiastic agreement of Jean Cavaillès to set up and run the occupied-zone section of the new network, which they decided to christen *Phalanx*.

Arlette Pineau greeted her husband after his six-week absence from Vichy with the news that she was expecting their second child in November. Of course, she knew where he had been, but his boss at the Ministry of Supply observed that he must have been very ill to have been away for so long and expressed surprise that Pineau had nonetheless put on weight since he was last in the office. Pineau would never be able to explain the glint of malice that crept into the secretary-general's eye when he went on to announce that the minister had decided to promote him to the top of his grade.

Reaction to de Gaulle's message was altogether more positive in the free zone, with union and other resistance leaders, including leading members of the pre-war government (whom the message blamed for France's defeat), seeing it as an effective rallying call to their movement. Pineau used the mobility offered by his job to excellent effect, not just in getting the General's communiqué widely promulgated in centres such as Lyons and Clermont-Ferrand as well as in Vichy, but in simultaneously recruiting informants to his network from the most fruitful of sources, including even a member of Pierre Laval's cabinet, who sent minutes of their meetings to Pineau via an intermediary.

As well as money, Passy had promised Pineau the services of a radio operator in Toulouse by the name of Fontaine, and it was with considerable pride that he knocked on his door for the first time to hand over a veritable sheaf of scrupulously encoded messages for transmission to London. Fontaine, a young man, received him with ill grace, acknowledging grudgingly that London had asked him to work for Pineau, but saying he hoped it was only temporary as they had promised him a network of his own. Far from impressed at the volume of Pineau's intelligence reports, he was horrified, saying it would take him at least five hours of transmission and that most of it should have waited for the next Lysander mission. Pineau was forced to admit to himself that he was probably right when London ordered Fontaine to stop transmitting when he was less than halfway through the pile.

More support from London arrived by parachute that summer in the shape of two additional radio operators who were also trained in the reception of parachute drops and Lysander flights. One, an earnest young priest, would be based at Limoges and the other, a bearded 40-year-old with the code name Lot, would operate from Lyons. Pineau hoped that Lot would be of particular use to him, as he had been told that the nearby Saône and Rhone valleys were especially suitable for aerial operations. He was disconcerted to find, however, that Lot seemed more interested in his own comfort and remuneration than the job of intelligence transmission. He argued that his dangerous task entitled him to eat in the best black market restaurants regardless of the fact that police officers were their best customers and the risk of arousing suspicion would be great. So Pineau continued to keep him on a tight rein and, although barely co-operative, he managed to run one successful parachute drop of courier and arms in the Beaujolais region.

Pineau began to be concerned that his network was not functioning as well as it could; not because of the lack of good intelligence, but because of the time it took to relay it back to London. The problem was especially acute for Cavaillès in the occupied zone where they had no radios and had to send their entire courier by messenger to Pineau. As he had been asked to organize the reception of a Lysander flight during the late August moon of 1942 and there was no designated return passenger, Pineau requested that he return to London on the flight to organize better lines of communication to and from the north.

Although the Ministry of Supply seemed quite happy for Pineau to be away from his office for weeks at a time so long as his reports kept coming in, and his wife resigned herself to another absence, Lot, the radio operator, was dead set against his departure. Pineau knew why; he feared that his boss would complain to the BCRA about his poor attitude. When the evening of the operation came, Lot stated categorically to the reception party that he had not received any radioed confirmation that the plane was coming. A little later, however, the BBC, in its coded messages, made it perfectly clear that the operation was indeed on. At the allotted hour, the party set off for the field close to the east bank of the river Saône, north of Mâcon, which they all knew well. It was Lot, in charge of marking out the landing area, who manned the torch at the touchdown end of the 'L' and who flashed the agreed recognition letter as the Lysander rumbled into view.

Seconds after landing, the plane, decelerating, suddenly slumped down into the ground to the sound of disintegrating metal. The next moment, the pilot was out of the plane, gesticulating wildly — the undercarriage had been completely shattered after he had hit a ditch two-thirds of the way along the flare path. There was no way that Lot could have failed to see the ditch when he marked out the field. Guy Lockhart, who was the victim of this unhappy landing, was not going to waste any time. He had no outward passenger, only courier, which he began to bundle into the arms of the Frenchmen around him, telling them in his strong English accent that he would join them on the road in a moment.

Minutes later, there was a loud explosion and the limping figure of Lockhart, silhouetted against his brightly burning plane, came running towards Pineau and his team. Having obeyed the order to set fire to an abandoned Lysander, he was now, for better or worse, putting himself in the hands of the people who had just brought about its incapacitation. As the group made their way silently but swiftly away from the blazing wreckage, visible for miles around, Pineau agonized over what he should do about Lot, trudging along by his side. In his memoirs, *La Simple Vérité*, he wrote:

> My hand was on my revolver. Did I have the right to kill this man? He was responsible for the accident; his betrayal was not to help the enemy but to save his own skin because he was afraid of how he would be judged by his bosses. He deserved to die, without a doubt. Any military tribunal would pass a death penalty. But here there was no judge, no council for the defence. As head of the network I was perfectly within my rights to execute any individual endangering an operation. But was he still a danger? If he had tried to run away, I would have shot him without any hesitation. He was just there, beside me, keeping pace. It would have been so easy simply to lift the gun to the nape of his neck and to press the trigger. But it would be killing a man in cold blood. I had never realized what it meant to make that decision to take a human life, let alone actually to carry it out...

They reached a level crossing and, full of remorse at failing in his duty as he saw it, Pineau knew that Lot would live. There were now other things to worry about: they needed to get to Mâcon without using the roads, which would be alive with police investigating the blaze, and Lockhart needed to put on some civilian clothes. The RAF man had remained surprisingly sanguine, considering he could easily have just been killed. Instead, with only a slight knock on his knee, he seemed almost to be enjoying the situation, treating it rather like a game.

The decision was taken to walk the ten kilometres to Mâcon along the railway line. When Lot announced that he would prefer not to go with them, Pineau ordered him, in no uncertain terms, to accompany the rest of the party and told him that if he really did not understand his situation, he would readily explain it. They reached Mâcon station without incident, although Lockhart was white with fatigue, and boarded a train for Lyons. Pineau disembarked with Lockhart on the outskirts of Lyons to take the pilot to the house of the underground journalist, Yves Farge, who agreed to hide him for a few days. Before he left the train, however, Pineau handed over a note for one of the party to give to a high-ranking Lyons policeman who was a member of the *Phalanx* network. Three days later, this note led to Lot's arrest and incarceration for black market activity.

Meanwhile, Pineau, who, via a messenger to his trusty Limoges radio operator, was able to tell London that their pilot was very much alive, had a plan which would get both him and Lockhart back to England. A few weeks earlier, Pineau had asked Fontaine to set up a seaborne evacuation for a number of people, including Cavaillès in Paris, who needed to reach London for training and other important liaison work. The operation from the Mediterranean coast near Narbonne was planned to take place in a few days' time. He calculated that two extra passengers should not compromise the mission.

Lockhart, refreshed after two good nights' sleep in Lyons, proved quite a handful for Pineau on the crowded train to Narbonne. He insisted on engaging fellow travellers in conversation and playing games with their children and, when Pineau whispered his concerns about his marked English accent, Lockhart dismissed them saying, 'I'll just tell them I'm a Canadian'. When the insubordinate Fontaine met them at their rendezvous in Narbonne, he became furious. He claimed he had no space for two extra aboard the Royal Navy-run felucca which was to make the pick-up and ferry the escapees to Gibraltar. He had planned for five: two politicians, an agent from another network, Cavaillès and himself. When Pineau asked who had given permission for him to leave France, he said he had contacted *BCRA* direct and, because they would not give him a network of his own and he refused to work as second fiddle, he was going to London.

The upshot of this heated exchange was that all seven would-be passengers took up a hiding place in the sand dunes close to Narbonne-Plage to await darkness and the arrival of the small boat that would get them out to the felucca from the beach. Fontaine had divided up the party into groups of one or two to aid concealment, and the plan was for them all to head for a flashed signal from a torch on the waterfront when the boat arrived. Cavaillès and Pineau were together and, after peering into the pitch blackness for a considerable time, they saw the signal and stumbled through the reeds and down the dunes onto the beach.

Suddenly, three pistol shots rang out. The two men froze. The sound had not come from where the other passengers were holed up. Somebody shouted something to the left of them and then there was another shout to the right. They had no idea who it was and could see nothing. Taking cover once again in the dunes, they decided to wait. The boat would surely stay out at sea until the commotion had died down. They heard some more shouting that seemed now further away, then silence. After half an hour, they crept out to explore the beach; there was no one; nothing. Cavaillès thought he saw a light go on then off again out to sea but, as they stood at the water's edge, straining eyes and ears, all they could discern was the sound of wavelets breaking modestly at their feet.

The late moon was coming up now and they knew its light would put paid to any further attempted landing so, bitterly disappointed, they assumed that the others were regrouping somewhere inland and set off along the road back towards civilization. Soon, daylight began to appear and, to avoid any police who may be out early on the road to investigate the shooting on the beach, they took cover in a thicket and slept. It was still early when they woke, but they were thirsty and decided it was now safe to go and look for a café on the road back to Narbonne. But they had broken cover too early. Barely a kilometre along the road, a police car drove past them, then stopped.

Although Cavaillès had all his correct papers, Pineau had sent all his back to Vichy via a messenger before leaving Narbonne for the beach. All he had was a false identity card belonging to someone named Berval. What were they doing out so early in the morning, the two policemen wanted to know, and were they aware that someone had shot at two customs men on the beach that night and then fled? Pineau and Cavaillès claimed they were on a walking holiday and had been nowhere near the beach, but it was when the search of Pineau's backpack revealed a pair of wet sandals that their story began to lose credibility. The two men, one of whose papers had shown that he was a Paris university professor, while the other claimed he was a Ministry of Supply inspector by the name of Berval, were whisked away in the back of the car, strongly suspected of being dangerous smugglers.

Their misery would possibly have been compounded had they known that all but one (the other network's agent whom they were soon to meet at the police station) in the escape party had made it to freedom. There are still conflicting reports about exactly what happened in the darkness, but it seems that one of the customs officers accidentally shot his colleague in the arm, and amidst the chaos, the two politicians, Fontaine and Guy Lockhart, made it to the felucca and eventually Gibraltar. Lockhart was back reporting for duty at RAF Tempsford on 13 September, less than a fortnight after his mishap on the Saône.

Pierre Brossolette, (left) arrives at the Free French intelligence headquarters at 3 Carlton Gardens, London, in the company of Charles Vallin, the politician with whom he escaped occupied France from Narbonne Plage in September 1942. (*Musée de l'Ordre de la Libération*)

There is an inexplicable omission in Pineau's account of his failed escape aboard the felucca on the night of 5 September 1942. Any visitor to Narbonne-Plage today will see a sizeable memorial to the successful evacuation of Pierre Brossolette with Charles Vallin from that spot on the self same operation.

Pineau certainly thought he had met everyone due to be taken out that night from among the dunes, so how he and Cavaillès missed the presence of Brossolette, whom they both knew so well, is a mystery.

CHAPTER 8: POZ 55

Marie-Madeleine Fourcade's Story — Part 1

December 1941

The familiar shape of a 1936 black Citroën *Traction Avant* makes lurching, tail-first progress through a landscape of soaring snow-topped mountains. The car is not under its own steam but is shackled to one of several flatbed trucks which form part of a freight train groaning and wheezing against the gradient towards the Franco-Spanish border. The letters 'CD' are clearly visible on the vehicle's sloping boot and, through the rear window, it is obvious that the back seat is piled high with sacks, packages and spare tyres.

Without any warning, the boot of the car springs open and a foot appears from inside, feeling gingerly for the wooden floor of the truck. It is followed by its twin and soon the stiffly unfolding shape of a man has emerged and is standing awkwardly beside the car, gripping the rim of the open boot tightly so as not to be bundled off the edge of the truck by the movement of the train. His breath is visible in the icy air and he stamps his feet on the planking and rubs a thigh with his free hand to encourage circulation. Slowly, he works his way to the back door of the car, opens it and begins to unclasp one of the sacks on the back seat. There is struggling movement inside the sack and a tear-stained, gasping face forces itself into the open air.

The face, with reddish hair swept back from it into a bun, belongs to a woman in her mid-thirties, whose striking good looks are scarcely dimmed by her distress. She is shivering fiercely, but regains some composure after several deep breaths of mountain air and, while not extricating herself from the sack, she massages and stretches every muscle she can. She exchanges some words with the man but then the train begins to slow, so she pushes her chin back down onto her chest and the man re-fastens the sack. He then makes his way back to the rear of the car and clambers once more into the boot, which he manages to pull tightly shut just as the train pulls into a station.

An hour later and the train is at last approaching the border at Canfranc. Its final stretch takes it into the long Somport tunnel. In the cacophonous darkness, a man slips out of the single passenger carriage behind the engine and makes his way cautiously back along the train, jumping from truck to truck until he reaches the black Citroën. The train emerges into the failing winter daylight, its brakes squealing as the lights of the frontier loom up ahead. The man is re-arranging the pile of tyres on the back seat, one of which had fallen onto the sack beside it.

'Stick it out,' he is saying, 'we're coming to the customs. Our friend will clear us very quickly. Be brave. Stick it out.'

Just before the train comes to a complete halt, the man jumps down from the truck and strides off along the track to where a group of railwaymen are gathered. Eventually, he persuades them that his car is a high priority and that they should unload it first from the train. In the process of unloading, all the tyres fall onto the sack and, while the border guards' torches play over the irregular shapes in the back of the car, its driver explains impatiently that he is on an urgent mission for Marshal Pétain and that he must get the three diplomatic bags and the tyres to the French ambassador in Madrid without further delay.

Slowly, the inquisitive group disperses, but now another uniformed figure, a customs official, has opened the back door and is reaching inside. Before long, his hands find the sack with its human contents and have figured out the unmistakable shape of a head. He addresses the shape as 'Schoofs' and expresses surprise that he is not in the boot as he had been told to expect. When the shape neither moves nor answers, he becomes concerned and begins to pummel it as if to bring it out of unconsciousness and begs it to speak. Suddenly a voice from the boot exclaims, 'Shut up!' and the customs officer recoils as if he has been shot.

From the corner of his eye, the Citroën's driver, now at the wheel, can see the German *Abwehr* official in earnest discussion with the Spanish border police inside their hut. But the sentry has just lifted the barrier and, needing no further encouragement, he accelerates away into Spain. After a succession of hairpin bends, the car eventually pulls up beside the road next to a mountain stream. Both the driver and the man who has extricated himself from the boot hasten to free their female cargo from its sack. She has finally passed out through the pain of her ten-hour confinement, but is eventually revived and they resume the long road to Madrid using a more conventional mode of travel.

The man responsible for this act of human smuggling was Commandant Jean Boutron, deputy naval attaché to the French Embassy in Madrid. He had been hand-picked by the Vichy government to reorganize its naval intelligence in Spain and was often involved in carrying the regime's baggage under diplomatic seal across the frontier. As Boutron had been aboard one of the ships attacked by the Royal Navy at Mers-el-Kébir in July 1940, his superiors were especially confident that he would not be inclined to have anything to do with the British in Madrid. Little did they know that, even before his appointment as naval attaché, Boutron had already been recruited by Commandant Georges Loustaunau-Lacau into his underground intelligence-gathering network, *Alliance*, with its direct links to the SIS. His value to the network was enormous, as he was able to hide courier bound for London in the diplomatic bag. He also helped another British-inspired intelligence group, 'Alibi', based in Madrid, and this latest border crossing had not been the first time he had carried one of its agents, the Belgian Jean Schoofs, in the boot of his car. But it was the first time he had smuggled a second person and used the diplomatic bag for such a purpose.

The fugitive in question was Marie-Madeleine Méric, successor to Georges Loustaunau-Lacau as leader of the *Alliance* network after his arrest and imprisonment by the Vichy authorities five months earlier. Her escape across the frontier had saved her from a similar fate, but not the majority of her key agents who had been betrayed by one of their number and were now languishing in a police cell. When Kenneth Cohen of the SIS French section in London heard about this severe setback to one of his most prolific and valuable sources of intelligence, he immediately despatched a member of his team, Major Eddie Keyser, to Madrid to meet the network head, someone they only knew by the code name POZ 55 and to bring them back to London.

Keyser, expecting to meet a hardened military type, was astonished to find himself confronted by a stunningly beautiful woman who, far from grateful for the offer of a respite from her gruelling activities in France, was determined to return there as soon as possible. This was not just for the sake of her beleaguered network, which she was determined to safeguard and rebuild, but because her two young children would be wondering what had become of her.

Marie-Madeleine Méric (better known nowadays as Marie-Madeleine Fourcade, following her second marriage in 1947), unlike most of the other main players in this story, seemed almost destined for a life of intrigue and undercover work from an early age. The second of three children — she had an older sister and a younger brother — she was brought up in the wealthy European colonial community in Shanghai, learning almost as much about the English culture and language as those of China and her native France. Her father was a shipbroker, but he also worked covertly, gathering intelligence as the Shanghai correspondent for the French government's *Deuxième Bureau*.

Marie-Madeleine was only eleven when, in 1922, her father died suddenly, having contracted a tropical disease, and the family returned to France. They settled in Paris where Marie-Madeleine finished her education at a well-to-do convent and the family enjoyed a life of considerable comfort, taking holidays at properties they owned in Villars-sur-Ollon in Switzerland and Mougins on the French Riviera. Although Marie-Madeleine displayed a marked talent as a pianist, she willingly abandoned any chance she had of turning professional when, at 17, she fell for handsome army officer Edouard-Jean Méric and soon married him. When he was posted to Morocco, she was keen to accompany him, satisfying, as it would, a taste for overseas adventure which she had acquired from her childhood in the Far East.

Again, in her young life Marie-Madeleine found herself close to the world of military espionage, her husband working as an intelligence officer among the quarrelsome North African tribes under French control. She would sometimes accompany him on horseback on his visits to tribal chiefs where, proud of her beauty and sharp-wittedness, he would involve her in his intelligence-gathering tasks. Marie-Madeleine was still not 20 when their first child, a son, Christian, was born in Rabat but, by then, the marriage had already begun to lose its shine. Edouard Méric's pride turned to jealousy as he found his wife to be the focus of admiration among many of his fellow unmarried officers. She, in turn, resented the reclusive existence he now attempted to impose on her and they frequently argued. The couple returned to France for a two-year posting in Antibes and, when Edouard was recalled to Morocco, Marie-Madeleine, who gave birth to a daughter in 1932, announced that she would prefer to stay in France to bring up her children. An irredeemable separation had begun.

Marie-Madeleine returned to the sanctuary of her family in Paris, where the care of her children could be shared and where she began to enjoy an active social life, often in the company of her older sister and her husband, high-flying army commandant Georges Georges-Picot. It was at one of their tea parties that Marie-Madeleine met both Charles de Gaulle and his contemporary from the Saint-Cyr military academy, Georges Loustaunau-Lacau. Both had made names for themselves as army intellectuals whose advice was valued by the top brass, including 'the hero of Verdun', Marshal Philippe Pétain, on whose staff they both served at one time. While both men deplored the government's apparent paralysis at the German occupation of the Rhineland in 1936, Loustaunau-Lacau's political concerns were far more extreme than de Gaulle's. He claimed he had evidence of joint Soviet and German military manoeuvres in the Russian plains and viewed every communist in France as a potential traitor to his country.

Marie-Madeleine was clearly intrigued by this man's energy and enterprise and shared his pessimism at France's ability to defend herself against the growing Nazi and communist threat. She therefore readily agreed, the day after their first meeting, to work with him in the clandestine task he had set himself of building intelligence networks against the Nazis and uncovering communist infiltration in the army. Even when, in 1938, Loustaunau-Lacau was dismissed from the army for becoming too involved with members of the outlawed ultra-right-wing *Cagoulard* movement, Marie-Madeleine continued to work for him as general secretary of the magazine publishing group into which his enterprises had metamorphosed.

At the outbreak of war, Marie-Madeleine was left to run the business almost single-handedly when her boss was remobilized and sent to the front line. There, so appalled at the state of the defences, he accused the high command of high treason and was promptly imprisoned. He was freed at his trial, however, and immediately asked for a new command. By then, though, France was all but overrun and his last piece of advice to Marie-Madeleine as he returned to confront the Germans was to head south in her prized black Citroën *Traction Avant* and he would rendezvous with her in his home town of Oloron-Sainte-Marie in the Pyrenees in due course.

So, with her children in the care of their grandmother on the west coast island of Noirmoutiers, and her maid beside her in the passenger seat, Marie-Madeleine joined the almost static exodus on the crowded roads out of Paris. The journey took several days, the early part of which was often to the sound of bombs and gunfire only a few miles away. For someone who had dedicated the last few years of her life to the task of alerting fellow countrymen to their vulnerability to such a fate, the agony of defeat was intense. 'You hoped for an earthquake that you might escape the shame', she recalled in her memoirs, 'you were glad of the pall of soot veiling the long lines of vehicles, four abreast, that suddenly blocked the great arteries leading to the south.'

The news at Oloron-Sainte-Marie was far from encouraging. Loustaunau-Lacau — or Navarre, as he was now more frequently known by his friends — had been wounded and captured and was in a German military hospital in Eastern France. Marie-Madeleine, together with a young publishing colleague of hers, Jean-Philippe Salmson, and his parents, who had also escaped to the Pyrenees, were utterly disheartened by the heavy concentration of German troops they had observed in the newly formed occupied zone. The widespread acceptance of defeat by those under Pétain's new Vichy government perplexed them. They were desperate to carry on the fight in some way, but were at a loss to know how to start.

The answer came with the shock appearance of Navarre himself. In typical swashbuckling style and in spite of unhealed wounds, he had eluded his captors while in transit by slipping out of one train and into another and had then made it across the demarcation line to his home town. By September 1940, he had installed himself, Marie-Madeleine and the Salmsons at the very heart of collaborationist France, Vichy itself. Once again, as in peacetime, his weapon would be the covert gathering of intelligence. Where better to carry this out than the new seat of French power where his past life gave him access to those with greatest influence, including the Marshal himself? Navarre took over the Hôtel des Sports in Vichy which, with Pétain's blessing, would become a reception centre and lodging for escaped or demobilized military personnel looking for a role to play in the new order. While Navarre would front up the *Légion des Combattants*, as the organization was known, he would put

Marie-Madeleine in charge of the underground element. Her sex was a perfect cover, he explained to her when she protested that no one would listen to a woman.

The plan was to recruit, from those who came to the Hôtel des Sports, men who could not accept the armistice and to organize them into a network of intelligence patrols on both sides of the demarcation line. Navarre, meanwhile, had made contact with the agent working for the Free French intelligence service, Pierre Fourcaud, and asked him, on his return to London via Spain, to explain to General de Gaulle and the British his intention to supply them with intelligence. While requesting resources to carry out his plan, he also made it plain that he saw himself as a parallel source of French resistance rather than one that was subjugated to de Gaulle, the need for independent command on French soil being paramount. To ensure his message got back to London and that he received a response, Navarre also asked Marie-Madeleine's brother, Jacques Bridou, another demobilized soldier recently arrived in Vichy, to find a way to London via Morocco and Gibraltar to duplicate the mission.

Meanwhile, Marie-Madeleine set about her work, dividing the country up into regions and allocating men to set up patrols in each one and working out lines of communication back to the Vichy headquarters. Her task was helped considerably by the widespread contacts of her military recruits from the *Légion des Combattants*, although any means of vetting new agents for potential duplicity were non-existent, something that would come back to haunt the network as time went on. By the early spring of 1941, patrols had been established in the areas surrounding Marseilles, Lyons, Dijon and Périgueux in the Dordogne area, where an undercover line crossing gave them access to Bordeaux and the Atlantic coast.

On her first return to Paris since the armistice, Marie-Madeleine was able to enlist the support of a number of people involved in Navarre's old intelligence-gathering and publishing organization, and to create their first cell in the occupied zone. Even at this stage, however, there were plenty of danger signs; the Germans had ransacked the offices of the old publishing business as soon as they had entered Paris, showing that they had wind of Navarre's pre-war activities. They also singled out Marie-Madeleine for an intimate search on both entering and leaving the occupied zone. She later discovered that the code on her *Ausweis*, obtained through a duplicitous Vichy contact, marked her out as a high security risk to the Germans.

A little while after the Paris adventure, Pierre Fourcaud arrived back in Vichy with the unwelcome message from de Gaulle that 'whoever is not with me is against me', and his consequent refusal to help Navarre in any way. Fourcaud was as dismayed as any of Navarre's team and promised them use of the radio (Romeo) he had smuggled into France for his and Gilbert Renault's use and insisted Navarre took half of the one million francs the British had given for his use. This was especially welcome, as Navarre and Marie-Madeleine had funded their entire operation themselves to date and had practically run out of money. The other good news from Fourcaud was that the British were highly sympathetic with Navarre's wish to remain independent of de Gaulle and wanted to meet him personally with a view to supporting his network directly.

Before such a meeting could take place, the network suffered its first betrayal. An air force glider pilot and one of the first recruits among the demobilized servicemen to be recruited at the *Légion des Combattants* turned out to be in the pay of a Gestapo agent based in Vichy. The first piece of information he handed over was the name of his closest air force comrade, Maurice Coustenoble, who had become Marie-Madeleine's right-hand-man. Coustenoble had managed to escape capture and, with his jet black hair dyed peroxide yellow, made it to the network headquarters to warn them that their cover in Vichy was blown.

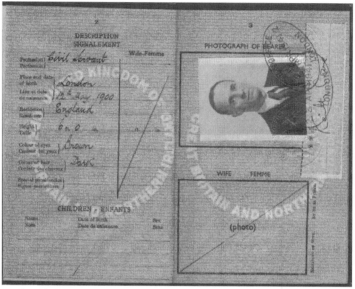

The photo page of Kenneth Cohen's false passport under the name of Keith Crane, issued in April 1941 for his trip to Lisbon to meet Navarre. (*Colin Cohen*)

The entire outfit retreated to the Pyrenees and set themselves up in a small hotel in Pau, where Marie-Madeleine had already established a colonel from the pre-war *Deuxième Bureau*, Charles Bernis, who had volunteered to collate intelligence reports prior to their despatch to London, once there was someone to receive them. Among the latest reports delivered to him by the breathless party that had descended from Vichy was a rumour among White Russians living in Paris that Hitler was about to turn on Stalin.

Soon after the network's enforced move to Pau, Navarre was contacted by a messenger for the British to say that an agent was waiting for him in Lisbon. Friendships that dated back to his trainee days at the *Ecole de Guerre* meant that his passage into and across Spain was assured, with no questions asked, by the head of Franco's *Seguridad*. Armed with the fruits of his network's intelligence-gathering, he spent three days in Lisbon with Kenneth Cohen, the SIS's head of French intelligence, where they agreed to co-operate fully and worked out a modus operandi. Cohen provided a radio transmitter for their exclusive use, codes for the encryption of messages and questionnaires to fill out about German military information across France. All of these, together with five million francs (worth about £25,000 in 1941), Navarre carried back to France across two borders in the French ambassador's diplomatic bag.

At last, the *Alliance* network, as it was now known, had a purpose to all the hard work and the risks its agents were taking. Moreover, it had more than enough money now to keep it going. Very soon, they had moved to a new headquarters in Pau, the Villa Etchebaster, a private house which gave them more freedom to come and go unobserved and allowed them ample space for their activities and to conceal the transmitter behind a mirror over a washbasin. The apparently bottomless source of money risked becoming a distraction to some of the network's recruits, however. Marie-Madeleine, on her second visit to Paris to deliver the questionnaires and codes to her agents there, noticed how much better dressed her head of patrol had become and that his estimated costs for carrying out his work seemed excessive. Later, he was found to have been using the network's money to engage in the black market and was frozen out of any further involvement.

Elsewhere throughout the network, though, there was palpable progress, so it came as a shock to Marie-Madeleine when, in May 1941, Navarre announced that he was leaving for Algeria and wanted her to take charge of the operation in France. For some time, Navarre had been encouraged to believe that the French army under Vichy control in North Africa was susceptible to a revolt by which it would transfer its allegiance to the British. His main ally in this plan was a virulently anti-collaborationist air force Commandant, Léon Faye, who Navarre had already sent to Algiers to drum up support among the military for such action.

The plot was either ill-timed or ill-conceived, because it resulted in both Navarre's and Faye's arrest, along with their co-conspirators. They were returned to France to await trial in Clermont-Ferrand prison, although Navarre, with the help of a sympathetic police commissioner, escaped his captors. Heavily disguised, he surprised Marie-Madeleine on a train to Marseilles, where she had planned to set up new headquarters, fearing that Pau's cover would be blown following the arrests. With typical audacity and believing the police would never look for him on home territory, Navarre persuaded her to turn back to Pau, where they would continue to direct operations together, both with false identities.

Throughout June and the first part of July, the network continued to grow. They had more than 100 people working for them with every area of the country covered and cells or informants operating within Tunis, Belgium, Italy, the Vichy *Deuxième Bureau* and even the *Abwehr* itself, thanks to Navarre's extraordinary influence and enterprise. Three more radios had also been smuggled across the border by Jean Boutron, who was now using Marie-Madeleine's Citroën as an official embassy vehicle for his journeys to and from Madrid. The operation was producing a large volume of high-quality intelligence back to London at a time when morale on both sides of the Channel had been boosted by the news of Hitler's power-sapping invasion of Russia.

But on 18 July the police, having followed Navarre's wife and daughter to a secret meeting he had arranged with them in Pau, recaptured their elusive quarry and carried him off to Clermont-Ferrand, this time ensuring his pre-trial incarceration. (Three months later, he was sentenced to two years in prison for leading the attempted revolt in North Africa; Léon Faye received five months). Once again, Marie-Madeleine found herself in charge of the network and, in spite of her concern that some of its members would find it difficult to follow the orders and direction of a woman, she was determined not to let such an effective intelligence-gathering machine disintegrate. She was also well aware that the Vichy police were hunting her down as a known accomplice of Navarre. Making it appear that she had left for Marseilles, she remained in Pau, but could not visit the Villa Etchebaster and relied on her closest lieutenants to bring her messages and reports for encoding to the hotel room where she was necessarily confined.

One such report was the devastating news that Henri Schaerrer, who, with Maurice Coustenoble, had become her most trusted aide, had been captured by the Germans. They had discovered him in the uniform of a German sailor having infiltrated a U-boat nest on the Gironde estuary in an attempt to supply accurate answers to one of the SIS questionnaires.

The fact that the Pau headquarters had remained unmolested since his arrest was enough to confirm Marie-Madeleine's faith in his courage to stay silent under torture.

The August moon marked the network's first parachute drop to be organized with the RAF. Together with some new, smaller radios and other supplies for clandestine work such as invisible ink and extra fine silky paper for messages, came an Englishman, Arthur Bradley Davies, whom they codenamed Bla. This Cockney, who spoke fluent French, had been sent by the SIS to show members of the network how to operate the new radios and to teach them revised methods of ciphering. That job done, he was to be escorted across the demarcation line and taken to Normandy, where he would set up a new, independent network.

Things could not have started less auspiciously for the Englishman. Firstly, his attire, chosen supposedly to blend in with the locals, caused helpless laughter when he was presented to the headquarters team at Villa Etchebaster. Marie-Madeleine, who made a rare visit there from her hideout to meet him, described the scene:

> Before me stood the most ridiculous, the most grotesque parody of a 'typical' Frenchman. He was attired as if for a village wedding — short jacket and waistcoat, striped trousers, a spotted cravat, a stiff shirt with cutaway collar beneath a little goatee beard, a pair of pince-nez and, as a crowning glory, a bowler hat.

Far worse, however, was that the man was dangerously ill. He had acute appendicitis and his life was only just saved at the local hospital. When he came round from the operation, he began to speak in English and Josette, the Villa Etchebaster housekeeper, pretending to be a concerned wife at his bedside, threw herself on him with kisses and much louder words of her own to drown out the incriminating language. As he began to recover, his minders grew concerned about his behaviour. He began to take advantage of Josette by playing the English-speaking game on purpose and, out of hospital, was surreptitiously helping himself to other people's meagre food rations. The agents were also all aghast at Bla's disregard for security. Surely, they felt, a man sent by the British, of all people, should not give his encoding lessons in a loud voice in the public park, nor exchange names and addresses with every visitor to the Etchebaster?

Marie-Madeleine wondered if London had sent this man deliberately to test them out. He stayed in Pau far longer than originally intended and, when he eventually set off for Normandy, he spent the whole train journey asking inane questions of his escort in a loud Cockney-French accent or fiddling with the radio transmitter he was carrying. At his destination, he vanished without trace. News did later reach Marie-Madeleine from London that Bla had established radio contact with them and that they were pleased with the information he was transmitting.

They must also have been delighted with the volume of intelligence emanating from the five other *Alliance* radios distributed throughout France by the autumn of 1941. As well as those at Pau, Marseilles, Nice and Lyons, a Paris transmitter was now up and running, the first direct link to London from the occupied zone. Another coup for the network came when one of its Paris agents arrived in Pau with a giant plan of the entire complex of U-boat pens newly built at St Nazaire wrapped around his body. Unfortunately, however, in this unending game of snakes and ladders, disaster always followed on the heels of triumph, this time in the shape of the arrest of six of the network's Paris agents, including Lucien Vallet, the radio operator. No one knew how the police had received wind of their operation, but at least the incriminating transmitter had not been discovered and it was the French police, not the Gestapo, handling the case.

Marie-Madeleine leaned heavily on her second-in-command, Maurice Coustenoble, at times of such harrowing setbacks. He even had an eerie knack of predicting disasters, having been certain, without any evidence, of Navarre's impending apprehension in Pau. A short time after that, an internal voice having told him that Admiral François Darlan, Pétain's hard-line deputy, would die by the revolver, Coustenoble resolved to carry out the deed himself to avenge Navarre's imprisonment. When he announced his plan to Marie-Madeleine, she forbade it on the grounds that assassination was beyond the remit of an intelligence-gathering network. Darlan did indeed die by a revolver just over a year later in Algiers when he was shot in a corridor outside his office by a 20-year-old member of the Resistance.

Now, on a November afternoon, Coustenoble came to her with another premonition, this time about an impending raid on the Villa Etchebaster. She agreed to let him burn all unnecessary records kept there, to give her what was left and to organize for the radio transmitter to be removed and hidden. Sure enough, the following evening, Jean-Philippe Salmson, who was due that night to return to Paris with a number of other volunteers to reinforce the depleted patrol there, rushed into Marie-Madeleine's room to say that all the members of his party had been arrested and the Etchebaster raided. Nearly everyone in the network in Pau, including Coustenoble, was behind bars except for him and Marie-Madeleine, and the police were looking for her everywhere.

Even Marie-Madeleine's mother, who had arranged to cross the demarcation line with the Paris-bound party, and Navarre's wife and son were in police custody.

The escape to Madrid in the diplomatic bag had been the only possible option left to Marie-Madeleine after this disastrous development. At least it provided a temporary respite from never knowing whether it was friend or foe knocking at the door, but it also brought still worse news about the network. In the first of a series of meetings with Eddie Keyser of the SIS (known to her as Major Richards), she learned that her Paris agents were all now in the *Abwehr's* hands, that the Lyons patrol had been betrayed by one of its members and in the Dordogne, where the network's parachute drops were organized, the entire reception team had also been picked up. (She would later learn that it had been the head of the Dordogne patrol, a man by the name of Lagrotte, who had not only betrayed his own team but had been responsible for all the arrests in Pau as well. He was, moreover, the person who tipped off the police about Fourcaud's and Renault's shared radio transmitter at La Bardonnie's château which led to the latter's arrest — proof, if it were needed, of the dangers of inter-network dealings).

The meetings with Keyser also gave Marie-Madeleine the opportunity to question him about the reliability of their envoy Bla. She had grown more suspicious than ever since she heard that he was seldom in Normandy but constantly appearing in Paris, pestering the families of the imprisoned agents there. Could he, she asked, be responsible for their betrayal? Having checked with his superiors back in London, Keyser still insisted that the man was sound, but assured her he would, nonetheless, be eased out of the *Alliance* network.

The conversations with Keyser also revealed that not all the courier from the network was getting beyond the British Embassy to London. One report to which Marie-Madeleine had been particularly keen to hear a reaction was about certain American and British firms that were still making deals with the Nazis through Swiss and Vichy intermediaries. It seemed that the ambassador, the former conservative cabinet minister Sir Samuel Hoare, had decided the document was not serious and had prevented it from leaving Madrid. Keyser promised that such interference would not happen again.

Marie-Madeleine returned to France once more as the contorted contents of Vichy's diplomatic sack. The task which lay ahead would, to most, seem an impossible one: revive a network whose heart had been torn from it while playing cat-and-mouse with the Vichy police, whose dossier on her was growing all the time. She was left in no doubt about how much the British needed her to succeed. Above all, it was intelligence on U-boat installations and shipping movement that they craved; anything that could help safeguard the Atlantic supply convoys and seaborne troop transportation would be vital in the coming months.

Marseilles was to become the new centre of operations for the *Alliance* network. It was in the back office of the vegetable shop there, used as cover by the still-unscathed local patrol, that Marie-Madeleine was reunited with the man known simply as 'Gavarni' who had been acting as her chief of staff in Pau. Although he had also been arrested in the police swoop, he had demanded to see Commandant Rollin, the chief of state security in Vichy, telling him that the network was dead, and agreeing to hand over their radios and all the money provided by London in return for the release of all the free-zone agents.

Once again, however, it was the presence of large amounts of cash which was clouding the issue. Gavarni, the first to be freed by Rollin, tried to persuade Marie-Madeleine that the *Alliance's* future was now working with Vichy's *Deuxième Bureau*. They were to amass vast sums of money by pretending to the British that the network was still working for them and in need of constant financial support.

Horrified by the corruption of one of her most trusted men, Marie-Madeleine nevertheless allowed Gavarni to return to Vichy to ensure the release of the other agents. Ceasing all further contact with him, she later discovered that he had only handed over to the Vichy police some 80,000 of the two million francs of network money in his care, keeping the rest for himself. The timely arrival of Léon Faye in Marseilles, newly released from his prison sentence, came as a godsend to Marie-Madeleine at a time when everything else was conspiring to drain her of confidence. News that her beloved Henri Schaerrer had been executed by his Nazi captors two months previously affected her greatly. Even her trust in the competence of her London masters was shaken when a parcel arrived through the post with writing scrawled all over the outside of its brown wrapping paper describing anti-aircraft sites in the Boulogne area. The agent who had sent it was using the SIS-recommended practice of writing his messages in invisible ink on the outside of a package — the least likely part of it to arouse suspicion in a search. Unfortunately, the ink supplied by London was substandard and had revealed itself in the heat during delivery. By a miracle, no postman had reported it.

The year of 1942 proved, if anything, more turbulent for Marie-Madeleine and her network than the previous one. Optimism grew in the early months thanks to the injection of

Léon Faye's dynamic involvement. As Marie-Madeleine's new chief of staff, he set about recruiting high-calibre fellow demobilized air force officers and, in a very short period, new regional patrols had grown up out of the ashes left by earlier denunciations. SIS HQ were particularly pleased to have so many airmen involved, as they would understand the special requirements of the Lysander pilots, who they were keen to start sending out on a regular basis for courier and personnel exchanges.

While all the new blood lent vigour to the enterprise, there were still parts of the old organization which were providing considerable practical value and experience. There was a direct radio link between Madrid and the Marseilles network HQ through which Jean Boutron had been able, among other things, to relay yet further unheeded warnings of the *Scharnhorst* and *Gneisenau*'s imminent departure from Brest. Marseilles had also organized, through two merchant ships which plied regularly between the French port of Sète and Barcelona, a regular means of delivering despatches to Spain. This means of communication later turned sour on the network after the skipper of one of the ships claimed that he had thrown a package entrusted to him into the furnace, as he feared a search. The package had contained two million francs which Marie-Madeleine had asked to be sent from her reserve in Barcelona.

The entire headquarters team in Pau was also brought back into the fold after their release by the Vichy police. Coustenoble, in particular, had been given a rough time in prison, being made to sit on the edge of a ruler for hours at a time to reveal the identity of his boss, but without success. He had managed to hide two radio transmitters before his arrest, and these could now go straight back into operation.

His courage under interrogation might have been all for nothing had not Marie-Madeleine the advantage of friends in high places. Her army brother-in-law, Commandant Georges-Picot, had, through his Vichy connections, heard that incriminating documents, traceable to her, had been handed to the police by a couple from Tarbes. These were the records that Marie-Madeleine had taken away with her from Pau during her escape across the Pyrenees and which she had hidden in the coal shed of the couple she thought she could trust. They were now in the possession of Commandant Rollin, head of security in the free zone, who happened to be a good friend of Georges-Picot. The latter had persuaded Rollin that he would bring his sister-in-law to Vichy to explain herself on the condition that she would not be thrown immediately into jail.

The first thing she had to account for was a sheet of paper with the words 'Darlan will die by revolver' scrawled repeatedly across it. This had, in fact, been the 'voice' speaking to Coustenoble and manifesting itself through his pencil onto the paper. Marie-Madeleine insisted that it was nothing more than the ramblings of a professed clairvoyant she had known in Paris who occasionally sent her these strange messages. She managed to convince Rollin that Pétain's deputy was in no danger from her or any of her acquaintances. It was impossible, however, for her to deny her involvement in an undercover network, as a list of code names of her agents were among the records. The police had already deduced that ASO 43 was Jean Boutron and he had been arrested in Madrid and put on a plane back to France. Rollin also accused her of having been to Madrid and back to make contact with the British, which she hotly denied.

Marie-Madeleine claimed that any radio links her group had had with London had been destroyed in the police raid in Pau and brazenly accused her interrogator of lacking patriotism by disabling a network set up to oppose a foreign occupation of his country. Throughout their interview, Commandant Rollin's attitude had swung from anger and frustration at his interlocutor's stubborn defence of her activities to one of grudging admiration and, at times, to something close to sympathy. His view, not unique among some of the powers of Vichy, was that, while he deplored the German occupation, resistance groups only made the task of handling the occupiers more difficult and any liaison with the British was a waste of time, as they would never be of any help.

The extraordinary result of Marie-Madeleine's summons to Vichy was a promise by Rollin of protection under a false identity provided by him on the condition that she ceased her activities and returned to her family and children on the Riviera. He warned that Admiral Darlan ran his own police force which was far more sympathetic to the Nazi cause and methods than his men. Jean Boutron, meanwhile, was sent to a prison in the Alps, partly for his own protection, since he had been followed by two *Abwehr* agents on the plane from Madrid who he was convinced had orders to kill him. He would later be sprung from jail by members of the *Alliance* in Grenoble and eventually escaped France aboard a submarine to Gibraltar.

It was Marie-Madeleine's daughter who eventually provided her with the pretext to leave the Riviera without arousing the suspicions of her brother-in-law or the Vichy police that she might be resuming her undercover work. The young girl needed to go to Toulouse for an operation which would keep her in hospital there for some weeks. It was only natural for her mother to accompany her and to stay there while she recovered. Through the sympathetic connivance of the head of the clinic where she was given a room to stay, she was able to establish a temporary headquarters there, receiving visitors from the network and setting up a local Toulouse patrol.

She was able to make a brief visit to Marseilles during that spring when she saw for herself how much Léon Faye had achieved in her absence. Marie-Madeleine had devised a new system of agents' code names, whereby every individual became an animal. She became *Hérisson* — Hedgehog — Faye was Eagle and Coustenoble was Tiger. There were now outposts of the menagerie in every corner of free and occupied France, including the forbidden north-eastern zone where Coustenoble had revived previously severed contacts. Valuable information was even coming from inside Italy thanks to the work of Colonel Charles Bernis in Nice who was in contact with anti-fascists in Turin. They were monitoring air force movements for signs of reinforcement of Rommel's desert campaign, which was in full swing at the time. This source would later obtain the timetable for different squadrons' departures for North Africa and the information was relayed back to London in time for their interception by the RAF, thus depriving Rommel of vital air support for his advance on Tobruk. The Marseilles patrol was equally important to the British desert war effort, giving details of German arms consignments transported across the Mediterranean under the disguise of French commercial shipping. Torpedo boats were also reported being sent down the Rhône into the Mediterranean in large numbers.

If all was going well for the rejuvenated network, the outlook was far more grim for the men of the old Paris patrol, half starved and under constant brutal interrogation by the Nazis in Fresnes prison on the outskirts of the capital. In spite of their misery, they continued to try to thwart their tormentors by smuggling out messages made with pinpricks on tiny scraps of rolled up paper when their families were allowed a rare visit to them. Lucien Vallet, who had been the patrol's radio operator, had written one of his messages in a code which only Marie-Madeleine could decipher. Coustenoble brought it to her while she was still in Marseilles and its content was shocking, if not entirely unexpected. In order to demonstrate to Vallet how much they knew about his activities, his interrogators had placed before him the radio transmitter that he had been using before his arrest but which had been sent to Bla for repair. How did the Germans obtain the radio, considering that Bla was still free? What was more, the entire patrol that he had set up in Normandy was now in German captivity and yet the Englishman himself was, according to London, still transmitting useful material to them on his own set.

Here was proof positive that the man was a German agent and Marie-Madeleine radioed London immediately to that effect. Their first response was simply to say that he was continuing to send excellent information. Utterly exasperated, Marie-Madeleine radioed again. A day elapsed until finally the following message arrived from London:

No. 218 for POZ 55: You were right stop Bla a traitor stop working for the Gestapo stop secure everything he knows about that is still intact stop we are issuing execution order stop Richards.

'Everything Bla knew that was still intact' included just about everyone involved with or visiting the Pau headquarters before his departure to Normandy. Shocked that London now expected them to kill the traitor that they themselves had put into their midst, Marie-Madeleine and her lieutenants nonetheless realized its necessity, even if most of the damage had already been done. In his transmissions to London, Bla had bemoaned his loss of contact with the *Alliance* network, so an attempt was made to lure him to a rendezvous in Lyons. He never turned up, but two *Abwehr* agents did and they nearly succeeded in grabbing Marc Mesnard, Marie-Madeleine's trusted treasurer, who had volunteered to meet Bla and lead him into the hands of the network.

This would not be the end of the Bla story. About three months later, by which time Marie-Madeleine was again permanently based in Marseilles, one of the *Alliance* agents, who had been trained with Bla in London, bumped into him at Marseilles train station. His story was that his old network had been smashed, that he had just avoided capture by the Gestapo and that he was now penniless and looking for a new network to serve. Told that he had come to the right place, Bla agreed to be driven by two supposed policemen to a house on the Corniche, where Faye was waiting for him. Before he carried out the execution, Faye wanted to extract as much information as he could from the Englishman about how much the Germans now knew about their network. Bla flatly refused to admit to any treachery, saying that he had no idea who Faye was and nor did he know any of the men holding him.

Marie-Madeleine had originally agreed not to be involved in Bla's despatch — her men felt it was inappropriate for a woman — but now Faye realized that his denials would become futile when face to face with the leader of the network. Sure enough, as soon as Marie-Madeleine walked into the room, a look of terror swept across Bla's face and his defiance turned into an immediate readiness to admit his duplicity. Originally, he had infiltrated British Intelligence on behalf of Oswald Mosley's fascists. His allegiance switched to the Nazi variety of republican fascism when he found himself excluded by social divisions within Mosley's movement. After he had left Pau, he spent all his time in Paris rather than Normandy and, with the help of his German masters, used his transmitter to send genuine information to London that they knew they already had, laced occasionally with something false which was sure to send them into unnecessary circles.

Frustratingly, although they could not stop him from talking, he told them very little they did not already know, but confirmed that he had indeed betrayed the Paris and Normandy patrols. The Gestapo had sent him to Marseilles with the express purpose of tracking down Marie-Madeleine which, if he failed, he should get himself to Algeria where he would carry out further undercover work for the Nazis. The one question he refused to answer was who his German contact was in London.

To kill someone you know in cold blood is no easy task, as Christian Pineau discovered, walking away from a wrecked Lysander beside the Saône. The attempts by Faye and other *Alliance* members to carry out London's orders on Bla would, in other circumstances, be almost comical. Explaining to Bla that they intended to send him back to England, to allay his immediate fears, they dissolved one of the SIS standard-issue suicide pills in a bowl of soup which Bla devoured, and which produced no ill-effect other than increasing his verbal diarrhoea. Next, they gave him a cup of tea with the same deadly ingredient. Probably through the foul taste of the tea, Bla showed now that he understood what they were doing, expressed his sympathy at the painful task they were having to perform and swallowed the rest in one gulp. This dose appeared to be as harmless as the last and failed to stop his talking, let alone his breathing.

In exasperation, and perpetuating the mythical plan to transport him to London via a submarine, they led him down a precipitous cliff at night to a small beach where they had arranged for a fishing boat skipper with gangster connections to pick him up and dispose of him while at sea. The fishing boat never materialized and, the next morning, Marie-Madeleine received an embarrassed account of how the Englishman was still alive. Finally, abandoning the humane approach, Marie-Madeleine decided that they should stage a proper hearing in front of her, Faye and the others. An indictment was read out to which Bla readily owned was true. Then, by the power of their execution order from SIS headquarters, they condemned him to death. Marie-Madeleine then left the proceedings and the next day, Lucien Poulard, one of Faye's lieutenants, reported to her that the deed had been done.

She never heard how it was done and was never party to an altogether different account of Bla's fate. According to Patrice Miannay in his 2005 *Dictionary of Double Agents in the Resistance*, Robert Alesch, a priest originally from Luxembourg and another SIS agent working for Germany who controlled Bla, reported at his trial in 1945 that he had provided Bla with 75,000 francs of SIS money to flee France. He later received a thank-you note from Bla who claimed to have settled with his wife and children in Bizerte on the Tunisian coast. If, through religious or other scruples, Faye had ultimately been unable to carry out the execution, he never owned up to it to Marie-Madeleine. His own eventual execution by the Nazis would preclude any post-war confession. It has to be said, however, that the only author to have been given access to SIS files, Keith Jeffery, reports no record of this alternative version of events in his 2010 book, *MI6, The History of the Secret Intelligence Service, 1909-1949*. In fact, he finds an enquiry from Bla's wife in 1944 asking of his whereabouts with a reply from the authorities that they had neither seen nor heard of him since 1942.

If the treachery of Bla and the failure of espionage essentials such as invisible ink and suicide capsules had shaken the *Alliance's* trust in the infallibility of His Majesty's Secret Intelligence Service, a new line of communication had opened up with London a few weeks earlier in this summer of 1942, which helped restore confidence in their ability to deliver. Up until then, they had relied on parachute drops for the delivery of men and material but, with the arrival of the Anglo-French Arthur-Louis Gachet by the same means, they had an RAF-trained Lysander landing expert in their midst. The network already had a patrol dedicated to aerial operations under the command of a 26-year-old air force lieutenant, Pierre Dallas, who had been investigating potential landing sites in both the Auvergne, west of Clermont-Ferrand, and on flat land beside the rivers Saône, Rhône and Ain to the north and east of Lyons. Dallas was a keen canoeist and, in landings close to a river, planned to make his getaway with incoming agents by paddle power, thus avoiding any roadblocks set up if the alarm had been raised.

The *Alliance's* first Lysander exchange took place on the night of 23 August from the comparative luxury of an actual disused airfield at Thalamy, near Ussel in the Auvergne. It was Guy Lockhart's penultimate operation for 161 Squadron and it successfully delivered Léon Faye to the Sussex coast. His return a month later was far from smooth. Thick cloud and heavy rain over the landing site close to where the rivers Rhône and Ain converged prevented any chance of putting down and the Lysander returned to Tangmere. The next night, the operation was on again, although the weather was hardly any better. John Bridger, at the controls, was forced to fly very low in near total darkness, relying on glimpses of the Loire, whose upstream course led towards Lyons and the target. When they reached the mountains of the Lyonnais, the plane flew below the level of their ridges as the pilot picked his way around their contours.

At the landing site, no signal could be seen through the mist and heavy rain until, to Bridger's astonishment, the expected letter 'A' was flashed from a field on the opposite side of the Rhône to the agreed target. In spite of this misunderstanding, Bridger brought the plane down, only for its right front wheel to sink up to its axle in mud. Faye disembarked, but the outgoing passenger, Jean Boutron, recently sprung from prison, was nowhere to be seen. He was, in fact, back at the *auberge* where they had been staying, as Dallas had judged that no plane could possibly land that night and had gone to the site with the outbound courier only as a precaution. Waiting now for Boutron to be fetched was out of the question, so Faye and the reception crew began to dig a furrow with their hands to free the sunken undercarriage. With the propeller at full throttle and the four men heaving on the fuselage, they eventually got the Lysander free and, within seconds, it was airborne again and on course for the Channel.

A similar missed opportunity occurred during the October moon when a new radio expert for the network, the Anglo-Spanish Ferdinand Rodriguez, was flown in to the Thalamy airfield, again by John Bridger. Marie-Madeleine's brother, Jacques Bridou, was the intended return passenger. He had been working with the *Alliance* ever since his return from his mission to London in late 1940 and was now keen to return there and offer his services to the Free French cause. Unfortunately, Dallas, who was to meet him at Ussel station and take him to the airfield, slept through his stop on the train and the two men arrived breathless at the landing site, only to witness the Lysander disappearing into the night sky. Arthur-Louis Gachet, Dallas's deputy, had arrived at the field separately and improvised a set of flares.

By the autumn of 1942, rumours were rife about major developments in both France and North Africa. The *Alliance* was only too aware of the increasing number of thinly disguised German agents operating in Marseilles and throughout the free zone. The last message Bla sent to Marie-Madeleine via his 'executioners' was that Hitler planned to march into the free zone on 11 November and that she should leave Marseilles before that date. There was good reason to believe him, as there were also signs that American and allied forces were about to land in Algeria. Hitler would badly need control of the south of France to resist any threat from across the Mediterranean.

At the same time, it became known that a key French military figure, General Henri Giraud, had recently escaped from the German fortress of Koenigstein, where he had been held since the armistice, and was now in Vichy. Although prepared to support Pétain, Giraud was clearly an embarrassment to the government, declaring, as he did, open opposition to the German occupation and urging Pétain to take up arms against them. This was at a time when, according to General Camille Raynal, one of the *Alliance's* moles in Vichy, Pétain had sent a telegram to Hitler promising his armed support against any allied invasion of France.

A message came from London asking Marie-Madeleine to sound out General Giraud and see whether he would make a Lysander flight to Britain. He was senior in rank to de Gaulle, and Churchill was desperate to find a more co-operative French ally to work with. Marie-Madeleine arranged for one of her best-connected agents, Maurice de McMahon, Duc de Magenta, a stunt pilot and head of her Paris operation, to meet the General, but Giraud had a deep-seated loathing of the British and he was determined to see France liberated without any British involvement.

During Léon Faye's subsequent visit to London, he was able to plant the idea of getting Giraud to North Africa instead where he could take command of French forces once the allies had made their landing in Algeria and Morocco and overcome any Vichy-inspired resistance. This suggestion was put to Giraud via the Americans and some tenuous links they had with the General who reluctantly agreed to leave France in a clandestine mission by submarine and be taken to Gibraltar to meet General Eisenhower just before the allied invasion. Giraud's one stipulation was that the submarine, necessarily a British one, should have an American skipper for his passage, such was his Anglophobia.

Responsibility for the mission, code-named Minerva, was given to Marie-Madeleine and her team who arranged an embarkation point close to Le Lavandou, where a small fishing boat would ferry the General, his son, two officers on his staff and a personal bodyguard out to the submarine, *HMS Seraph*, on 3 November. Although eventually postponed for two nights, the mission went as planned and Giraud was delivered to Gibraltar two days before the invasion began on 8 November. For some reason, he had presumed he would be given supreme command of the operation and, when told that General Eisenhower was holding the reins, Giraud decided not to accompany the invasion fleet but to observe the outcome from Gibraltar. Although the allies fairly soon took control of the key targets of Casablanca, Oran and Algiers — thanks, in part, to anti-Vichy resistance cells in Algeria — there were nonetheless nearly 500 allied and 1,300 French soldiers killed in the various engagements. When Giraud finally crossed the Mediterranean, he discovered that Admiral Darlan, on a chance visit to Algiers, had been put in overall charge of French forces in North Africa by the allies and he had to accept second-in-command — at least until Darlan was assassinated the following month.

Giraud had, in fact, ordered a second submarine operation to follow the night after his embarkation, as he expected a number of generals to follow his lead and join him in Gibraltar. This additional request caused a flurry of radio transmissions between Madrid and London to arrange the operation and would have disastrous consequences for the *Alliance* network. Marie-Madeleine knew that she and her team were running an ever-increasing risk, as German detector vans, disguised as French police vehicles, were now appearing in towns throughout the free zone, especially in Marseilles. Such was the price on her own head that Marie-Madeleine could only make brief visits to the headquarters there, returning either to Toulouse or to the seaside hideout near Le Lavendou, where the submarine evacuees gathered.

It was during one of her visits to La Pinède, the villa in Marseilles now serving as their headquarters, that the police made their move. Not one of the generals that Giraud was expecting to follow him had turned up in Marseilles and, so as not to waste the opportunity of an escape route to London, Marie-Madeleine was organizing a substitute party, including her brother and Jean Boutron. Last minute messages to London had been enough to lead the detector van to the door and, before they had time to destroy any evidence, French police, led by a bespectacled Gestapo agent brandishing a revolver, were in the house. It soon transpired that the French policemen were extremely reluctant players in the raid, resenting being forced by the Vichy government to round up their countrymen on behalf of the Gestapo.

An extraordinary scene ensued whereby every time the German's back was turned, one of the French policemen assisted Marie-Madeleine in her desperate task of hiding or destroying network documents. Unfortunately, they could not destroy everything, including the most potentially damaging of all, which gave frequencies, call signs and locations of every transmitter in use by the network throughout France. It was taken, along with the six people arrested at the villa, to the headquarters of the *Surveillance du Territoire*. These included Léon Faye, Marie-Madeleine and her brother Jacques, who had arrived at the villa at the worst possible moment, during the raid, to say goodbye to his sister before leaving by sea that evening.

Fortunately, there was no sign of any Germans at the police headquarters, and a mood of wanting to help their prisoners wherever possible prevailed among the officers. News of the successful allied landing in North Africa arrived during their interrogation to the joy of the *Alliance* members and their captors alike. Faye had been summoned to Vichy, where he was confident he would persuade Pétain and Laval, apparently thrown into panic by the developments across the Mediterranean, that now was the time to take up arms against the Germans, forestalling their almost inevitable invasion of the free zone. Meanwhile, realizing the network's transmitter details could not simply be destroyed as it had been seen by the German Gestapo agent, the police inspector in charge and Marie-Madeleine colluded in making what appeared to be an identical copy, except that the information on it was false. This one act would save the network and also many lives.

As well as the good news about the allied landings, Marie-Madeleine also received word from Dallas, via one of the sympathetic policemen who had raided her headquarters, that the second submarine embarkation had gone ahead successfully. On 11 November, came the news they had all been dreading — German forces had marched across the demarcation line. This altered everything. Firstly, it sealed the fate of Léon Faye, who very quickly found himself in prison, his proposition considered nothing short of treason by Vichy's puppet rulers. Secondly, it meant that, as soon as the Nazi advance party had reached Marseilles, the French police would be forced to hand Marie-Madeleine and her fellow prisoners over to their new masters.

But there was such repugnance at the German invasion among the Marseilles police that they took it upon themselves to conspire with members of the network still at large to stage a fake ambush of the police van carrying the prisoners to Castres gaol. So, by midday of the German invasion, Marie-Madeleine and her friends were once again at liberty. Liberty would have a different meaning for them from now on, however. Before, even when captured in the previously free zone, they could hope for a degree of sympathy from the authorities and a chance to negotiate their release. Now, capture would almost certainly mean torture and death, particularly for Marie-Madeleine, whose arrest had become a key objective for the Germans.

In London, Kenneth Cohen had been following his network's recent fortunes with deep concern and, when he received news of Marie-Madeleine's escape, he ordered a Lysander flight for her immediate evacuation to London during the forthcoming moon. Such was his and his whole organization's admiration for their 'Hedgehog' that he and others from the office went in person to Tangmere to greet her on the tarmac. As Peter Vaughan-Fowler's plane taxied to a halt in front of them, instead of the single graceful shape of Marie-Madeleine, no fewer than three swarthy-looking men extricated themselves with considerable difficulty and cramp from the rear cockpit. They turned out to be the three Corsican policemen who had been driving the police van which had set Marie-Madeleine and the others free. She had promised them a passage to England in return for their assistance and was herself in no mood to leave her post in France at such a critical moment. Barbara Bertram always cherished the memory of the trio's wide-eyed arrival on her doorstep at Bignor, each clad in a peculiar assortment of clothes. She immediately christened them the Marx Brothers.

CHAPTER 9: KEEPING HOUSE IN SUSSEX

When the war ended and normal family life resumed at Bignor Manor, Barbara Bertram found to her dismay that she could not sleep. As an accusing silence enveloped the house each night, all the elements of her recent fevered life continued to run frantic circuits inside her head. Her subconscious brain could not accept that she was no longer ruled by the demands and anxieties of the moon periods. It therefore re-created them for her in a cacophonous fusion of sounds and images: unintelligible waves of excited French conversation; the gramophone scratching out Jean Sablon's *Je Tire Ma Révérence*; smiling or anxious faces of men and women, many now mutilated and dead at the hands of torturers; the roar of a Lysander passing dangerously low; the clatter of washing-up in the sink; the clink of bottle against tumbler; the shrill summons of the telephone; cars arriving in the drive as dawn broke; the thump of darts hitting their target; and endless piles of vegetables to prepare.

To remedy his wife's insomnia, Tony Bertram suggested that Barbara unburden all that tormented her at night onto paper. As a writer, he understood the relief that can come from translating the nebulous content of one's mind into the familiar shape of words on a page. Barbara followed his advice and produced a vivid piece of writing which she entitled '*C'est on, C'est off — what it was like*'. Whether this monologue was ever intended for publication is uncertain, but it would have been too sensitive a piece for 'The Office' to have allowed its airing immediately after the war. Her son Tim has continued to keep it under wraps since his mother died in 2004, so it appears now for the first time. The extracts which follow give us the sound of Barbara's own voice and a clear sense of how she felt as she went about her special housekeeping duties.

Barbara Bertram as depicted by the artist Paul Nash. (*The Bertram Family*)

I must get up — it's no use not — but I must make a list first of what I've got to do. Reception soup; Reception Pie; make beds; pud for dinner; pud for Reception; ring up boys — poor darlings. I suppose they must stay at school over the weekend. If c'est off they could sleep somewhere and if c'est on Mrs. Pentecost might have them but I think Tony's right really, it's dangerous having them here. I must dig up leeks — Oh it's no good just thinking, I must write it down after breakfast. If only I hadn't got to listen for the telephone all day.

Bother, Caroline doesn't seem to have a drop of milk this morning, I suppose she doesn't get enough to eat — what can I give the rabbits? I might pinch a swede if there's no one about. It's cold and beastly, I wish I'd put a coat on — and it's going to rain. Beds. Tony said it would be a double to begin with but you never can tell. That's six French, two drivers, Tony and probably John. Six and two's eight and two's ten and me, eleven. That's three in our room, three in the guest room, the drivers in the drivers' room, us in the boys' room and John in the drawing room. No, I think I ought to be kind and put two French in each room and Tony and I can muck in with John in the drawing room, there won't be much night anyway. Cigarettes. How on earth can I get enough? Beer. I think there's enough whisky and gin for the moment. Flowers, lots in the garden but I must pick them soon. I've had lots from France. Lily-of-the-valley on my breakfast plate on May 1st picked in France the night before. Cooking. That'll have to have a separate list later. Wash and iron. I hate table napkins. Get in veg. I'd better finish the list later. I wish I had time to dig today, the earth's just right. I ought to put in some more beans too. I must add to the list: Get in wood and coal. I'd better light the fire at about two.

Thank goodness Tony is bringing them down, they'll be punctual. Those awful flaps when they're late, especially the night Stephen was killed — I mustn't think of that — and I went over to Tangmere to show them the way and the Lysanders stood up like giant dragonflies and they were all so cheerful and then the pilots came out like silent grey priests and got in and started the engines and one of them backfired letting out flames — it's no good trying to have clean hands when there're so many potatoes to peel. Let's think how many we'll want, eleven, better say twelve, there may be an odd high-up. They're large, so two each, that's twenty-four for dinner and twenty-four for Reception, Lor! Forty-eight. I must get the stove alight soon or the water won't be hot. Forty-seven. No, I suppose later will do, I'll finish the spuds first. Forty-six. I ought really to wash my hair. Forty-five. That's three done — one sixteenth. I must stop counting, it'll drive me mad. Forty-four. Thank goodness the butcher comes today and I've got a hare, it's not bad, only I must skin it sometime. Forty-three. They'll have to have chocolate cake again for pud. Luckily it's not often the same French and the others don't matter. I wonder which drivers will come. They do work hard. Jean was marvellous explaining New Yorker jokes to the Colonel.

What's the time, half-past ten. I must go into Petworth and finish the Reception potatoes later. Cigarettes, beer, cake if possible, catch Perry-the-paper-man. Perhaps I can get some sausages, anything there is. What shall I do if Tony doesn't ring up soon? I should have to go to Petworth directly after lunch, no, it has to be after two. Oh hell, Caroline's loose. Why can't I tie her up properly? Come here you brute. I do hate this heavy, cold chain. Curse the goat, I believe Tony's right, she's more trouble than she's worth but it is nice having extra milk and an occasional kid. I hope it's not getting foggy. The night Stephen was killed — that Reception Pie. I could only say over and over again to myself, 'what's happened, what's happened?' and poor Tony trying to talk naturally to the two arrivals and they were terribly shaken too and poor Mary, the driver, whose husband had been killed recently. And then at last when the meal was over and I got Tony alone and I could say 'What's happened?' 'Stephen's killed and McBride and Berthaud and Cazenave.' That's all he said and then he flopped into bed. And Robin back that night. He came later and brought the half-burnt courier, all bloodstained.

No wonder the crash of two Lysanders in the small hours of the morning of 17 December 1943 haunted Barbara as she lay awake in the weeks which followed the war. It had finally brought the grim reality of her secret war right to her doorstep and a young man she had known since he was a baby had been among those killed. That December moon had not begun well for 161 Squadron. The first operation was the one from which Jimmy Bathgate never returned (see Chapter 5) and then bad weather forced two further missions to turn back unfulfilled. One of these had been an attempt by the squadron's commander, Wing Commander Bob Hodges, to pick up one of his own men, Robin Hooper, who had been stranded in France since the previous moon when his plane had become irretrievably bogged down in a field near Niort in western France.

On the night of 16 December, the weather was better and the forecast promised a clear passage to and from France, although there was a slight chance of some fog forming on the English south coast later in the night. Hodges therefore made preparations once again for a flight to a field some forty miles south of the Loire, near Parthenay. His outward passenger was an agent for the Belgian government in exile, François de Kinder. Meanwhile, a second operation, entitled Diable, was also planned for the same night using two Lysanders, in which Stephen Hankey and Jim McBride would return Georges Charaudeau, the head of the SIS's Madrid-based network, Alibi, to the French countryside near Châteauroux, along with five of his fellow agents.

Barbara had good reason to remember this particular departure, as it was the only time she went to Tangmere to witness the start of an operation. It happened because one of the cars bringing three of the agents down from London arrived late at Bignor. It was not one of the usual FANY drivers but a man she did not know who had got lost trying to find his way through the un-signposted Sussex lanes. In order to ensure their prompt arrival at the Tangmere cottage, they took Barbara with them to show the way. When they reached the aerodrome gates, they realized they had no pass for her, so she crouched low by the passengers' feet so as not to be seen. They arrived as the pilots and passengers for the other planes were just walking out across the tarmac to climb on board — they were in a hurry to get off so as to beat any fog on the return journey.

In fact, they set off so early that, when Bob Hodges began to circle over the French landing site, the reception party were only just arriving and he had to wait while they hastily set up the flare path. The landing, exchange of passengers, take-off and homeward flight passed without incident and in the clearest of moonlit visibility. But approaching the English coast, instead of the dark shape of land, a thick, white blanket lay spread out beneath them. Tangmere radioed to them that there was currently about 500 feet of moderate visibility beneath the cloud but that it was deteriorating rapidly. Relying on his instruments alone, Hodges made his blind approach to the runway as the Lysander descended through some 1,000 feet of dense fog. The ground appeared suddenly 300 feet below them, allowing the pilot just enough time to adjust his approach for a conventional runway landing.

Delighted though he was to have successfully retrieved one of his squadron's top pilots from potential torture and death at the hands of the Gestapo and to have got home in the nick of time, Hodges could not celebrate. The other two Lysanders were still on their way home and the cloud base was falling all the time. He made for the control tower where both Hankey and McBride were already in radio contact as they approached across the Channel. With thick ground fog imminent all along the south coast of England, planes returning from operations all over the continent were being diverted to Woodbridge in Suffolk, where visibility was slightly better and where special paraffin burners were in place along the runway to disperse the fog.

But that was no option for the two Lysanders whose fuel tanks were close to empty. In other circumstances, Hodges would have been happy to order his two pilots to sacrifice their aircraft and to bail out. But their passengers — they had two each — were without parachutes, so they had somehow to bring their planes down intact. As they were both due overhead at roughly the same time, Stephen Hankey was told to land at the neighbouring naval airfield at Ford while McBride began his approach on Tangmere. With both pilot and control tower relying entirely on instruments, McBride was guided onto his final approach. Visibility on the ground was now only 500 yards, but he arrived over the end of the runway at the perfect altitude and heading for landing. At this moment, however, he saw the red light on the top of the runway controller's caravan and mistook it for hangar obstruction lights. He radioed sharply, 'You are flying me into the hangars', and opened up the throttles to go round again. Once more, he came in on a final approach, receiving assurances from the controller that he was set for a successful landing. Then the radio went dead. No plane emerged from the fog; there was utter silence.

Hodges, Hooper and several others made their way to the end of the runway and then began to cross the heavily ploughed fields that lay under the final approach path. Eventually, they saw an orange glow through the fog which, as they drew close, became the sight they had been dreading — a fiercely burning Lysander on its nose, the pilot trapped in the cockpit and obviously dead. A man and a woman stood beside the wreckage, clearly in shock and utterly disoriented. These had been McBride's passengers, Marcel Sandeyron, a garage owner from Pont de Vaux on the Saône who worked for the *Azur* network, and a female agent known only by her code name, Atalas. They had miraculously survived the crash unscathed and were later taken back to Bignor by Tony Bertram for a mournful reception pie.

This was only after Tony had carried out an even more unenviable task. He had been called to a hillside to the west of Ford aerodrome where Stephen Hankey's aeroplane had hit a tree as he attempted to land. Tony had been asked to identify the three charred bodies in the wreckage, as he was likely to have known them all. Apart from their close friend, the pilot, there was Albert Kohan (alias Berthaud), a White Russian turned Free French resistance leader who, on his earlier wartime visits to England, had become hugely popular with both the pilots and the SIS conducting staff. The third corpse was of another previous visitor to London, Jacques Tayar (alias Cazenave), leader of the *Electre* intelligence network and a pivotal player in the radio communications systems set up between France and London.

Much to her distress, Barbara Bertram was unable to attend Stephen Hankey's funeral which was held three days later, as she had an important doctor's appointment in London for her younger son, Nicky, which could not be changed. She did, however, drive Stephen's widow Elizabeth to Brookwood Military Cemetery in Surrey a few days later for the burial of the two Frenchmen who had died with him. Both men had been guests at Bignor Manor twice previously and Barbara would have felt their loss almost as deeply as that of Stephen Hankey.

No doubt the bloodstained courier brought from the crash site would also have contained some kind of gift from France for the Bertrams, as, despite all their other concerns, it was an unfailing courtesy observed by all returning agents. For one man, André Carudel, an agent in charge of pick-ups for his network, it was a point of honour to send a gift of some description to the Bertrams on each of his exchanges. Carudel was well known as a jockey in France before the war but being half French and half English, was recruited, like Tony Bertram, into the Durham Light Infantry when his call-up came. Tony had subsequently been responsible for Carudel's move to Secret Intelligence duties in France, his bilingualism being a valuable asset. It had been André-the-jockey, as Barbara referred to him, who had seen to the lily-of-the-valley arriving on her breakfast plate for Mayday morning.

Barbara had an understandable fascination for anything that had come fresh from the mysterious and dangerous world of occupied France. Often, the agents arrived at Bignor with their shoes caked in mud from the field of the night before. After they had cleaned them outside the back door, Barbara would collect the mud and sow mustard and cress in it so that she could tell her guests that they were eating something grown on French soil.

Telephone again. This must be Tony.

'Hello (yes, it's The Office). Hello darling. Six. Four men and two unattached females. O.K. see you later.' For once it's what they thought it would be. That's eleven, easy. I'd better make the beds and leave the camp beds till later. Are there enough sheets? I doubt it. I hope they don't notice that I generally give them used sheets, I expect they're too tired to bother.

Tony didn't say what time dinner would have to be. I'd better ring the pilots. It's about time we had another pilots' party. They have to be over at Tangmere by nine. That means dinner at 7.30. They'll arrive punctually, at least Tony's lot will. John will be late of course but that won't matter. They'll want tea. I'd better go to Petworth. Lor! I've left the soup on. Thank goodness I hadn't started. I know I shall leave something on one day and we'll have nothing to eat.

Je tire ma révérence, dada, dadi, dada ... et voilà tout. How silly not to be able to remember all the words. I shall always think of that party when I hear that and Octave listening to records for hours on end. He's dead too. I wonder if his wife still teaches the deaf and dumb. What is the good of coming to Petworth? I can never get anything. What's the good of six buns? But it's no good pretending I've got ten children, they know I haven't. That's the cigarettes, the cake if possible and the sausages. I'll get the beer at the pub by the station. How lovely the river is. I wish I had been able to go with them when one of the drivers took a party on the river. I must take the boys in the holidays. I hope there won't be too much on that moon, they do so hate having to turn out of their room for the Hullabaloos. I hope Nicky's all right.

I'd better make a final list of things I can't do till the last minute. Finish beds. Cook meat and veg. I can get the table laid now — eleven. That means five down one side and four the other and one at each end, a squash but not impossible, we've been nineteen. It'll mean the ping-pong table-top on the dining table. The fires. I'd better do the kitchen stove first. I hate getting coke, I hate getting coke, I hate... Catch Perry-the-paper-man, oh dear, I've missed him. I must do it tomorrow. Good, there's enough coal in, we only need wood. I'd better do it properly and get three barrow-loads. Unless I just get in enough for tonight and get the French to help in the morning. No, if they're new they'll be late up and off to

London directly after breakfast. I'd better do it. Cigarettes, matches, flowers, soap and towels in the bedrooms. I'd better make John's bed up on the sofa now and leave the camp beds.

I do hope this op will be successful. It's so awful when the same people come back having failed to find the field or something. They're tired and miserable and have to go through it all again. And the time when the plane turned over and burnt. Poor Lestanges. I hope his burns heal all right. And the awful haunted look of the ones in the second plane who saw the first plane burning and couldn't help and had to come back and go out again the next moon. And we thought that all three and the pilot had been killed but it turned out it was only the pilot. And Lestanges brought back the stamps for the boys I'd asked him for and he'd been desperately ill with his burns all the time.

I must milk Caroline and feed the animals before they come. Poor Duff, he never gets a walk nowadays. If this lot doesn't get off they may go for a walk tomorrow but lots don't like walking. I don't think Manuel really liked it when we raced him up the Downs. Stephane walked, and the Colonel and Garnier — I wonder if he's all right, poor Claude, it must be awful not knowing what happened to his father — and of course Michael, Michael the second, the first was a Pole, one of the original Hullabaloos, and the third was a General. I should never have got the garden dug that year if he hadn't helped in Tony's old mackintosh and hat.

I must get tea. We simply haven't eleven cups with handles. Oh well. Some of the Hullabaloos look so ill and strained. Brossolette did when he arrived with Jacques Robert. He was grey all over, Pierre-le-gris we called him. And I had to keep them here for two days and then drive them to London. And the electricity broke down and we went down to the Guest House for dinner because I had nothing to cook on and Jacques — Popeye — would make awful remarks about all the old ladies there. Now that's everything done except changing and washing. What can I wear? I wish I didn't hate myself in trousers, then I needn't wear stockings. I haven't put the flowers in the bedrooms, lor, here they are!

The drawing room at Bignor Manor, c. 1941. The sofa and armchairs often doubled as beds when the house was full of agents. (*The Bertram Family*)

It is not always possible to identify the agents Barbara is referring to in her monologue. Unfortunately, 'the colonel' or 'the general' could be any number of the officers who passed through Bignor Manor. Secrecy, still scrupulously observed by MI6 more than seventy years since the end of the war, meant that it was impossible to find out the true identity even of 'John', Tony Bertram's fellow conducting officer. In fact it was only as a result of the publication of the first edition of this book that John's identity was revealed when his daughter, Caroline Babois, attended an author's presentation of this book at the inaugural Petworth Literary Festival in November 2011. She had been researching her father's war record and this had led her to the Bertram family and *A House for Spies*. Her father was John Gentry who held the rank of Royal Navy commander, working for Kenneth Cohen as his primary interlocuter with the Free French and the *BCRA*. A keen sportsman, he had worked in south west France in import-export from 1925 until the outbreak of war. Between May and June 1940 he had given his services to the Naval Control Board in Bordeaux, helping hundreds of British citizens board ships for home ahead of the German invasion. He escaped to England himself on board *HMS Beagle*, the last ship to leave Bordeaux.

Many of the agents Barbara knew only by their Christian names and these were often pseudonyms, so the Octave she talks about, for instance, remains unidentified. For others, however, she used their real names, or at least a pseudonym which was either well known or which, through a certain amount of detective work, can lead to the real person behind it. The 'Caroline' of the extract above was, of course, the goat, and 'Duff', the family's Dalmatian; Manuel, who did not enjoy walks, on the other hand, was Captain André Manuel, Colonel Passy's right-hand man at the *BCRA*. He was a frequent visitor to Bignor, as it was here that de Gaulle's secret service staff had their first opportunity to debrief returning agents. It was a point of some contention between the British and French services that *BCRA* officers were not allowed to meet their own men straight off the plane at Tangmere. The British claimed that security prevented the likes of Passy and his staff from access to the air base, but Passy believed that it was because the SIS wanted it to appear that they valued the agents' work more than their Free French counterparts and also because they did not want the *BCRA* to meet the French agents who were working directly for the British.

'Stephane', who did enjoy his exercise on the South Downs, was Stephane Hessel, a German Jew who took French nationality in 1937 and, having joined de Gaulle in London in 1941, was sent on a clandestine mission in France just before the allied invasion in March 1944. He was captured by the Germans and became one of the few to have made a successful escape after being sent to a concentration camp. After the war, he became a distinguished diplomat for France and contributed to the drafting of the Universal Declaration of Human Rights in 1948.

A later chapter will reveal the story of 'Garnier', another of Barbara's keen walkers who had struck up a strong friendship with Stephane Hessel during his two visits to London. She would not have known his real name, Christian Pineau. The Claude she refers to is his eldest son whom he arranged to evacuate to England via a Lysander flight in April 1943 'to protect him', as Pineau wrote in his memoirs, 'from the imprudences of a seventeen-year-old.' Claude's youngest brother, Gilbert, was left to wonder all his life about why he, aged ten at the time, and his other two older brothers from his father's first marriage were not considered at equal risk and allowed to remain in France. Gilbert has clear memories of being given secret messages to carry in his clothing on behalf of *Libération Nord*, his father's undercover newspaper, when travelling in and out of Paris.

The two 'Michaels' Barbara recalls are both identifiable; 'the Pole' would have been Roman Czerniawski, founder and leader of the Paris-based *Interallié* network who was flown to England by John Nesbitt Dufort in October 1941. He was parachuted back to France later that month only to be arrested by the *Abwehr* a few weeks later. Thanks to the treachery of Mathilde Carré, a member of *Interallié*, the network was destroyed, but Czerniawski bargained with his captors, agreeing to return to England as a German agent. Once back in London, however, he agreed to become a double agent on behalf of the allies and eventually played an important role in deceiving the Germans into believing that the invasion of France would centre on the Pas de Calais rather than the beaches of Normandy.

The second 'Michael' was Michel Pichard, who was sent out to France by the *BCRA* in January 1943 to assist Gilbert Renault in the *Confrérie Notre Dame*. He would later return to London and transfer from the *Renseignements* (Intelligence) to the *Action* branch of the *BCRA* and take control of all their parachuting activities. Pierre Brossolette and Jacques Robert have already been discussed in this book. Brossolette went on to become a pivotal player in uniting the majority of resistance networks under the Free French banner. He made four Lysander flights in the course of his work for General de Gaulle, so became very well known at Bignor Manor. Jacques Robert was a jovial, robust character with a distinguished record as a tank regiment lieutenant responsible for destroying some thirty enemy armoured vehicles during France's short-lived resistance against the German invasion. Known affectionately as 'Popeye', he was first recruited by Gilbert Renault in December 1941, but later set up a separate network in Lyons (*La Phratrie*) after evading a Gestapo hunt for him in Paris.

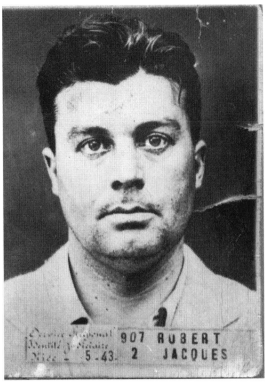

Jacques Robert, (Popeye) photographed by the Vichy Police after his arrest in Nice in April 1943. He escaped four days later. (*The Bertram Family*)

Robert survived the war, escaping his eventual capture by the Vichy police and reaching London once again, where he trained parachutists who would be dropped into France as the allies advanced to bring in resistance fighters into the action against the Germans. Soon after the invasion, he was himself parachuted behind the lines and fought with the *maquis* for some two months. Brossolette would not live to see the liberation of his country. During an attempt to leave France on yet another mission, the boat he used to escape from the

Brittany coast in February 1944 ran aground in bad weather. He took refuge with a local resistance fighter, but was arrested the next day after a routine police check. It did not take long for the Gestapo to realize they had caught a man they had been hunting for a long time and he was taken to their headquarters at 84 Avenue Foch in Paris where he was interrogated and tortured for two-and-a-half days. When he would not tell them anything, he was thrown into Fresnes prison before being brought back to Avenue Foch for a further ordeal. Seizing upon a moment of inattention by his captors, Brossolette, who doubted his ability to stay silent for a second session, raced towards an open window and fell five storeys to the cobbles below. He died that evening from his injuries.

'Poor Lestanges' was, in fact, Lieutenant Jean Lacroix. Barbara had mentioned to him at dinner before his departure from Tangmere on the night of 10 February 1944 that her son Tim had just begun a stamp collection and would be thrilled if he could bring back some stamps from France on his next visit to Bignor. He was to be flown with two other agents to a field about ten miles south-east of Bourges in central France. His pilot that night, a young Australian, Flight Officer John McDonald, was on only his third Lysander mission, the first two having been flown within the preceding week.

On reaching the landing ground, McDonald aborted two approaches before going round again for a third attempt. He had probably forgotten one vital action needed before landing, which was to switch the fuel mixture control from 'weak' to 'normal'. This would mean he was unable to throttle back fully and could explain why he touched down much too fast. The Lysander sped beyond the flare path and ran into a patch of plough, where it flipped upside down and burst into flames. The two other agents were thrown out of the rear cockpit more or less unscathed, but the pilot and Lacroix were trapped in the burning fuselage. The heat prevented the reception party from getting near the plane, so they bundled the two dazed survivors away before anyone came to investigate the blaze, and left the other two men for dead.

When the Germans eventually arrived at the scene, they found only the remains of John McDonald. Somehow Lacroix had extricated himself from the wreckage and, finding himself alone and in excruciating agony from his burnt arms, staggered off in the direction of the nearest village. There, he put himself at the mercy of the priest who, knowing that the local doctor was a Nazi sympathizer, pushed Lacroix some five miles on his bicycle to a convent nursing home where his burns could be treated. The Mother Superior took on the responsibility of caring for him herself, locking him in a room and allowing a rumour to spread that the person confined was one of her nuns who had become pregnant.

Thanks to the priest, contact was made with members of Lacroix's network who were able to arrange a flight out of France for him during the next moon. He was still in a very bad way as he clambered out of the Lysander that had brought him back to Tangmere but, before he boarded the ambulance waiting to take him to East Grinstead Hospital, he handed the conducting officer a package, asking him to give it to Barbara. These were the stamps he had promised to bring back. When Barbara visited Lacroix in hospital, however, he could remember nothing about any stamps.

'Hello, how are you, it's nice to see you again. *Bonjour, monsieur, comment allez-vous? Bonjour Madame.*' I wish I knew what I really ought to say to sound friendly.

'Hello, darling. Yes, everything's O.K. You have to be there at nine, dinner's seven-thirty. *Entrez, Madame. Vous fumez? Et vous?*' It's idiotic to be so tongue-tied. All I do is to push cigarettes into their faces and grin.

'*Du lait, madame, du sucre?*' I wonder why they always repack as soon as they get here. '*Laissez-moi voir vos chemises, monsieur. Vous êtes sûr qu'il n'y a pas de marque? Ah, si, il y a de marque.* Pass me the Milton, Jean and here's some scissors. You do that case while I do this one.'

'*Vous ne fumez pas? Encore du gin, madame?*' Talk about Martha. Luckily Jean's being marvellous as usual and let's hope people won't notice I never talk. I hope there's enough rum. I hate giving out rum just before they leave, it's so grim, like an execution.

'Are you nearly ready for dinner, darling? It's about time, we won't wait for John. Oh, here he is. Late as usual, John. I suppose you want a drink. All right, but hurry as dinner's ready.' I hate the going in to dinner, I'm so bad at it. I never know their names or where they should sit if I do and they're so miserable because I don't place them. I wish they'd just sit down anywhere. Thank goodness they're fairly quick today and the soup's still hot. 'What's the weather like, John, is it still clear?' Oh dear I hope it's not cancelled. What would happen if I dropped the dish carrying it in? If it happened in the kitchen I'd scoop it up and say nothing, but I suppose they'd hear the crash. Oh, the telephone.

It can't be off, it can't be off, it can't ... it is, c'est off. I can see by Tony's face. How awful for them. I do hate these last minute cancels. We shall have to try and be gay tonight. They're amazing how well they take it, it must be an awful strain. This means lunch, dinner and Reception Pie tomorrow anyway and if c'est off again lunch and dinner perhaps for days. I shall have to go to Chichester. I suppose it's better to have it cancelled now than when they're at the aerodrome which has happened sometimes. Rémy and Michael the second went over twice — all screwed up to go and then plonk — 'Yes, of course I'll play darts. No, I think I'm wanted to make four for bridge, you've plenty for darts without me.' How damp the cards are. I must do something about that cupboard. '*Deux piques*'. I hope they're not too good, I've really no idea how to play. '*Je passe*'. I'm sure that's wrong, I probably should have said four clubs or something. Oh lor, I wish they wouldn't have the radio on all the time. 'No, John, I'm not interested in your silly game, I'm playing a serious one, run along. *Trois careaux*'. The beds are all right except the camp ones. I must switch on the bedroom fires at about ten. '*Trois coeurs*'. Oh why has he gone on, I shall have to play the hand and I've got nothing.

'Chalk? It's in that box. Oh isn't there any? I'll get some from the boys' room. Can you wait till I've finished this hand?' What did I come up for? Oh yes, chalk. I hope there is some. How lovely and quiet it is up here, I wish I could go to bed. I must get the boys to tidy this cupboard next time they're home, it's impossible to find anything. I hope Nicky's all right. 'Here you are. Who's winning? I'm doing rather badly I'm afraid. I never have anything above a four'. I wish I could stop smoking. I feel all rough and dry inside. '*Deux piques*'. Tomorrow I can kill an old hen for lunch. No, it had better be for dinner, it'll take ages to cook. We may have to fall back on corned beef for lunch unless perhaps we have last night's Reception Pie and I make something else tonight if c'est on.

'*De la bière pour vous, Madame? Vous ne l'aimez pas; vous aimez du thé peut-être? Mais non, pas du tout.*' Oh lor, the cups haven't been washed up from tea. 'Oh thank you, you are dears. I don't know what I should do without you. No, there aren't eleven cups with handles.' Really the drivers are wonderful. Thank goodness the water's hot.

Oh dear, I wish they'd go to bed. Luckily Tony talks, it would be awful if we were both dumb. Thank goodness, they're moving. '*Vous êtes ici, madame. Bonsoir, dormez bien. Et deux messieurs ici, et deux là. Le petit déjeuner quand vous voulez — de neuf heures jusqu'à midi.*'

'John, you're on John's bed. Yes, of course it's wrong that you should have a comfortabler [sic] bed than me but you always do sleep there and I'm all right here.' For goodness sake stop talking and go to sleep. Camp beds are most horribly uncomfortable. Let me think about breakfast. There're plenty of eggs so that's all right. I'm glad I changed to ground coffee, that's one nightmare less. Popeye ground it for me and ate a bean because he was so pleased to have real coffee again. If the police had asked him and Brossolette for their identity cards that time I was taking them to London and got stopped for speeding, I wonder what I could have done. I might lie my way out of it now but that was right at the beginning.

How foggy it is. I hope it still is when they wake up, then they'll see why it was off. If they come down in bits we could have boiled eggs but we haven't enough egg cups for all at once. I think I'll risk it, they never do come down all together. There's someone now. Oh good it's Tony. 'Morning, darling. Did you sleep? Oh well enough, a bit cold. Is anyone else up yet? There's some coffee ready if you'd like some.' Oh, here's someone else, I must put the eggs in. '*Bonjour, Monsieur, vous avez bien dormi?*' Oh lor, here they all are.

I don't think I shall suggest taking anyone to Chichester. It's quicker alone. I must get petrol and oil. I hope they remember to send my petrol coupons punctually, I've only three gallons left. Bother, I haven't filled in the Food Office forms. If they ever really look at them they must think it odd that sometimes I have thirty-three main meals in a day. Good, there's the keeper with lots of rabbits. I'd better buy six if he'll let me. That's marvellous, what luck. There's the cathedral. How marvellous, a salmon. Now we're all right for ages. I must hurry back or I shan't have lunch ready in time. They may have decided to do something this afternoon. What a lovely day, I wish there was time to enjoy it. It looks like fog again tonight though. I'd better stop at the pub — they're sure to be there. 'Hello, darling. Any news? C'est off, I thought it would be. We'd better have a pilots' party, hadn't we? I'll ring up when I get in. No, I won't stop. I'd better see to things'. C'est off. Poor things and poorer still the ones waiting over there perhaps hidden in a barn.

I must ring up the pilots at once. 'Extension 86 please. Hello, this is Barbara Bertram, can some of you come over tonight? Oh, four or five or six but you'll have to wash up and bring some beer, about seven o'clock. Goodbye.'

Good, here they are back. 'Lunch will be ready in two minutes'. I do hate this liquid paraffin for the salad but I suppose it's better than nothing. '*Asseyez-vous, messieurs. Vous avez joué aux fléchettes? Qui a gagné?*' This meat's tough and tasteless. I must get in veg for tonight. 'Thank you, it would be lovely to get the washing up done if you really don't mind. The pilots will help tonight but I do hate it when they throw the plates from one to the other, we've only got fourteen and three cracked ones.'

'No, I'm not coming for a walk after all, darling, I'd rather get things ready. Yes, I'll try and have time for a rest.' Of course I shan't. I'm glad Duff's getting a walk. If there's someone here between the moons it's better for him, at least he gets as far as the pub every day. Pierre-the-peasant was a marvellous man. That letter from his wife was one of the most touching things I've ever heard. So clever of her to say all she wanted to — just the things he wanted to hear — without it appearing that she was writing to him at all. And the work he did in the garden. Stacks of grass and nettles for Caroline and everything dug and tidy as it's never been before. And then he scythed the Armstrongs' grass and carried it up on his back. But after dark how lost he was, he sat and held my knitting wool and played it out as I knitted.

Gosh, I must hurry and get tea, they may be back at any moment. I'd better make hot buttered toast as we've got all that butter from The Office. 'Hello, Duffy, was it a lovely

walkies? Tea's just ready. Will you organize a wood-getting.'
'*Du lait, Madame, du sucre?*' I'm like a gramophone record. 'All
right, I'll play. You two against John and me. You start. Good,
forty away'. How silly this is, I shall have to go in a minute
and see about things but it seems unfriendly never to play.
'John, if you're going to play as badly as that I shall stop.
There, that's the way to score, I've left you double twelve'. I
wonder if I ought to get out the drinks yet. Perhaps it's a bit
early and they seem settled down and Tony's reading — I
won't disturb them yet. I hope the pilots remember the beer.
'All right, John, I was only putting the soup on. What do we
want? Sorry, you must have jogged my arm.'

Here are the pilots. Good they've brought lots of beer.
Here it is beginning again just like all the pilots' parties. What
a lot of pilots there've been, Guy and Mac and Peter and
Robin and Hugh and Bunny and Stephen and McDonald and
Mac something else, and Andy and Dinger and ... I must stop
thinking, so many of them have been killed. '*Du whisky ou du
gin, Madame?*' Oh dear, I've forgotten to milk Caroline. It's
always a mistake to play darts when there's a big night, I
always forget something. 'No, you can't play ping pong till
after dinner. I've laid the table already.'

How nice the pilots are. I wish the boys were here. If this
op's put off much longer it'll be next weekend and the boys
must come home. They've been here with big crowds
sometimes; that Christmas when Manuel was supposed to
come and we waited and waited. 'Tidings of comfort and joy'
but there was no joy. Val tried to go out and Manuel tried to
come in and Passy and Brossolette came down and the
Christmas tree was all ready with the French and English flags
on top and the boys were so excited and couldn't understand
why we were all depressed and Passy brought us all lovely
presents. Oh dear, I mustn't dream. '*Du pain, Madame?*' I must
put the coffee on but I'll make them wash up before we have
it. 'Do be careful.' Oh I do hate it when they throw the plates
like that but they get it done beautifully quickly. 'Oh, you want

to play ping-pong, all right. One love, two love.' How can Robin sit and read with all this noise going on? 'Five-ten, change.' There's one pilot playing patience.

I wish I could remember people's names better, I know most of the earlier ones and the ones that have been several times. Of course I don't know if they're their real names. Faye was the one who brought me the first bottle of scent, a lovely Sciapelli bottle and oranges from Algiers, he came several times. And he's been arrested. Marie-Madeleine was here with him and we went to Horsham and she bought us twelve little glasses because she had broken one of ours and that boy, Dorling, I think, who sent Tony books, he's been arrested too — I mustn't go on thinking. '*De la bière, Madame?*' 'All right I'll play darts if you want me to but I shall be bad, I warn you.' I wish they wouldn't excite Duff like that. 'Down Duffy, down.' They'll get hairs all over their trousers, he'd better go in the kitchen. 'Come on, lovely for Duffy.' Poor Duff. Oh dear, how dirty the house is. I really must try and clean it a bit in the next dark period.

There's Elston come for the pilots. I hope they go quickly. It's awful the way I always want people to go. I love having the pilots but I'm tired. 'Another beer before you go, Bunny? I'm just taking Elston some.' It's silly the way he won't come in when there's a big party. Oh, they've started to sing. 'You must come in, Elston, and help sing. *Alouette, gentille alouette.*' I wish I knew all the words, I ought to by now. I must rush up and switch on the bedroom heaters. I wish they'd go, it's half past twelve. Good, they really are moving. 'Goodbye, goodbye.' Now let's hope the rest will go to bed. '*Une cigarette, Madame? Encore de la bière, Monsieur?*' Good they're going up. 'No, John, I will not smoke or drink ever again and now I'm going to undress in the dining room and then come in and get straight into bed and go to sleep and Tony and you are not to talk at all.' I shan't wash or do my hair. Heigh, ho. 'Goodnight, I'm asleep.'

I wish I were. There's a wrinkle under me and the rooms all smoky and stuffy. It was a good party, we've had lots of good parties. The first one Stephen came to was a good one — I wonder if he knew he was going to crash, I expect he did but I don't suppose his passengers did, I wonder if they'll ever conquer the fog difficulty. I hope this lot gets off tomorrow.

This part of the monologue, as well as depicting the camaraderie that existed between agents, pilots and SIS conducting officers, is a roll-call of some of the most significant players in the allies' undercover campaign to secure strategic information from occupied France. The occasion Barbara recalls when Rémy (Gilbert Renault) and Michel Pichard twice got as far as Tangmere before the operation was called off took place in September 1942, Renault's third and final stay at Bignor.

Clearly, Passy had a human side, as Barbara testifies with the story of Christmas 1942, when he and Brossolette waited in vain at Bignor for the return of André Manuel. He, like so many of the French, was full of warm appreciation of Barbara's attentions, describing the manor in his memoirs as '*un* home délicieux' and recalling the charming welcome and toothsome food that Barbara reserved for her departing and arriving guests. He was, perhaps, a little more suspicious of Tony Bertram's bonhomie which, he considered, disguised a psychological examination of each agent, the results of which would be keenly received by his SIS bosses.

A month after his fruitless Christmas vigil, Passy returned to Bignor to await Manuel's delayed return once more. This time, at least, the weather allowed the operation to go ahead and 'Pick' (Pickard) successfully landed his outgoing passenger, Pierre Brossolette, in central France, near the town of Issoudun. This was, however, the occasion when Pickard's compass sent him drastically off course on his return flight with Manuel and René Massigli on board (see Chapter 5), and Barbara, Tony and Passy spent an anguished night together as the Lysander became increasingly overdue. It was not until 8 o'clock the next morning that a call came through to say the missing party had turned up at Land's End.

Passy was himself able to appreciate the sense of relief experienced by so many of his agents on their dawn arrival at Bignor Manor when, on 16 April 1943, he was brought back from a seven-week mission of his own in France. The mission, organized at General de Gaulle's request, was to appraise all resistance groups in the north (occupied) zone of France, both intelligence- and action-oriented, of the General's military and civil directives. With the help of Paris-based Pierre Brossolette and de Gaulle's key representative in the former free zone, Jean Moulin, he would prepare to establish a National Council for the Resistance, covering the whole of France.

When Winston Churchill was told about Passy's intended mission, he immediately forbade it, saying that it was far too risky to send someone with as much knowledge of allied undercover work in France as Passy. De Gaulle argued that other men with almost as much knowledge as Brossolette had already been allowed to operate in France, and Churchill eventually relented on the condition that Passy kept a cyanide capsule on his person at all times (hidden in a signet ring), which he would not hesitate to use upon capture by the Germans. One of his most dangerous moments was during a meeting he had called in Paris between Brossolette and Moulin when the two men fell out with each other dramatically, each accusing the other at the top of their voices of ambitious self-interest and almost coming to blows. Passy's entreaties for them to calm down were in vain — Germans occupied other parts of the building — and it was only through good fortune that no one came to investigate the disturbance.

The 'Val' to whom Barbara refers could claim to have been even more frustrated than his fellow house-guests during the Christmas of 1942. His real name was Vladimir Bouryschkine, a White Russian brought up in Paris and the USA and an agent for MI9, the branch of the SIS specializing in creating escape routes for crashed or escaped allied servicemen. On two consecutive December nights, his Lysander pilot made it all the way down to the *Alliance's* landing ground at Thalamy, east of Ussel in the Auvergne, in very difficult flying conditions, only to be confronted by fog at their destination. He did eventually make it into France by parachute in March 1943, but not before a total of nine aborted attempts to get him there.

There was better luck for the *Alliance* network during the January moon of 1943, when John Bridger was able to land at Thalamy to deposit a Belgian agent and take off again with Léon Faye on board together with Henri-Léopold Dor, a liaison agent for the network and almost certainly the 'Dorling' Barbara remembers. He, like many of the *Alliance* network, was from an affluent background, having been sent to study law at Cambridge by his father, a distinguished Marseilles maritime lawyer. Those who believe that a tendency existed until quite recently for MI6 to put their trust in people from the higher echelons of society would not have been surprised to see the *Alliance* — their foremost intelligence network in France working exclusively for them — made up of such well-heeled and cosmopolitan individuals as Marie-Madeleine, Léon Faye and Henri-Léopold Dor. The likes of Sir Claude Dansey would have felt particularly comfortable dealing with such people and even Barbara, with her childhood exposure to the high life, clearly appreciated the refinement of the gifts they brought her and Tony.

Barbara's concern about Dor's arrest was justified. He had, in fact, fallen into the hands of the Italians who were occupying Nice in early 1944 and was subjected to interrogation by their secret police. He was given the *giro* treatment, which meant being tied to a chair and, deprived of all food and drink, spun round incessantly for thirty-six hours in an airless room lit by powerful arc lights. When the spinning finally stopped, he was beaten savagely on the head until he passed out. Regaining consciousness, he found he was losing his memory and was genuinely unable to give his interrogators any answers. Instead, he astonished them by pulling himself to his feet and spinning himself round, then launching his head against the stone wall of the cell for good measure to hasten total amnesia. He succeeded in giving nothing away and when, at Italy's exit from the war, he and others from his network were handed over to the Gestapo, the Italians forgot to pass on their police dossiers, and the Gestapo, with no evidence for a prosecution, let the men go in a gesture of contempt for their former allies. Dor therefore survived the war and eventually settled in Britain.

Although torture was scarcely the favourite topic of conversation at Bignor Manor, occasionally Barbara's guests did broach the subject with her, including Marie-Madeleine who, during her eventual lengthy stay in England, came down to Bignor to meet an incoming agent. She and Barbara sat up all night talking and torture was one of the things they discussed. Apparently, the tough subjects did not withstand the treatment as well as the intelligent, sensitive ones. One returning agent who had survived torture told Barbara he had tried to visualize the pattern of spots on her Dalmatian, Duff, to take his mind off what was being done to him. Often, it was the smaller things which were more difficult to endure. Extraction of teeth and nails or pins pushed into a woman's breast were worse than beatings, hanging by the wrists, electrocution or near drowning, which at least induced semi-consciousness after a time. If you could survive the first quarter of an hour, you would be less likely to crack thereafter.

Perhaps the agent of whom Barbara had the fondest memories was Pierre Delaye, the man she called Pierre-the-peasant. At least he was spared torture, although she would never see him again after he left Bignor. He spent a whole month at her house as he had been told he needed to practise his radio operator skills there before he was ready to join Christian Pineau's newly-formed network, *Phalanx*. Originally a farmer, he served as a captain in the French army during the early part of the war before becoming a prisoner of war in Germany. At one point, he went on hunger strike with a number of other prisoners, saying he was doing it for his son.

He managed to escape the prison camp and eventually reached Britain via the USSR and was recruited by the *BCRA*. After his training at the hands of the SIS, he was parachuted into the Beaujolais region of France early in January 1943 and proved almost immediately to be the most reliable and efficient radio operator and co-ordinator of airborne missions Pineau could have wished for. On 11 May that year, Delaye was transmitting from a house in the small town of Loyettes on the Rhône, east of Lyons, when the Germans arrived at his door, having been tipped off by a local inhabitant. He fled the house on a bicycle, but was caught and killed in a hail of bullets as he tried to cross the bridge over the Rhône. The last time he had seen his wife and child was when he left to fight at the beginning of the war. Locals from Loyettes remember the sight of his German assassins beside Delaye's corpse devouring a twenty-eight egg omelette which they had ordered the local auberge to make for them in celebration of their coup.

Eight o'clock. Lor, I'm late. Anyway they'll be later. I'll have to take Caroline to the Billy soon. Last time one of the Michaels held her in the back of the car, if there's nobody here I shall have to walk her and it's miles. I'll give the chickens dried stinging nettles — Pierre-the-Peasant told me about that. Oh dear, people are moving about and I'm not nearly ready. '*Bonjour, vous avez bien dormi?*' Poor things it's awful how we all pretend they're just paying an ordinary visit here and all the time they must know they may be arrested and tortured as soon as they get to France. 'Hello, darling. You all right?' We never seem to have a chance of talking to each other during a moon. 'Any plans?'

I hope they decide to go to Brighton or somewhere, then I needn't get lunch. 'Yes, of course I can manage lunch here, much nicer.' Oh dear, I hope I sounded sincere.

'Hello John, you're early for you. Coffee? Everyone's down except the drivers.'

They deserve a lie-in; often driving all night and amusing the French all day. And that moon when Peggy was busy getting engaged to Jimmy and she had to play bridge with his letter proposing to her in her pocket and him ringing up every minute for an answer. Their wedding was fun, I hope they'll be happy. And Rachael married into The Office too.

'No, I don't think I'll go for a walk but I'll meet you at the pub perhaps.'

I wonder what the pub really thinks. And there was that awful moon when I was so ill and Tony and a lot of them went to the pub and I went down to bring them back for lunch and I could hardly stand. Luckily the drivers were kind and insisted on me going to bed when we got back and it was 'off' so that was all right. I wonder if it would have been a girl.

That would have been lovely but I suppose I should have had to give up the job, so perhaps it was just as well.

It really does look hopeful. Oh dear, I'm as bad as the French. We always tell them not to look at the sky here in the morning as it means nothing. I do hope c'est on. Eddie's supposed to be coming with a fresh lot tomorrow and it's so awfully difficult if two parties are here and can't meet. We've only had that once so far and that time in spite of all our careful planning and timing, I found them all in a huddle in the bathroom. It must be awful to know you're going to be tortured if you're caught. I wonder more don't kill themselves, I hate having to sew poison into their cuffs, it feels almost as if I was helping to murder them.

Here they are. '*C'était bien au bistrot? Vous avez gagné aux fléchettes?* No, no-one's telephoned. Lunch is ready when you are.'

I hate this time when we're just waiting for the telephone and everyone pretends they're not and then when it rings there's suddenly an icy feeling of tension and everyone stops breathing.

The telephone! Good, c'est on, I can tell at once from Tony's face; if John answers the phone you can't tell. Everyone looks so pleased. I wonder if they really are. Now I suppose they'll start packing and re-packing all over again. And Tony will have to give out papers and money and revolvers again.

'Oh, give her a shilling. Yes, that's heaps.'

It's awful the way she always comes Red Cross collecting when there's a flap on. Oh dear, Caroline's all entangled in her chain. Good, Tony's doing her. It's nearly tea time. I'd better do the animals first. I wish there was ever enough good food for them. In the summer I must try and find time to glean again as I did last year, that gave them lovely corn for ages. There's a Lysander coming over. I'd better tell the others. Oh I hope he won't come too low. I suppose it's one of them thanking us for last night's party, but I wish they wouldn't;

he's coming much too low, it must be Peter. How enormous it looks. He's coming round again, I wish he wouldn't, I wish he wouldn't. He was only a few inches above the church that time. Good, he's going. It was awful the time I went out to wave to a Lysander and it wasn't, it was a German plane and they tried to machine-gun me. I suppose I ought to have known by the sound that it wasn't a Lizzy.

'Did they say what time they wanted them over, Tony? O.K. We'd better have dinner at seven then.' That means potatoes on at six-thirty, switch on oven at five-thirty — '*Vous n'avez pas du thé, Monsieur*'.

Wine to warm soonish. I wish Tony wasn't giving out the things so early, they'll have nothing to do later. 'More tea, John?'

I do hate the radio on all the time, I wish they wouldn't. The French news is nice, and *Les Messages Personnels* and *Les Français parlent aux Français* and *Ici Londres*, but this perpetual music, it must drive Tony dippy when he's trying to cope with money and things. I wish that man wouldn't walk up and down all the time too. Poor thing, I expect he's all on edge. There's one man quietly reading as though nothing was happening. I'd better start the drinks early.

I shall have to change all the beds about, I suppose. I wish I knew what was coming in. I bet John won't tell me even if he knows. I wish he wasn't so maddening when I want to know anything.

'John, how many and what sexes are expected? Beast. Of course it matters to me.'

'*Un whisky, Monsieur ou du gin?*'

I must go and see to things. Tony and the drivers can do the drinks.

Soup's done, veg done, pud done, only the meat to do and the table. Eleven again. Plates to warm. We haven't enough plates or bowls for soup, it'll have to be a mixture. It's ridiculous The Office not sending us down any crockery. We've never had much and now there's hardly one unchipped plate. I'd better do the blackout while I remember. Let's see there are nineteen not counting the drawing room windows. Eighteen, seventeen, sixteen, I really must mend this one it takes longer to put up than all the rest, fifteen, fourteen, oh dear, another one broken.

There, that's done. I'd better see how they're getting on.

'No, I don't think I'd better play. I'll have to see to things in a minute.' They're given their revolvers and things and then they play darts against the door of the secret cupboard. I wonder if there's enough coal and wood for tonight, I hope so, oh and coke. I'd better get that now before it gets any darker. I hate getting coke, I hate getting coke — oh shut up repeating things. Oh lor, someone's had a bath and used all the hot water. I hope it heats up before I have to wash up. 'Dinner's ready.'

It mustn't be off tonight …

'*Du pain, Madame, du sel?*'

Oh dear, waves of talk keep washing over me without me hearing a word, I must be getting tired. I hope I shall answer intelligently, I just can't attend at all. How cheerful they all are. If Tangmere or The Office ring up during dinner it'll be the last straw. I wonder what the exchange thinks we're up to. All these calls to and from London and Tangmere often in the middle of the night. I must go and get the coffee and then the rum. Oh dear, so like an execution. I wonder what it's really like to be tortured — I mustn't think of that, I wonder if they do.

'*Un peu de rhum, Monsieur?*' I try to smile to make up for being such a dumb idiot. Oh dear, Tony's just going to tell them it's time to go. I wish it didn't make me feel sick. What a lovely night. It's cold though. '*Au revoir, Monsieur, mais pas ce soir.*' Oh dear, I've said that so many times, I hope it sounds fresh. '*Au revoir. Je vous reverrai après la guerre à Paris. Au revoir, au revoir.*' They've gone. I wish I didn't feel sick.

There is no doubt that Barbara's task would have been nearly impossible without the help she received from the FANY drivers, especially when operations had to be cancelled through bad weather. These women were hand-picked for their ability, discretion and demeanour and, although they were ostensibly used as drivers, they invariably had a more important additional undercover role assisting with the training and preparation of SIS and SOE agents for their missions behind the lines. Of the thirty-nine FANYs who themselves volunteered as agents, a third died in German concentration camps with Violette Szabo and Noor Inayat Khan perhaps the most famous examples.

The Peggy that Barbara refers to in this piece is undoubtedly Peggy Van Lier, who would have known only too well what her passengers would be subjecting themselves to on the other side of the Channel. Her father was a Belgian businessman, her mother was South African, and she had herself worked as an agent in Brussels as a member of the Comet Line, operating in conjunction with MI9 and organizing the repatriation of hundreds of downed allied airmen via Marseilles, the Pyrenees and Spain. The cover for her organization was a Swedish Red Cross canteen providing food and clothes for poor children in Brussels. The escape line was betrayed in November 1942, however, when an English-speaking German posed as a British pilot, and Peggy, among others, was brought before the SS. Her cool head saved her, the German interrogator believing her story and letting her go.

Although she had been determined to resume her undercover work in Belgium, MI9 felt it was too dangerous for her to continue and insisted that she should herself be smuggled out of Europe along the Comet Line. On her eventual arrival from Gibraltar at RAF Hendon in January 1943, she was met by a dashing Coldstream Guards officer,

Jimmy Langley, a senior figure in MI9. Langley, who lost an arm at Dunkirk and was captured, had made his own way across France, having escaped from a German military hospital, and reached England in 1941. He and Peggy made a handsome pair with much in common to discuss. They quickly fell in love and Barbara was a witness to the moment the relationship became official.

The answer to who Rachael was and whom she married from The Office might be traceable in the forbidden files of MI6 but must otherwise be left hanging. The 'Eddie' who would be bringing the next lot of agents to Bignor is fairly certain to be the same Major Eddie Keyser who was sent out to Madrid by his boss, Kenneth Cohen, to meet Marie-Madeleine Fourcade after her painful train journey to the Spanish border. Cohen himself, whom Barbara was only allowed to know as 'KC', made several visits to Bignor himself, to greet some of the bigger fish landed by the previous night's Lysander flight.

> I do hope they have joy. I can't bear it those nights when the same lot come back having failed to find the field. I mustn't worry. I'd better start tidying up. Three glasses of whisky undrunk. I shall pour them back into the bottle. No one will know. Papers and bullet boxes must be burnt. Razor blades, cigarette packets, a hat, a glove, oh, why am I smoking again? My throat's dry already. Oh lordy lord, I wonder if they've got to Tangmere yet. There, that's the glasses washed and sort of dried, they'll have to do. Manuel helped me dry up the night he came down to meet Passy and Brossolette. The next morning those three had breakfast early before the rest were down and I was so tired I couldn't understand a word they said. I don't think I was meant to, there was an atmosphere.
>
> I'm getting on, there's only the plates left and they can dry themselves. I'd better re-lay the table then cook. There's not much left to do, only Reception Pie itself and the salad. I

wonder if they meant to leave this sack of *vivres* behind. I hope so. I'll put it in the larder and hope for the best. What a mess the bedrooms are in. Marie-Madeleine helped me make the beds the night she was here to meet someone. I wonder if they're over France yet. I wonder what happened to the three funny policemen — the Marx Brothers — we've had a lot of policemen. One left his ring behind. I wonder if I shall ever see him again to return it. And one man dropped his identity disk in the lav and I fished it out and gave it to John and it was awful because he didn't want The Office to know who he was and I betrayed him.

I shall only half undress. I must set the alarm for three forty-five. Tony said they might get back by four and I hate being woken by the telephone. Lor, it's nearly one already, I must get to sleep quickly. How nice it was when Madame Grenier came and he came down from London the next morning to meet her and they talked and talked politics all day and far into the next night. And when he was here with that conservative old Colonel and they got friendly together. And all the children we've had, Popeye's and the Petits' and three or four older boys — I wish we'd had all Rémy's children. And some of the women have been so unlikely; beautiful young girls who have done such brave and dangerous things and quite old ones and some who even look like cinema spies — a sort of double bluff. I must go to sleep. John's quite right, this bed's awfully cold and the pillow smells of his foul hair grease...

I thought it was the telephone for a minute. I must make up the fire. I hope it's kept in the kitchen stove, then I can lie down again till the telephone rings. It's cold. I mustn't sleep again. It's silly to have woken myself so early, they're always later than Tony says except when they've failed to find the field. I wish it didn't make me feel sick and breathless waiting for the telephone. That night I fell down the stairs hurrying to answer it, I thought I was really hurt. How awful it would have been if I had been. I'll never sleep upstairs again on those nights. There it is, quick. 'Hello, darling. How many? Four single men and a married couple. Good. I'll be ready for you. O.K.'

Four and a couple. How do I do that? Oh, easy. The couple in our room, two men in the guest room and two in the boys' room — poor boys. I hope Nicky's all right.

The heaters, the soup, the potatoes. It's silly to hurry they can't be here for half an hour. It's mad the times I give them bacon and eggs for Reception Pie but they seem to enjoy it so much.

'Well, Duffy, have you woken up too? Cold, isn't it?'

I wish they'd come, I hate waiting for them. There's the car door; oh lor, I feel so sick. That slam of the car door which says they've come always makes me feel sick. I must go to the door. What a lovely night. The moon's so bright, I hope it won't matter showing a light for a few minutes. Here they come. It's so silly of me to greet them here when they always have their hands full of parcels and they try to take off their hats and shake hands and they can't and we all get all tied up. '*Bonsoir, Monsieur, bonsoir, comment allez vous?*' I'm glad he's come back.

'*Bonsoir, bonsoir.*' There I am tongue-tied again. Why can't I greet them properly. '*Entrez, entrez, un whisky, une cigarette?*'

Thank goodness there are none of the terrifying sort, not even the woman. Oh dear they've got presents for us. '*Merci, Monsieur, merci bien.*'

Oh dear, I feel so grateful and I can't express it. It's amazing the way they bring us all these things. Books and wine for Tony and all my scent and stockings and brooches and things and a badge a General gave me; luckily Tony thanks them properly, they'll just have to think I'm a nit-wit. How bewildered the new ones look. I wish Duff wouldn't overdo his welcome but perhaps he makes up for me. 'Reception Pie's ready when you are darling.' Oh dear, they'll expect me to tell them where to sit. I seem to be always ladling out soup. I hope there's enough bread. 'The wine's in the kitchen, darling.'

Tony's looking tired and no wonder. It's lovely how appreciative they are, I expect they're dying of hunger. Oh dear, the conversation's coming at me in waves again. I hope they go to bed directly they've finished.

'*Du sel, Madame, du pain?*' It's fatal if they once get into the drawing room. I must be firm with them and show them upstairs straight away. Good, Tony's moving.

'*Voici votre chambre, Madame. Deux Messieurs sont ici et deux là. Dormez bien. Vous avez des pyjamas et rasoirs? Le petit quand vous voulez.* Good night, drivers, sleep well.'

It's nearly six, it's hardly worth going to bed. 'I'm going to have a bath. You go to bed. I'll come in later. Just help me with our camp beds, darling. I hope you're not in a hurry to get off this morning, John. Good. Go to bed and don't talk when I come in.'

If only everyone would stop talking. How lovely a bath is I shall wallow. Let's think. It's six, I could get to bed by six-twenty and I needn't get up till about eight-thirty. Oh yes, it's worth it. Lor, I'm tired, I must set the alarm or never wake up. Thank goodness John and Tony are asleep. I wonder what the ones who went out are doing. I don't suppose they're in bed.

Damn the clock, I can't find it to stop it ringing. I hope it won't wake Tony and John. Goodness, I feel awful. Bother, I forgot to get my clean clothes from my room; oh well, I suppose it doesn't matter. There's the telephone.

'Hello, oh hello, yes, everything's lovely. Five male, one female. Is it important because he's still asleep? They're having lunch here and leaving, I hope, directly afterwards. O.K. I'll tell him. Goodbye.'

There's another op tonight. If c'est off I hope they decide before they leave London. Ugh, how stuffy the house smells. I wish I'd cleared away before going to bed. If I open the windows it'll be freezing when they come down but I must for a bit. I hope some come down soon then I can wake John and he can start 'huddles' nice and early. It must be rather fun for them waking up and seeing England for the first time — it's a lovely part of England for them to see. I shall have my breakfast now in peace. Oh good, they're bumping about, I must wake Tony and John.

'Good morning, darling. They're moving. You must care, wake up. And you too, John. Yes, I know it's cold. Tony! Don't go to sleep again. Oh do wake up, both of you. I can't stand over you all day. I want to get this room tidy for "huddles" too.'

Poor things I expect they're tired but it's no good sympathising with them.

'*Bonjour, Monsieur. Vous avez bien dormi? Vous êtes le premier. C'est joli par ici n'est pas? Du café? Oui, c'est du vrai.*'

They still look rather dazed but cleaner. Who was that one who shaved off his moustache as soon as he arrived, before Reception Pie? We really ought to have more than one bathroom but luckily they can all wash in their rooms, except the drivers. The house is really too small all over.

Good, the fire's still alight, I shall only have to blow it. That's the best of wood. I shall need more wood for tonight. I wonder if they want more coffee, I'd better go and see. I wish they weren't all talking so much. Lor, how late it's got. I'd better begin lunch. I wish the last two would come down, it's nearly twelve.

The telephone! Good, c'est off for tonight. Oh good, oh good, I can go to bed at seven.

'Will you have to go up with this lot, darling? Good. We can have a lovely evening.'

Only three or four more hours of talk, talk, talk. Good, here are the last two...

'*Du café, Madame, du sucre?*'

It isn't so much that I don't understand when I'm tired, I just don't hear, it's all one blur of noise. That dark boy looks terribly tired. I hope they let him rest — I mean make him rest.

It must be beastly for them being searched when they get here. I suppose it has to be done. I hope Tony's remembered to take their French money and metro tickets and things to give the people going out. There's the last 'huddle' over, now we can have lunch.

Oh dear it's not only the talk that's coming at me in waves but people are all blurry too. It's odd how much I like this job, it's really rather a nightmare, but I wouldn't give it up for anything. I hope the thought of France won't always make me feel sick and the Marseillaise won't always make me cry.

It must seem to them that our rations are ample. How nice they all are and how careful of our things, hardly anything's been broken. How I must try and say goodbye friendlily. Some of them are oddly dressed for London, how they will enjoy buying new clothes.

'*Au revoir, Monsieur, au revoir, Madame, au revoir, au revoir.*' How tired the poor drivers must be. 'Goodbye, John. Stop talking and go, can't you.' Dear John, he'd be so surprised if I was nice to him. There, they've gone.

'Well, darling, are you very exhausted? No, I'm not going to rest. I shall dig till tea time and I shall go to bed at seven. Go and have a lovely read.' How quiet it is in the garden.'

And so Barbara ends her cathartic portrayal of a moon period at Bignor Manor. Considering the extraordinary mixture of types sharing such close quarters in such tense circumstances, it is remarkable how even-tempered the house parties usually remained. Even if her French comprehension sometimes failed her, Barbara's antennae were nonetheless well-tuned in detecting unease and discord. The 'atmosphere' that she sensed during the 'huddle' between Passy, Brossolette and Manuel following their mission in France had not been imagined. In his memoirs, Passy recalls his and Brossolette's deep displeasure with Manuel's conduct while they were away. 'We were extremely cold towards him', Passy recalls, 'as he had completely neglected us during our time in France. By what we considered to be plain inertia on his part, he succeeded in slowing down and disrupting the plans that we had begun to put into action, particularly in the important area of transmissions.'

Such was the anger of his returning boss that Manuel handed in his resignation the following day. Although Passy's 'brotherly friendship', as he put it, for Manuel would not allow him to leave the *BCRA* altogether, he did relieve him of his duties as deputy and replace him with Brossolette.

Other differences surfaced at Bignor from time to time, not least between those of divergent politics. One elderly, aristocratic and reactionary French colonel was forced to share his breakfast table with a communist politician and activist, Fernand Grenier, whom Renault had persuaded to fight with de Gaulle and had brought from France to England with him in January 1943. It is his wife that Barbara refers to above who came over by Lysander to join him the following June. Awaiting her arrival at Bignor, Grenier spent his time exchanging angry glares with the colonel until, one day, they accidentally met on their separate walks in the surrounding countryside. To Barbara's relief, they returned to the house reconciled and full of admiration for each other. On another occasion, a party of six, delayed for several days, were so antagonistically divided that, to separate them, Tony was forced to take three on an outing to Brighton, while Barbara escorted the rest to Chichester. One of Barbara's trio was so tense that he could only walk up and down the drawing room all day, driving everyone else to distraction. For one alarming moment, she thought he was about to make a gift to her of his prized purse, made, he had assured her, out of the skin of an assassinated German.

As well as some more welcome gifts received from grateful refugees, the Bertrams occasionally benefited from weight restrictions imposed on the baggage of outgoing agents. The 'vivres' that Barbara refers to being left behind would have been a sack of luxuries such as chocolate, butter and cigarettes, all useful currency in France for rewarding helpers. These would have to be sacrificed, however, if there was too much else to take out and Barbara's catering was duly enhanced. One sad reminder of an artist among her guests was a new box of oil paints which he had to leave behind because of its weight. The man was arrested and shot soon after his return to France, so Barbara gave the paints to one of the Bertrams' many distinguished artist friends, Oliver Hall, RA, whose nearby studio had recently been destroyed in a fire.

Bignor Manor must have felt a very strange place to the children who were whisked out of the imminent clutches of the Gestapo and landed in Sussex. The two Petit boys, airlifted in the same moon in the nick of time by Jim McCairns with their mother and their father Max, arrived at Tangmere having been horribly airsick. For two nights, the family had been hidden in a barn until, in the dead of night, the boys found themselves being bundled into an aeroplane where they had to lie at their parents' feet with all the luggage on top of them. When they arrived at Tangmere and heard a language they could not understand, they thought they were in Germany and were petrified.

As for the Robert (Popeye) girls, Chantal aged 6 and Marianne aged 3, whose July 1943 arrival in England Barbara also recalls here, they had been told before their departure that they would go to sleep in France and wake up in England thanks to the powers of the Holy Ghost. The sleeping pills they had been given wore off, however, and as Hugh Verity's

Lysander made its recognition signal above the field in France, both girls leapt to their feet, clapped their hands and shouted gleefully, 'Here comes the Holy Ghost! Here comes the Holy Ghost!'

Barbara's fond memories of these visiting children are a reminder of how much she must have felt deprived of her own for such long periods during the war. Her recurrent call of 'I hope Nicky's all right', was understandable. Her younger boy was an epileptic and it must have been doubly difficult to rely on the care of others during that time. In the summer of 1947, Barbara suffered what she describes in her memoirs as 'the only tragedy of her life'. Nicky, then aged eleven, had gone out with his bike having finished his homework and did not return for his supper. As concern for him grew and darkness fell, the growing number of searchers could find nothing. It was not until 9 o'clock the next morning that one of the local Bignor farmers came to the Manor with the shocking news that they had found the boy dead. He had climbed a ladder to the top of a haystack, fallen head-first down a vertical aeration vent between the bales and died of asphyxiation.

CHAPTER 10: A NETWORK BETRAYED

Gilbert Renault's Story — Part 2

No one, not even Gilbert Renault, had been impressed by the man Pierre Julitte had chosen as his own replacement as co-ordinator of all the *Confrérie de Notre Dame* network's radio transmissions after he and Renault left for England in February 1942. So concerned were the team of Paris radio operators about the incompetence of their immediate boss that they had asked François Faure, in charge of the network during Renault's absence, to relieve him of his duties immediately, but Faure had preferred to await Renault's return.

So, on 23 March, in a small house in the western Paris suburb of Chatou, the scrawny, goat-featured individual they all only knew by his pseudonym, 'Phoebus', was hunched over a transmitter, giving a somewhat inept demonstration on the use of the Morse code to Paul Gloriod, a recent recruit to the network. Gloriod had not been the only operator to point out to Phoebus the risks he was running by insisting on a work schedule which had their transmissions to London going out from the same addresses at the same time every day. Now, as he sat and watched his instructor tapping out coded messages, something prompted him to move to the window. A canvas-covered truck was moving slowly up the street towards them. It continued on past the house, turned round and then, when almost opposite, the driver pulled up, climbed from the cab and began to poke around under the bonnet.

Although it was already too late, Phoebus broke off his transmission and he and Gloriod set about a frantic attempt to hide as much compromising material as they could. The Germans were at the door now, while others had broken down a gate into the garden to surround the building. The mistress of the house could delay answering the banging at the front door no longer and she and the two men were immediately herded into the kitchen to be searched. Although they had somehow managed to secrete nearly all the evidence of their activity, including the transmitter, Phoebus had not had time to rid himself of an uncoded version of a message he had just sent out and a notebook containing a list of the pseudonyms of fellow agents. Both items would prove to be of immeasurable value to the Germans. They were able to match up the uncoded message with the coded version that their monitoring had captured, thus enabling them to break the code being used by the network. As for the names in the notebook, it was not long before their interrogators had persuaded Phoebus how much better off he would be if he translated them into actual names and addresses.

At 2 a.m. on 25 March, André Cholet, christened 'Lenfant' by Gilbert Renault when he recruited the wireless technician into the *CND* as a radio operator four months earlier, is sleeping soundly in his Paris apartment when the doorbell begins to ring incessantly as though it were a fire alarm. His wife staggers to the front door, opens it ajar and is shoved backwards on her heels as three men in civilian clothes burst into the hall, each brandishing a revolver. She is pushed violently aside as they make for the bedroom. There, they shout at her husband to get out of bed and when he asks why, one of them slaps him twice across the face and informs him he is now in the hands of the German police.

Husband and wife are interrogated separately about the whereabouts of their transmitter and the apartment is haphazardly ransacked but nothing is found. Cholet is allowed to go and kiss his ten-year-old son goodbye in the next-door bedroom before returning to his wife's side. The policeman in charge informs Cholet that they are already holding Phoebus and tell his wife that she should persuade her husband to tell them what they want as they have ample alternative means of extracting information from reluctant informants. She says nothing and the policeman who has been rifling through Cholet's wallet throws the money it contains into her face before pocketing it.

Before her husband is led away, Cholet's wife goes to the door of her son's room to tell him to come and give his father one more hug. The boy refuses, saying he has already said goodbye, so Cholet leaves the apartment with his escorts, never to return. (Far from indifferent to his father's departure, the boy was terrified of leaving his bed in case the Germans decided to search it. Beneath his bolster, he had a notebook containing the addresses of all the other agents which Cholet had been able to pass to him as he said his farewell).

Two and a half hours later, it is still dark and Cholet's fellow radio technician and *CND* agent, André Crémailh, becomes aware of a series of dull thuds which, through the earplugs he is wearing to help him sleep, sound a bit like a bombardment. He ignores them for a while, but they get louder and eventually he realizes someone is at the door. The same aggressive Gestapo trio force their way into his flat as soon as he turns the lock and ask him if he knows André Cholet. He replies that of course he does, they are workmates and have known each other since they were seventeen. Immediately, they set to work, searching every room, but succeed only in finding two sets of radio headphones. Crémailh just has time to throw his washing things along with two tins of jam and a bar of chocolate into a case before being escorted out of the apartment.

Later that morning, Crémailh's fiancée, Madeleine Laurent, lets herself into the same apartment. Finding everything in disarray, she immediately guesses what has happened. Knowing all his hiding places, she loses no time in burning all the incriminating documentation, including copies of reports sent to London and transmission plans for each of the frequencies used by Crémailh. Then she organizes a neutral rendezvous with Mme Cholet and with others she knows who are attached to Renault's Paris headquarters. She soon learns that it is Phoebus who is directing the Germans to every address he knows. She then returns to her fiancé's home to ensure she has not missed anything compromising and, while she is there, a key turns in the lock and two plain-clothes policemen enter.

Her tactics are far from conciliatory, demanding to know what right the men have to be in the property. They counter by telling her that she has no right to be there herself, the apartment having been requisitioned. In spite of their threats to arrest her, she demands to know what it is they hold against her fiancé and where they have taken him. Giving nothing away, the policemen push Madeleine out through the front door and tell her that she might get a letter from him in two or three weeks' time.

Crémailh, meanwhile, is incarcerated in cell 53 on the ground floor of Fresnes prison. He is kept there for five days on a diet of acorn soup and with a mattress so filthy that it is like sleeping on black oilskin. It is 1 April when he is eventually taken by car to the Hotel Cayré on Boulevard Raspail which the Gestapo are using as an interrogation centre. Also in the car is another of the Paris radio operators, Roger Duthoit, who can only mutter about killing himself. When it is Crémailh's turn for interrogation, he is faced by a panel of five men. One, who appears to be in charge, says nothing throughout the session. Two others ask all the questions and the remaining two record the questions and answers on their stenographs. Their haul of radio equipment and documents lie at their feet.

Crémailh has had five days in gaol to work out the story he is going to tell. Yes, he knows Cholet. Being in the same business, they often exchange spare parts and it was at Cholet's workshop where he met someone known as 'Guy' (Pierre Julitte's pseudonym). This 'Guy' came to see him a few days later and asked him to join an undercover network. Crémailh says that he refused point blank but that Guy would not take no for an answer and put him on a reserve list, expecting him to change his mind. That is why his name appears in Phoebus's notebook.

The fact that Crémailh has not been active for the network for several weeks helps to give his story some credence with the Germans. He has, in fact, been the most vociferous critic of Phoebus's working methods and has said that he will only resume transmitting if the network adopts a schedule of his devising. It is a copy of this schedule, among other documents, that his fiancée was able to destroy before the Gestapo's second visit to his apartment. Her actions, together with the Germans' inability to disprove Crémailh's version of events, will eventually save her fiancé's life.

Similar scenes to these were being acted out all over Paris, with all ten of Renault's team of radio operators led away to a Fresnes prison cell. Sipping a very acceptable white Saumur in the Geay farmhouse kitchen after his hasty evacuation from the field where he had just been deposited back into occupied

France, Renault knew that he needed to be in Paris as soon as possible to survey the extent of the damage.

The journey to the capital was not without incident. The first problem was Robert Delattre, alias Bob, the man who had been in charge of the Lysander operation and who was to accompany Renault back to Paris along with another of the network's agents. The copious quantities of Georges Geay's wine he had consumed both before and after the event had exacerbated the mortification he was feeling at the near-disastrous landing when Guy Lockhart's aircraft became bogged down in mud. Bemoaning the fact that the pilot had overrun his landing strip, the incident had induced such obstinate despair in Delattre that Renault and the others had to physically force their drunken comrade through the farmhouse door and onto the road to the nearest station.

Their route took them unavoidably past the illuminated gypsy encampment which had so confused Lockhart from the air. However, the *gendarme* on guard at the gate seemed to show no undue interest in the nocturnal pedestrian party that traipsed past him, all of them heavily laden with baggage and one wishing him good day as he zig-zagged unsteadily from one verge to the other. Even the *Wehrmacht* proved inattentive when one of their officers chose to share Renault's and his companions' compartment in the train to Paris. Having placed his own bag on top of the case containing the radio transmitter Renault had brought from England, he even failed to notice an exclamation of, 'Oh! I'm sorry, excuse me', uttered in English by Renault as he woke up suddenly having accidentally elbowed his neighbour in the ribs. Clearly, he had not fully readjusted to his return to France.

Rapid adjustment was essential if he were to survive more than a few days back in Paris. Having received all the dismal details of his radio operators' capture from Jacques Robert (his acting second-in-command in Faure's absence), and ensuring that there were no more agents whose whereabouts Phoebus could possibly know, Renault set about issuing new tasks and questionnaires that he had brought with him from London. He spent a whole day going through his new instructions with one particularly valuable agent, Roger Dumont, his *Luftwaffe* specialist, the man who had provided the vital information needed to bring success to the Bruneval raid a few weeks earlier. It therefore came as an appalling shock to Renault to discover that Dumont had been picked up by the Gestapo only an hour after he had left him.

Dumont had had no contact with the radio team and, in his utter distress at the news, Renault racked his brains to work out how the Gestapo could have known about him. Then he realized that there had been just one brief occasion when Phoebus had been brought to an apartment belonging to Dumont's assistant in the *Luftwaffe* section, Lucienne Dixon, and the two men had met. By sheer ill fortune, when Phoebus, clearly warming to his task, had sent the Gestapo to the apartment, thinking it belonged to Dumont, only Dixon's young son was there, but he innocently directed the plain-clothes men to the restaurant where the two agents happened to be dining with about six other friends. Dumont was led away at the end of his meal and Lucienne Dixon was picked up later at her apartment.

If these further blows were debilitating to Renault's morale and that of his closest associates, they did not allow them to paralyse their activities. Knowing that Dumont would have been carrying the key to the studio where he kept all his plans of German airfields, and other documents that could lead directly to Renault and his team, Robert and another agent were sent the morning after the arrests to break into the studio and remove all possible evidence. There were also individuals who needed to be taken to comparative safety, south across the demarcation line. Those successfully smuggled across included an agent, Jean Tillier, who had been arrested at the same time as Lucienne Dixon but subsequently released. Also among them were the wife and son of André Cholet, whom the Gestapo would have had no qualms about taking as hostage in their attempts to extract information from their captive. Madeleine Laurent, André Crémailh's fiancée, in equal danger, flatly refused to leave Paris and instead would become a regular caller at the Gestapo's offices, demanding to know where her man was being held so that she could deliver food packages to him. Her persistence paid off when, a month after his arrest, a suitcase of delicacies was delivered to his cell.

Such was his trust in his captured comrades' silence under torture that Renault also began to plan the revival of the Paris radio operation, with a request to London to parachute another six transmitters onto a site in Brittany. Robert Delattre was the only radio expert now operating in Paris, and the flow of intelligence coming from all the network's provincial cells for onward transmission to London was as abundant as ever. Good new operators were very difficult to come by, however. One man whom Robert had had recommended to him from another blown network was clearly so scared about being caught while making transmissions that he pretended he was unable to make contact with London. In fact, he had not been transmitting at all and seemed to have joined the network only to benefit from the wage it paid him. The man was soon ejected from the occupied zone, his escorts doing nothing to disabuse him of his mistaken belief that he was being taken into the countryside to be executed.

Only the weather saved the network from another disastrous consequence of incompetent undercover work. Renault had asked one of his earliest and youngest recruits, known only by his code name Lebreton, to identify a suitable site in northern Brittany where the replacement radio transmitters could be dropped by the RAF. Renault had always harboured doubts about the motivation of Lebreton, but he had been responsible for bringing Alphonse Tanguy, one of his most effective agents of all, into the network, so he decided to entrust him with the parachute operation. It transpired that the dropping zone identified by Lebreton was a stretch of land where *Wehrmacht* troops exercised three nights a week, and the safe house he had chosen nearby was a hotel where he was unknown to the proprietor and which had recently become the headquarters of a new German division that had been formed in the area.

Robert Delattre, arriving on the night of the proposed drop and discovering the absurdly dangerous situation his colleague had managed to contrive, had time only to dash to the site, ready to flash the 'no' signal when the British bomber arrived. Fortunately, a strong wind had got up over the Brittany coast and the pilot made the decision to abort the mission while still over the Channel. This was, in fact, doubly fortunate as, unbeknown to Renault, the British had decided to drop François Faure back in France along with the radios. Afterwards, when a furious Renault asked Lebreton why he had not reported the unsuitability of the site, the young man answered that it was because he was afraid Renault would cancel the operation and he had so wanted to witness a parachute drop.

On the whole, however, the success of the *CND* was in large part due to Renault's sound judgement of character. Mostly, he found people utterly dedicated to him and his cause with the discretion and courage essential in the business of clandestine intelligence-gathering. One such agent he valued above many was his personal liaison man, Paul Mauger, the 18-year-old he had taken on in May 1941. Renault regarded him almost as his eldest son and he was treated as a much-loved member of the family by Edith and the four children. Now Renault wanted to reward the young man for his year's invaluable service, carrying messages and courier throughout occupied France, by giving him a passage to England where he could fulfil his ambition of joining the Free French air force.

The plan was to send him, along with Jacques Robert, who was due some training, in the next Lysander operation, which was planned for the late April moon. Pierre Brossolette, however, still working under Renault, had recently returned from a mission in the free zone with what he described as highly important information about the re-emergence of the political parties in Vichy France. More through force of character than with a compelling argument, he persuaded Renault that the need for him to take Mauger's place in the plane to get this information to de Gaulle was paramount, so the young messenger bravely swallowed his disappointment. He was told that he would not have to wait long for his passage to England, as Renault, snowed under with intelligence material, was hatching plans for the network's first seaborne evacuation with the help of Alphonse Tanguy in Brittany. Meanwhile, the Lysander exchange of agents in the field near Saint-Saëns went ahead without any major hitch, while Barbara Bertram's mischievous twosome, Robert and Brossolette, sank into the beds at Bignor Manor which had been occupied the night before by their outward-bound counterparts, François Faure and Christian Pineau.

With Mauger soon to depart, Renault needed a new liaison agent and agreed to take on another very young man, Pierre Cartaud, who had been working in the same capacity for Jean Fleuret, the ex-Bordeaux harbour master and prolific source of marine intelligence in the south-west. Cartaud came with a glowing recommendation from Fleuret, who had practically brought the boy up himself alongside his own son. This was partly because Cartaud had a lifelong fraught relationship with his father. As a member of the Nazi-sympathizing *légion des volontaires français*, the father had told his son that he suspected him of Gaullist involvement and that he would not hesitate to denounce him if ever he discovered proof. A move to Paris for Cartaud should be a safer option for all concerned.

And there was much for him to do. Even if the means of transmitting intelligence back to London via Paris had been severely curtailed by Phoebus's betrayal, the network was bigger and busier than it had ever been, with courier needing delivery from fifteen regional cells involving some 2,000 agents covering the entire occupied zone, including Belgium. Renault was especially pleased to be able to collate a report on the success of the Royal Navy and commando raid on the dry dock at St Nazaire on the night of 27 March. It was not until Churchill was shown extracts from this report that the British knew for certain that enough damage had been done to the dock gates to prevent its use by the *Tirpitz* and other heavily-armed successors to the *Bismarck* for the foreseeable future. It was not long, either, before the point of the raid and its successful outcome was known by those in France who listened to the BBC's nightly French broadcasts. Until then, German and Vichy propaganda had dressed up the attack as a feeble attempt at invasion which had been summarily repelled.

One effect of St Nazaire, where British commandos had actually been seen to set foot on French soil and engage German troops in close combat, albeit with heavy losses, was to rekindle a desire among some Frenchmen to be ready to join the fight when the real invasion came. And although the British secret services continued to draw a very clear distinction between their intelligence-gathering and their saboteur functions, the Free French had a different perspective by April 1942. Passy's organization, which controlled Renault and other networks in France, was no longer called the *service de renseignements* (Intelligence Service), but was now the *Bureau Central de Renseignements et d'Action Militaire* (Central Office for Intelligence and Military Action). From de Gaulle's point of view, the niceties of separating intelligence work from undercover armed action were far less important than keeping as much as possible of the resistance movement under one banner and control, whatever its means of expression.

However, Renault, who was still wary of inciting action against the occupier before an allied invasion became imminent, was beginning to see he would increasingly have to involve himself with those looking to prepare for armed conflict as time went on. To that end, he promised financial help and radio links to London to a Colonel Alfred Touny, the head of a newly formed resistance movement known as the *Organisation Civile et Militaire*, with whom he had been put in contact and who impressed him with his obvious leadership qualities.

The *OCM* began life as an intelligence-gathering network, but had ambitions (which it would later fulfil with distinction) to develop into an armed organization. Its immediate value to Renault's network was that it already had a well-established cell operating around Caen, one of the few areas where the *CND* was sparsely served. One of its agents, René Duchez, was responsible for perhaps Renault's greatest intelligence coup of the war. By posing as a decorator, he gained access to the commander's office at the Caen headquarters of the German military engineering organization, Todt. There, he found a map which marked in great detail the positions of all the defences, shelters, underwater obstacles, beach barriers, passages and phoney mine fields along the entire coast of Normandy's Cotentin peninsula. Having been smuggled by Duchez out of the Todt offices, the map found its way back to Renault for him to ensure its safe passage to London at the next possible opportunity. Renault was receiving so much material at the time that he had no idea of its significance and it was only much later that he learned that the plan for the 1944 allied invasion of Normandy was largely shaped by information carried on that map.

Pierre Brossolette's connections with the old political left allowed Renault to pursue another initiative, which he hoped would avoid some of the dangers of allowing allied arms supplies to fall into the hands of ill-disciplined or ill-intentioned resistance groups. Brossolette introduced Renault to the secretary-general of the national teachers' union, Georges Lapierre, who was very receptive to Renault's plan to involve pillars of local communities such as teachers, doctors and priests in ensuring that the armed groups ready to rise up in the support of an invasion were manned by the more responsible citizens of their locality. Lapierre was able to provide a number of sympathetic and influential contacts from among his colleagues and Renault put Jacques Robert in charge of the enterprise, knowing that he was much better suited to action-oriented undercover work than to the intricacies of intelligence-gathering, collation and encryption.

As well as encouraging Renault to branch out into the realms of armed action, General de Gaulle now realized he needed to broaden the political base of the Free French movement beyond even the unions and to attempt to bring at least some of the militant communist resistance organizations under his banner. A meeting was therefore arranged between Renault and Georges Beaufils, one of the leaders of the very effective, if ruthless, *Francs-Tireurs et Partisans*, a network with close associations with the French Communist party. The two men established an instant *rapport*, but Renault wanted to question the organization's terrorist-like tactics of assassinating isolated German officers and soldiers. Even if it meant they could seize their weapons, the inevitable reprisals which followed the death of a German meant that ten usually innocent French citizens would be gunned down as a result. And with every such execution, Beaufils replied grimly, another fifty or one hundred Frenchmen and women would volunteer for his organization. Renault agreed, as a first gesture of rapprochement, to arrange an RAF arms drop for the *FTP* as soon as possible.

Renault must have realized that the risk of his betrayal grew in direct proportion to the rate at which his influence was spreading across the resistance effort in occupied France. He sensed that it was no longer safe for Edith and the children to be with him in Paris and arranged for them to be moved to a country house near Baud in Brittany. Although this was comparatively near their home at Vannes, none of their family or friends was to know they were there, given the Gestapo's call at Renault's mother's house in the autumn of 1941. The reason for sending his family to that part of the world was his ultimate intention to get them to England by sea using the relay he was setting up between the Royal Navy and Tanguy, who had just acquired a small fishing boat in Lorient.

But it would not be the contacts Renault was making outside his own network which would endanger him and his family so acutely over the next thirty days or so; the threat would come from events and people much closer to home. Renault's existence in Paris during mid-May 1942 was one of long periods in the network's Champs Elysées headquarters of working through sheaves of intelligence material, sorting out what needed photographing for microfilm, what needed encoding for urgent radio transmission to London and what could wait until the next physical transfer of courier by air or sea. These sessions would be interspersed with frequent rendezvous with his agents, all of which would take place on the streets or in the cafés and restaurants of Paris. Not only did Renault choose a new venue for every assignation, he committed the date, time and place to his phenomenal memory, shunning any written record wherever possible.

For one such rendezvous on 15 May, Renault asked his second-in-command, François Faure, whether, at the last minute, he could take his place as he had an important task to finish off. The meeting was to introduce Georges Facq, the man Renault had just chosen to replace Roger Dumont as his *Luftwaffe* specialist, to his inspector of provincial agencies, Etienne Legraverend, and two agents based at St Brieuc on the north coast of Brittany. Unbeknown to everyone, the two Bretons had been under surveillance by the Gestapo for the past fortnight and now they had led them to Paris and the heart of their network.

Faure, Facq and Legraverend had left the meeting and were walking along the Boulevard du Montparnasse when a large Mercedes pulled up beside them. Ten armed Germans surrounded them and ordered them into the car. Faure dropped the package of courier he had just been given by Legraverend and attempted to kick it under the vehicle, but it burst open and the Gestapo men pounced on the documents as they blew about the pavement. He also realized he was carrying a small notebook recording all his rendezvous, as, unlike his boss, his memory was not sufficiently reliable. Somehow, he managed to extract it from his pocket and hide it under the seat of the car without being seen.

François Faure, alias Paco, Gilbert Renault's second-in-command. (*Musée de l'Ordre de la Libération*)

Although the Germans found the notebook later that day, it was after the next appointment that Faure had marked down, a meeting with Renault for lunch at midday. When Faure did not turn up for that meeting, it did not sufficiently disconcert Renault for him to change his plan for a later get-together, again including Faure, at the famous Restaurant Prunier on the Avenue Victor Hugo, where one of Renault's agents worked as *maître d'hôtel*. Fortunately, when two plain-clothes German policemen, one tall and blond, the other small with brown hair, arrived at the restaurant asking for M Morin (one of Renault's pseudonyms), his name was not on the list of tables booked as the party had taken a private room. While the two Gestapo men waited in the main dining room, the restaurant manager was able to escort Renault to the door after his meal without him being seen.

With growing concern at Faure's failure to appear at their second rendezvous, Renault made his way to the Gare Montparnasse, where he was to catch the night train to Lorient with Delattre. Here, they would make the final arrangements and radio contacts with London for the first maritime liaison operation planned for 20 May. Delattre was not the only person to meet Renault on his way to the station. Some of his closest associates were there to break the news of that morning's arrest. Utterly shocking though it was, Renault decided to continue with his trip to Brittany. Trusting implicitly that the three men would give nothing away to their interrogators, he nevertheless instructed his Paris team to find a new headquarters and to remove all the incriminating papers from Faure's office and a transmitter which was kept at Legraverend's. They were also to warn everyone who might have appeared in Faure's notorious notebook. It very nearly did for the chief of the network's Lyons agency, who was stopped just before he entered a café where a dozen Germans were waiting for him with Phoebus among them to help them to identify their prey.

From now on, things only became worse. The sea operation in Brittany whereby Renault's beloved Paul Mauger would at last make his escape to England, taking the long-delayed courier with him, came to nothing. The plan had been for an exchange to take place off the coast between Tanguy's tiny fishing boat, *Les Deux Anges*, and a much larger vessel manned by the Royal Navy and disguised as a French trawler. Firstly, an engine failure on Tanguy's boat made them miss their first pre-arranged rendezvous, then the entrance to the harbour at Lorient was closed after the RAF dropped mines on their way to a bombing raid on St Nazaire. It would be another month before the next operation of this type could be arranged, so Renault, Mauger and Delattre returned disconsolately to Paris.

Max Petit, who had stepped into Faure's shoes as second-in-command, had received news from London of an intended parachute drop while Renault was away. As well as some more transmitters, they wanted to send another radio operator for use by the *CND* along with a special agent, René-Georges Weill, and his own dedicated radio operator whose mission was to build links with the communists. The parachute operation to the north of Paris, organized by Robert Delattre, went according to plan but, on his return to the Gare du Nord, Delattre was asked by the French anti-black market police to open a brand new suitcase he was carrying along with his own. This was not his own case, but one which Brossolette had sent specially from London and was full of English cigarettes and other luxury goods which were probably to be used by Weill in his dealings with the communists. Delattre had also hidden one of the new transmitters in this case.

On finding the transmitter, the French police decided this was a job for the Gestapo but, while Delattre was being led away, one of the policemen made a sign behind his back to indicate that this was his prisoner's opportunity to flee with the offending suitcase. The escape did him little good. He had arranged an earlier rendezvous for the same evening with Renault and had told Weill to meet him there too. What he had obviously forgotten was that he had details of the appointment in his personal suitcase which he had been obliged to leave at the police post when he had been detained at the station. Delattre and Weill arrived at the rendezvous together about fifteen minutes early. Delattre's younger brother, Pierre, approaching from another direction, witnessed the two men being apprehended by plain-clothes police. They were led to a tramway hut, where Delattre smashed one of the windows and fled down the street. The police opened fire and stopped Delattre with a bullet in his arm. What the brother had not seen was that, inside the hut, Weill had slipped a cyanide capsule into his mouth and had died even before Delattre had made his attempted escape.

Weill's death had not been entirely in vain. He happened to have a passing resemblance to Renault, and the Gestapo, who would have had a reasonably accurate description of their most wanted man from the infamous Phoebus, were convinced at that moment that the limp body they slung into their car was Renault's. Therefore, when he arrived at the meeting point, only Delattre's ashen-faced brother was waiting for him, telling him to remove himself as quickly as possible.

If Renault seemed to lurch from one extraordinarily narrow escape to the next, others in his team were not so fortunate. And what was more, the Gestapo were now demonstrating that they had a new source of information which was leading them directly to the homes of many of the network's key agents. While two managed to avoid capture, each sensing that something was amiss before they entered their front door, six more were led away for interrogation. Among these was Paul Mauger, who had been picked up on an errand to look for the man who had replaced him as Renault's personal liaison assistant, Pierre Cartaud. Cartaud had failed to make a recent rendezvous and had, in fact, been the first to be hauled in in this new wave of arrests. Gradually, by a process of deduction, Renault realized that, of all his people in captivity, there was only one who could possibly have directed the Germans to so many addresses — Cartaud.

Even after the war, the circumstances of Cartaud's arrest never became clear and Renault agonized frequently whether it was under interrogation that this young man from Bordeaux decided to talk or whether he had decided to betray the network because he secretly harboured his father's ideology. Whatever the reason, one of those his information led to and who suffered grievously at his treachery was the man who had treated him as his own son, Jean Fleuret. Although Fleuret survived deportation, his wife died in a concentration camp and his son Marc, Cartaud's best friend, was never seen again after his arrest. Whatever Renault's doubts, it would seem from an account given by Fleuret of his interrogation after the war that Cartaud's treachery was premeditated. The Gestapo brought Cartaud himself into the interrogation room where he gave an extravagant Nazi salute. When his old benefactor hurled abuse at him, Cartaud simply rebuked him for denying him the freedom to live out his own convictions. Cartaud's ultimate tally for victims would be sixty agents arrested; fifty-two deportations to German concentration camps; fifteen deaths in captivity; two executions; and two disappearances.

The strain was now beginning to get to Renault. The thought of so many people who had put their trust in him now having to withstand mental and physical torture to ensure his and the network's safety was a constant torment. Although Cartaud had never been to the flat near the Pont Mirabeau where he was now living, he expected and almost hoped for an early morning call from the Gestapo. But he still had a network to run. The backlog of intelligence from the provinces was now becoming critical. Although he still had the use of one radio operator in the shape of Olivier Courtaud, the man recently parachuted in with Weill, the only safe house for transmissions unknown by Cartaud was 100 miles outside Paris. Even the return of Brossolette and Robert from England, parachuted into the free zone on 8 June, seemed more of a complication than a relief. However, when he arrived in Paris, Brossolette informed him that Passy had asked him to take on a role outside the *CND*, working to bring the re-emerging political factions together under de Gaulle.

Robert handed over a letter from Passy when he returned to the capital. It contained a formal order to Renault to return to England with all possible haste and to bring his wife and children with him. He was to hand over the running of what was left of his network to Robert. The latter was somewhat taken aback when Renault informed him that he would obey neither order. He would leave France only when he felt directly threatened by the Gestapo — in his eyes, Passy had mistaken his recent reports of the string of arrests as a collapse of the whole network. It was only the central operation and perhaps Bordeaux that had been badly affected. The framework was still intact. As for Renault's replacement, he would not be handing over to Robert, should he have to leave France, but to Max Petit, whom he considered to be far more suited to the task.

Considering his fatalistic mood, this was a surprising act of defiance from Renault. He felt, though, that it was the least he could do in return for his captured comrades' suffering to stay at his post demonstrating his faith in their heroic refusal to give him away under torture. It was only at the news that his two sisters, Maisie and Isabelle, installed in his old flat in Paris (which Cartaud knew well), had been arrested that he finally woke up to the fact that he and his whole family were now in grave danger. Surprisingly, perhaps, both Maisie (who was actively involved in the network's administration), and Isabelle (who was not) were released after their interrogation. However, it might have been because the Gestapo hoped they may lead them to their brother. Through an intermediary, Renault learned that his sisters had claimed their brother was a good-for-nothing who had fallen out with his family long ago. Their interrogators demonstrated that they knew much about Renault, including all his pseudonyms and that his wife and children were hiding out somewhere in Brittany. They were very keen to know the names and ages of the four children, something their aunts could hardly pretend not to know.

All this convinced Renault that the Gestapo were hoping to flush him out by capturing Edith and the children and holding them as hostages. It was high time for him to leave Paris, gather up his loved ones and get them to England somehow. First, he had to empty his flat where he kept a trunk containing all the courier waiting to go to London as well as the network's entire archive. Managing to squeeze all the courier into a single large suitcase, he arranged for the trunk with its remaining contents to go to an address in the Avenue de Neuilly, where cousins of his would look after it. One other precious possession which he was determined not to lose was the head of the statue of the Sainte Vierge, still wrapped in the paper in which it had been carried in the Lysander in March. He deposited this at Jacques Robert's mother's house, where he found his thwarted would-be lieutenant fully reconciled with his alternative task of developing Renault's plan for community-based armed resistance.

It now remained for Renault to get the suitcase, himself, his radio operator, Olivier Courtaud, and a transmitter to Brittany where, with the help of Alphonse Tanguy, he would organize a seaborne transfer with the Navy for his family, his courier and himself. Renault ensured that his baggage was despatched separately and his radio operator travelled in another part of the train so that, even if he was arrested in transit, his family and the courier might still make it to England. By the evening of his departure from Paris on 12 June, the stress of the past weeks had reached crisis point. He had looked so pallid in the restaurant where he, his cousins and other friends had dined before the night train that some of them insisted on accompanying him to the station. Renault described the scene thus:

> In front of the beautiful Baumann florist, I suddenly become dizzy. My legs go from under me and I feel as though I am about to fall senseless to the pavement. Nicole [one of his network aides and a close friend] holds me up by an arm, encouraging me in a low voice to keep walking. At last we get to the station. We're at the platform and the train is there, about to leave. I have a ticket for the *wagons-lits* bought the day before at Cook's. A German officer is sitting on the lower bunk, a boot in one hand and a slipper already on one of his feet. He politely wishes me good evening. The guard approaches and asks me for my ticket and my identity card. They ask for the card to stop people trading illegally in *wagons-lits* tickets.
>
> He compares my face with the photo on the card and asks, 'Are you monsieur Morin?' It's true! I've only gone and used the card with the name of Morin on it — the Morin the

Germans are hunting down, knowing that it is the same person as Rémy, Jean-Luc and several other false identities. All they needed to do was to check down Cook's passenger list ... 'Yes, I'm Morin,' I reply, 'you can see from my card.'

I get back down on to the platform and Nicole whispers, 'Courage'. A whistle blows. The train lurches forward. My brave comrade throws her arms around my neck and kisses me. Not knowing what that night has in store for me, I savour the freshness of a woman's embrace. As I step up onto the train I can feel one of Nicole's tears on my cheek.

In spite of everything, the journey produced no further horrors for Renault, and the next morning he was reunited with Edith and the children at their hideout near Baud. Tanguy had been at the station to meet him and Courtaud and very soon they set about planning the family's escape. Tanguy's fishing boat was now based at Pont-Aven, a small inland port up a tidal river to the west of Lorient. Courtaud had made contact with London and they had agreed to send their Royal Navy-operated Breton trawler, N51, to an offshore rendezvous at 6 p.m. on the evening of 17 June. The plan was for Renault, Edith, Catherine (twelve) Jean-Claude (eleven) Cécile (seven) and Michel (eighteen months), together with a young agent, Alain de Beaufort, working with Tanguy whose cover had been blown, to hide on board *Les Deux Anges* early that morning. They would then put to sea when all the other local boats would be leaving the estuary for a day's fishing.

As the Germans' habit was to search every other boat, the risk of being caught was extremely high. On the night before the family were due to set out, Renault stood over his three eldest children as they slept, wondering what fate he had brought upon his family. He had recently heard an account of a young teacher who was tortured in front of his wife and four-year-old son. When he would not talk, they grabbed his wife and began to torture her, to the terror and horror of the small boy. When she would say nothing she was led out, carrying the boy in her arms, both of which had been broken, and hurled onto the pavement outside the prison. Then they arrested the man's mother and father for similar treatment. But, reflected Renault, was it really any better for them just to wait around to be discovered in their own country, which they surely would?

The day of the escape did not begin well when the boy with the horse and cart who was supposed to be taking them from their hotel in nearby Riec-sur-Belon to Pont-Aven overslept. It meant that *Les Deux Anges* was the last boat of all to arrive at the estuary mouth checkpoint. The Germans had thoroughly searched the penultimate boat but let Tanguy off with a cursory glance at the crew list. Maybe it was the extremely modest dimensions of the boat that had persuaded them that it could not be carrying anything extra of significance.

Little did they know that there were seven human beings and three boxes of some of the most valuable intelligence material ever to make it out of France secreted in various corners of the vessel. Edith and Cécile were in one of the stern lockers (measuring 6 ft x 3 ft x 30 in) while Catherine and Jean-Claude were in the other. Renault, meanwhile, lay among petrol cans in the forward hold with de Beaufort beside him and his baby lying along his chest. Edith had armed Renault with a bottle of milk so that he could silence Michel at crucial moments but, as they lay alongside the jetty with the Germans aboard, the baby pushed the bottle away peevishly and was about to cry out. Renault happened to have been given a packet of chocolate sweets by Edith's thoughtful landlady at Baud and a supply of these miraculously induced little more than a contented sucking sound.

The cramped ordeal was by no means over even if they had overcome the most dangerous moment as the little fishing boat motored out to sea. German planes and patrol craft were constantly around them as they fished for conger eel along with the rest of the fleet. No one but the crew could be seen on deck and the stowaways had to endure nearly twelve hours in their hiding places until the 6 p.m. rendezvous. Edith and the children, apart from Michel who had his regular bottle and remained remarkably sanguine, felt horribly seasick throughout. It was with unspeakable relief that Renault heard Tanguy announce, close to the agreed hour, that a trawler that did not look like a local to him was in sight near the Glénan islands. As the two vessels drew nearer, a patrolling German Heinkel flew straight towards *Les Deux Anges* and passed within sixty feet overhead before losing interest and veering away.

The trawler was, indeed, the Royal Navy and the joy of Gilbert and Edith Renault at the safe transfer of their children and courier aboard the *N51* was matched only by the jubilation of the vessel's commander Sub-Lieutenant Steven Mackenzie and his crew at having found them. The trawler seemed palatial to the Renault family after *Les Deux Anges* and all but Gilbert collapsed onto bunks to recover from their stifling confinement and nausea. The journey to the Isles of Scilly would not be straightforward. It involved anchoring off the south Brittany coast for the night so that they could time their Channel crossing under cover of the next night's darkness. Twice on their passage north the next day they were closely scrutinized by German naval vessels, but were not stopped. On the first occasion, they happened to be close to some buoys marking someone's crab pots and pulled alongside them to haul them in to show that they were innocent fishermen. They were soon on their way again, free of suspicion and with a good supply of spider crabs for everyone's lunch.

There was a great sense of euphoria on the morning of 19 June when the trawler, now in British waters and flying British colours, drew close to the Isles of Scilly. An RAF air escort consisting of two Coastal Command Beaufighters was overhead and the three eldest children were out on deck for the first time, the colour back in their cheeks. They waved at the pilots as they passed low overhead in a playful display of aerobatics. Suddenly, there was a gasp from everyone on board when one of the planes, having just made a low pass over the boat, hit the sea and sank immediately like a stone. All there was to recover were two wheels which had floated free. The two airmen on board were never seen again. It was a shocking end to the Renaults' extraordinary escape and even a guard of honour lining the deck of the motor torpedo which had come to take them to the mainland from Scilly, its speakers thumping out a Sousa march, could not have easily erased the trauma of witnessing two such pointless deaths.

Neither could the Renault family's deliverance from France, against all the odds, allow Gilbert Renault any lasting sense of relief. To his astonishment, when he first reported to the offices of the BCRA at 8 Duke Street, London, he found himself under suspicion as a double agent. It was Maurice Duclos, of all people, Renault's fellow pioneer agent and friend, who had aroused the suspicions of the French counter-espionage officials, suggesting to them that it had to be more than good fortune that had saved Renault from so many narrow escapes, both when Duclos' own Paris network was blown and while the CND was suffering so many arrests. Even the high quality of the intelligence Renault was continually sending to London seemed almost too good to be true, and it was only by providing a lengthy account of his experiences and answering to a detailed interrogation that he was able to clear himself.

Meanwhile, bad news about Renault's network continued to assail him. First, he heard from Max Petit that his sisters Maisie and Isabelle had been picked up again by the Gestapo. This time, there was no sign of their re-release after questioning and, as Renault was fairly certain the Germans knew nothing about Maisie's role in helping the network, it could only be a hostage-taking ploy. And if that were so, his mother and other siblings were equally vulnerable. Renault felt dreadful that he was safe in England while his innocent wider family were at such peril on his behalf. Both Passy and his British intelligence counterparts believed, however, that any return by Renault to France would threaten the entire intelligence system and that his value to them was now at the London HQ. He had already persuaded the SIS cipher experts to use a new system of coding which would dramatically abbreviate radioed telegrams from France, thus denying German detector vans the time they needed to track down operators at work. His knowledge of all the sources of information was also invaluable in the business of grading and distributing information from his network.

But Renault was convinced that, without his presence in France, many of his outlying agencies would begin to seize up and, in any case, he could not suffer being out of danger when members of his family and so many of those that he had recruited were at such risk because of him, if they were not already in the Gestapo's hands. His controllers eventually relented and organized for him to be disguised as a much older man with a false hump on his back and plastic make-up on his face and set up a trawler operation to Brittany for a link-up with *Les Deux Anges* in September 1942. All went smoothly until the moment Renault and his new liaison assistant, Michel Pichard, prepared to make the transfer between the trawler and *Les Deux Anges* off the French coast. Tanguy had not accompanied his crew on this mission and it was the skipper, therefore, who shouted up to them that it was not safe to come aboard or even to pass over the courier. The Germans, he said, were searching every boat and were particularly suspicious of his. All that Renault could do was receive the courier from France and explain with considerable discomfort to his disappointed shipmates that he and his assistant would be returning with them to England.

Renault's surprise reappearance in London can have offered scant relief to Edith's emotional strain, especially as it was obvious that her husband had not abandoned his attempts to regain French soil. This time, he and Pichard would head for Sussex to put their faith in the services of 161 Squadron during the late September moon. This was Renault's third and final visit to Bignor Manor, but he was disconcerted to be recognized instantly and warmly greeted by Barbara Bertram on his arrival. His own children had taken several minutes to realize that they were in the presence of their father after the SIS make-up expert had applied a clear substance to his face, which, when dry, became rubbery and contorted his features, making him appear much older and quite ugly. Barbara later put her ability to see through the disguise down to the fact that she was partially deaf and always looked at people's mouths to lip-read. Renault had refused to have teeth taken out to alter the shape of his mouth and was therefore easy for her to recognize. Tony Bertram did his best to restore Renault's lost confidence in his disguise by pretending that he had told Barbara to expect him.

For two consecutive nights, Renault and Pichard said their farewells on the doorstep of Bignor Manor only to return from Tangmere an hour or two later because of adverse weather. On the second occasion, the station commander, reckoning that there was only a twenty-five per cent chance of the landing area being free of fog, made the unprecedented move of asking Renault himself to decide whether they should take off or not. (This would have been Peter Vaughan-Fowler's very first mission). Renault always questioned himself after his decision to turn down this last opportunity of the moon period to return to France, whether it was made for the right reasons or whether the presence of his family in London and a fear of what awaited him in France were undue influences.

However he may have felt on his second return to Bignor, this extract from his memoirs shows how life chez Bertram helped to ease some of the frustrations he and Pichard were feeling:

> Mrs Bertram would do everything herself, getting up very early, going to bed last at night, attending to a thousand needs of her guests while at the same time looking after her two children, her chickens, her rabbits, her goat, her garden and yet still ready for a game of bridge or darts.
>
> Those returning to France, nervous, impatient, irritable, often had to stay with her for several days. Her happy smile never left her, effortlessly winning the hearts and gratitude of her guests. She would never allude to the task that lay ahead of them (a forbidden subject under her roof), but many left her with renewed courage.

Back once again in London and seeing the haunted look on his wife's face, Renault promised her there would only be one more attempted departure and, if that failed, she would not have to face another farewell. For a second time, therefore, contact was made with Alphonse Tanguy for another attempted offshore operation. The response came back that they would try it for 15 October, but that they could only take one man. Renault soon understood the reason after he had leapt from the Royal Navy trawler onto the lively deck of *Les Deux Anges*. There was only one place where there was a chance that the Germans would not look in their now comprehensive search of every vessel entering port, and that was a narrow sail locker set beneath the stern decking, with a tight-fitting lid. Its opening was only 50 c.m. wide and Renault was told to lower himself into it and then to slide along beneath the deck so that none of his body would show should someone open the lid.

In these stifling, claustrophobic conditions, and enveloped by engine fumes, Renault escaped detection in spite of a lengthy inspection aboard by the Germans, during which time he lay ready to push a suicide pill into his mouth at any moment. When he eventually reached Paris, he found the situation little changed and his comrades such as Max Petit and Olivier Courtaud delighted to see him once they had got over his disguise which, in their eyes, with the bristly moustache and round, steel-rimmed spectacles, made him look like a German. Petit, whose gentle strength of character and coolness under pressure had ensured the survival of the network during Renault's absence, had become extremely concerned about the safety of his wife, who was Jewish, and his two boys in France. The Lysander operation of the previous month, which Renault had called off at the last moment, was to have brought them to England. Now Renault wanted to reward Petit by sending him together with his family on the next airborne operation, due at the end of November. The story of Jim McCairns' first

Lysander mission in Chapter 5 details how the family made it to safety.

While Renault had succeeded in getting them out in time, there was nothing he could do for his own family. The news he had been dreading soon reached him from Brittany: the Gestapo had seized his sexagenarian mother, his brother Philippe and his remaining three sisters, Hélène, Jacqueline and Madeleine, all of whom were brought to Fresnes prison in Paris where the other two Renault sisters were already enduring the misery of incarceration in a damp, rat-infested cell. It was an agonizing time for Renault, impossible as it was for him to offer them any comfort even though they were so close by. Their torment — and his — would last until February 1944, when the Gestapo decided to release Madame Renault and the three Vannes-based sisters from their Paris gaol. It would be far worse for Maisie and Isabelle who were deported to Ravensbrük concentration camp and were finally freed by the Red Cross on 23 April 1945. Philippe Renault died in Germany a month later from the effects of his deportation.

For more than two months, Renault worked hard in Paris, setting up a new headquarters and recruiting willing hands to help him in the business of receiving and preparing intelligence reports. By now, he was also acting as an important middleman in the process of rapprochement between de Gaulle and the resistance fighters of the left. His strong rapport with the young leader of the *FTP*, Georges Beaufils, had encouraged him to hand over a million francs of his network's own resources to provide for the families of workers whom the *FTP* had reason to believe were about to be sent to work in German factories. The workers in question had agreed to join the maquis if their families were taken care of.

Renault soon realized that he could provide only a fraction of what his militant friends required. He persuaded them that the only way of ensuring an adequate flow of funds and arms was by sending a representative of the French Communist Party to England, where he could sit alongside de Gaulle on his National Committee in London. So strongly did he believe in this course of action that Renault undertook to arrange the representative's clandestine passage and to accompany him personally to ensure its accomplishment. It meant persuading Passy in London to set up another seaborne meeting off the Brittany coast, but it is unclear how much Renault explained about who his important companion would be. It seems that de Gaulle was utterly taken by surprise when a leading French Communist arrived in his offices to sit on his committee, even though he quickly understood the value of such an important alliance.

No lesser authority than Moscow had sanctioned the departure from France of Fernand Grenier, the man they had delegated to represent the Communist Party among the Free French. Grenier was in a sorry state when Renault met him at the Gare de Montparnasse for their journey to the Brittany coast. Since his escape from a French internment camp, he had been kept in close confinement to avoid recapture. His exhaustion was such that he passed out on the bus he and Renault took from Quimper to Pont-Aven — Renault feared that he had actually died. He recovered sufficiently, however, to be squeezed into the sail-locker aboard *Les Deux Anges* with Renault beneath him, his legs resting on the revolving propeller shaft. They missed their first attempted rendezvous with the Royal Navy trawler, as it had taken them too long to get out to the Glénan islands in the adverse January weather. But on the second day, Renault and his precious cargo (which included the wildly impractical gift of a five-foot-tall potted azalea for Madame de Gaulle) were safely delivered into the hands of the Royal Navy and eventually to the English mainland.

Although he had appointed a trusted agent, Jean Tillier, to take over his role as leader of the network during his latest departure from France, Renault had no doubt that he would be returning, telling his Paris comrades that he would see them all within a month. In fact, it would not be for nearly another eighteen months that he again set foot in France. With Passy undertaking his own mission to Paris in the early spring of 1943, he insisted that Renault remain in London so as not to jeopardize too much vital knowledge at once. Even on Passy's safe return, there was reluctance at the *BCRA* to allow Renault back into the field of action, so valuable was his efficient and experienced administration of the ever-growing traffic of intelligence emanating from his and other networks in France.

The sense that he was abandoning his comrades weighed heavily on Renault, however, and it made him morose and ill-tempered with his wife and children. And although the *CND* continued to produce abundant high-quality material, it also began to sustain severe body blows. Firstly, news came of the arrest of Jean Fleuret, head of the all-important Bordeaux agency who, in spite of being identified by the treacherous Pierre Cartaud, had evaded capture up until that moment and had expanded his intelligence-gathering reach to the Mediterranean coast, crucial since the German invasion of Vichy-controlled France. Later, in June 1943, the trusty Olivier Courtaud, by then in charge of all the network's radio transmissions, had the misfortune to be picked up in a raid on his Paris apartment block when the Gestapo had been looking for a member of Jean Cavaillès' action-oriented network, *Cohors*.

Then, in November, total disaster struck the *Confrérie de Notre Dame*. Jean Tillier had appointed a friend of his, a professional tennis player and coach, Robert Bacque, to replace Olivier Courtaud as his chief radio co-ordinator. By this time, the German radio detector service had become so effective that the network had forbidden any transmissions from Paris. Bacque chose to ignore the rule he was supposed to be enforcing and was arrested in mid-transmission at his mistress's flat, not far from the Elysée Palace. It appears he had no stomach for a session with the Gestapo. He withstood the first couple of blows about the head, but needed only one look at the bathtub filled with ice-cold water (into which naked subjects were immersed to the point of drowning) to crack. He volunteered to write a lengthy report giving names, addresses and functions of every individual he had encountered in the *CND*, as well as details about headquarters and safe houses. Unsuspecting agents encountered arrest and ambush throughout Paris and beyond. Alphonse Tanguy, possibly Renault's most effective and loyal recruit of all, who played an even more central role after his leader's departure for England, was shot and killed by German police. They were lying in wait as he entered the office above a garage where Robert Bacque kept his radio headquarters.

This final betrayal meant that the network died alongside Tanguy. Renault returned to France on the evening of 22 June 1944 on the same Normandy beaches near Arromanches where the allied bridgehead had been established barely a fortnight earlier. His mission then was to revive old intelligence contacts and create new ones, so that the advancing armies would know where German troops were concentrated. One of those who landed with him from the same boat was Kenneth Cohen, who recorded the moment in his memoirs:

> Soon after D Day, I crossed the Channel in an MTB accompanied by André Manuel, Rémy, and three or four other Free French ex-agents who were returning to France more or less conventionally for the first time since the fall of their country. We disembarked onto the breathtaking Mulberry piers. 'I lift my hat,' said Rémy 'to the nation which could organize this!' A miracle followed. As he spoke, there clambered up the pier that familiar but formidable sight — Winston Churchill in boiler suit and with a cigar! Swallowing my fears, I saluted and explained my companions. What the PM was up to I never found out but his Churchillian French will certainly be long remembered by these returning French officers whom he greeted with much warmth.

The statue of *Notre-Dame des Victoires* which stands in the church of *Notre-Dame de* France off Leicester Square in London. Gilbert Renault salvaged the head when the church and statue were bombed in 1942 and took it to Paris via Lysander to have it remodelled. (*Thomas Wake-Walker*)

Later, in August, Renault was among the first to enter Paris, where he was able to secure much of the Gestapo's archive at their Avenue Foch headquarters. Among the papers he discovered was Robert Bacque's infamous report to his Nazi captors. Five months later, using his position as a colonel in the French army, he saw to the export of three large and heavy crates from Paris to London. These were the three sections of the statue of the *Notre Dame des Victoires*, reconstituted by a Paris sculptor thanks to Renault's salvaging of the head of the original. The statue still stands in the church of Notre Dame de France in Leicester Place, London WC2.

CHAPTER 11: THE ROAD TO BUCHENWALD

Christian Pineau's Story — Part 2

12 November 1942

Christian Pineau and Jean Cavaillès stood at a crowded bar on
Toulouse station concourse, a cup of insipid coffee in front of
them. The two gendarmes guarding them had seen no harm in
allowing them something warming on this chilly morning as
they waited for their connection to Limoges and the
internment camp that awaited them. A radio was on in the bar,
giving news of German armoured divisions advancing down
the Rhône valley — they would be in Marseilles before
nightfall.

As soon as word spread of the allied landings in North
Africa and the subsequent unopposed Nazi invasion of the free
zone, attitudes among officials and citizens of Vichy France
had shifted almost instantaneously. All those who had believed
Pétain had been playing a double game against the Germans
felt confused, if not deceived. Anyone such as Pineau and
Cavaillès, imprisoned for opposing Vichy rule, were perhaps
not such traitors after all. Certainly, their two escorting
gendarmes confessed to a degree of embarrassment at having
to treat them as prisoners, although it was clearly more than
their job was worth to let them escape 'accidently on purpose'.

As he leaned against the bar with his coffee, Pineau felt a tug
at his elbow. Beside him stood an old friend from his days with
the unions, Marius Vivier-Merle, now working for the
Resistance. 'Where are you going? Are you on the run?' he

inquired briskly. Pineau gestured towards his guards and told him to keep his voice down. He explained he was on his way to an internment camp at Limoges and discovered Vivier-Merle was catching the same train. He would be getting out earlier, at Cahors, where he was visiting the distinguished union leader and pacifist, Léon Jouhaux, who had been put under house arrest there by the Vichy government. With no clear idea of how he would achieve it, Pineau told his friend to wait at Cahors station, where he would do his best to meet him.

One of the guards asked Pineau what he had been saying to the man he assumed was a stranger next to him, but seemed satisfied with his explanation that they were just talking about the Germans, as was everybody. Once installed in their compartment on the Limoges train, the guards relaxed visibly. They had safely negotiated the change of trains at Toulouse without losing either prisoner and were now on the final leg of their escort duty. Pineau asked to go to the lavatory as the train got under way. He wanted to see how attentive they would be and, sure enough, one of the gendarmes accompanied him and stood guard outside the door. Pineau had spotted Vivier-Merle in the next-door compartment and occasionally his friend would wander down the corridor glancing discreetly at them through the glass.

Claiming the prison food had given him severe stomach problems, Pineau asked once more to go up the corridor just as the train was leaving Montauban. Again, a guard went with him. At midday, the train pulled into Cahors and Vivier-Merle passed their compartment on his way to leaving the train and cast an anxious, inquiring look in Pineau's direction. Both guards had begun to eat their packed lunch as the train stood in the station, and Cavaillès, oblivious to any imminent false move by Pineau, had followed suit with a sandwich he had with him. As the train began to move, Pineau leapt to his feet, indicating through gestures that he was about to throw up all over their lunch.

'Go on then,' said one of the guards, 'you can go on your own this time.'

It took Pineau less than two seconds to dash towards the WC and then to throw open the adjacent door and leap out of the gently accelerating train. Unharmed, he made his way back along the track towards the station where, to his relief, Vivier-Merle was waiting patiently on the platform. He gave his ticket to Pineau, who had no identification and no money, and paid for another himself at the barrier. The terms of Léon Jouhaux's house arrest must have been remarkably lax as there seemed to be no problem in the two men going straight to his front door and taking refuge there while Pineau changed his clothes, shaved off his moustache and took a reviving glass of wine with his illustrious former colleague.

As good luck would have it, another trade union friend of Jouhaux, a Luxembourger by the name of Pierre Krier, was at the house and he undertook to escort Pineau to the village of Mercuès where he lived, some seven kilometres to the west along the river Lot. Even though they took a back-lane route to the village, avoiding the main road, Pineau only just avoided detection by hiding in some farm buildings when a car approached them. His companion, who remained on the road, coolly informed the policeman who stopped his car beside him that he would certainly let them know if he ever saw a man with a moustache and a grey suit.

The village lay on the opposite side of the Lot from their route, so they rolled up their trousers to their thighs and waded across the river. Pineau was then led to an abandoned house that lay beside the river, where he was to stay for a few days until the manhunt had relented. Still wet from the river crossing and unable to light a fire for fear of drawing attention, Pineau settled down alone, shivering under some blankets and waiting for night to fall when Krier had promised to come with some food.

Although Pineau could not repress a sense of triumph as he lay in his hideout, having regained his freedom after some two months of incarceration by the Vichy authorities, his feelings were mixed with a sharp tinge of guilt as he thought of his brother-in-arms, Jean Cavaillès, by now languishing behind the locked gates of the internment camp. When he and Pineau were picked up on the road back from Narbonne-Plage after their failed seaborne exfiltration, they would doubtless have been released soon afterwards had Pineau not been carrying a false identity. Cavaillès' papers had been in perfect order and it was only his association with Pineau that had led to his imprisonment.

Pineau was still haunted by the look of reproach on Cavaillès' face as he had heard his comrade explaining to the *Surveillance du Territoire* inspector why they were near the beach at that time in the morning. Cavaillès had not been party to an earlier conversation between Pineau and the inspector when the latter had shown considerable sympathy with their plight and a willingness to let them off as lightly as possible. He assured Pineau that there was no firearms charge to answer — one customs man had shot the other by accident — and he already knew from the other agent he was holding, Jean-Pierre de Lassus Saint-Geniès, that an attempted operation with the Royal Navy had taken place. As he had to explain his false identity, Pineau had decided to retract the unlikely story of a university professor and a senior civil servant choosing to sleep under the stars on a camping holiday and confessed that he and Cavaillès had, indeed, been trying to get away by sea. Both, he claimed, had received an unsolicited approach by the Free French, asking them to join their cause in London. Their patriotism had made them accept the invitation which, deep down, the Marshal himself would surely have condoned.

Satisfied with this story, the inspector assured them that their likely fate was to be sent to a guarded residential camp from which, with good contacts, it would be fairly simple to gain release. Meanwhile, he agreed to ensure delivery of a letter from Pineau to his wife with news of his misadventure. Through her father, Bonamour, who had been working under cover with Pineau for some time, the *Phalanx* network would thus also get to hear about it. Unfortunately, the inspector's optimism on his prisoners' behalf had not reckoned with the wrath of the Vichy military justice department who, on receipt of his report, ordered that the three would-be escapees be locked up in Montpellier military prison to await trial for breaching national security.

Conditions in the prison were pitiful. Pineau shared a darkened, filthy cell with de Lassus Saint-Geniès, where they were fed on a diet of nearly raw chickpeas and where nights were spent brushing a variety of crawling insects off their faces and from their hair. Among their fellow prisoners, who they saw during a brief daily promenade in the courtyard, were men, some of whom had been working as agents for the British and others for the Germans. When Arlette Pineau, now heavily pregnant, was eventually allowed a visit to the prison, she was shocked to find a pale and emaciated version of her husband, pathetically grateful for the small package of food she had brought him. In spite of his pallor, she surprised her husband by being happier than he had seen her for some time. The reason, she explained, was that at least now he could come to no further harm.

Tristan Bonamour du Tartre, Christian Pineau's father-in-law and second-in-command of the *Phalanx* network. (*Gilbert Pineau*)

Any hope of lenient judicial treatment was dashed by Pineau's interview with a virulently Vichyist colonel charged with investigating his case for the Montpellier military tribunal. The colonel asked Pineau how he could believe he was serving his country by attempting to join up with traitors. Surely he was aware that Monsieur de Gaulle had been condemned to death in his absence and that he, too, could therefore be liable for the same sentence. Fortunately, this was an extreme view amongst Pineau's captors and, with the help of the lawyer allocated to the case (who confided to Pineau that he was a member of the *Combat* resistance movement), five years' imprisonment would be the likely outcome of their trial. Meanwhile, they were moved to the more comfortable 'political' section of the gaol.

The new regimen allowed the three men much more spacious quarters consisting of a room with four beds, a table and chairs and freedom to use the adjacent ablutions at their leisure. A fourth prisoner who shared their room was clearly a stool pigeon planted by the authorities. His presence did not, however, deter Pineau from re-establishing contact with his network. Visitors were allowed for two hours every day and, as well as his wife, Pineau was able to receive Bonamour, his father-in-law, who he appointed as leader of *Phalanx* in his absence. Meanwhile, Cavaillès had been visited by a professor friend of his who belonged to *Combat* and who, with other local resistance contacts, threw down an unsolicited challenge to the three prisoners' audacity.

It arrived in the shape of a packet inside a shopping bag which Arlette — who was never searched because of her delicate condition — had been asked to take in on one of her visits. Had she known what was in it, she would probably have left it behind. The package, intended as their passport to freedom, contained a hacksaw, a length of thin cord and a tube of sleeping pills. Only Cavaillès showed enthusiasm to go through with the proposed escape, but the other two felt duty-bound to support him in spite of their severe misgivings. Unfortunately, their pessimism was justified. The cord, to be thrown to accomplices beyond the perimeter wall, never came into use. The sound of sawing on the bars of their window was enough to wake the whole prison, not least Boulivard, their stool pigeon cell-mate, for whom three sleeping pills dissolved in his bedtime tea were hopelessly inadequate for their intended purpose.

He threatened to shout for the guards as soon as he realized what was happening, and short of killing him and risking being found with his body the next morning if their escape failed, there was nothing they could do but to stop sawing. Their rate of progress was such that it would have taken them at least two hours of work on the bars to get out, by which time their accomplices would have long given them up. Although Boulivard wasted no time the next morning in telling his guards about the failed escape, Pineau had been able to hide the offending implements (later smuggled out by Arlette), and, knowing that the prison governor was far from unsympathetic to their predicament, negotiated with him to let the matter rest on condition that no further such attempts were made.

As time passed, Pineau had to content himself by writing a play, while Cavaillès worked on his book on philosophy. Meanwhile, reports reached them about how the network continued to function smoothly under Bonamour's stewardship, with new agents recruited and a series of successful parachute drops carried out. While pleased to see his creation thriving, Pineau found the proof that he was not indispensable a little hard to take and became increasingly frustrated by his exclusion. These feelings were immediately dispelled when, one day, the prison governor came to give them the news of the allied landings in Algeria and Morocco. He was as delighted as they were and predicted that they would soon be set free.

The following day, however, the mood changed when news broke of the Germans' entry into the free zone. There was now concern for the political prisoners at Montpellier, as the Nazis would show them no mercy when they arrived. The case against de Lassus Saint-Geniès had never been so strong, and he was allowed to leave prison. Unable to do the same for Pineau and Cavaillès, the authorities nonetheless got them on an early-morning train ahead of the advancing occupation, their destination the internment camp near Limoges. Of course, only the unfortunate Cavaillès would arrive there.

The price of freedom for Christian Pineau was a severe fever contracted after two days in his damp, cold riverside hideout. He was still in a sorry state when his father-in-law arrived at Pierre Krier's house, where he had been taken when it was considered safe to do so. After spending a few more days there, Bonamour and Pineau, avoiding Cahors, made a circuitous railway journey to Lyons, the centre of the *Phalanx* network's operations. Pineau noticed a marked change to the place since the arrival of German forces. Nazi uniforms now exclusively filled black-market restaurants that had once been frequented by locals, untroubled by Vichy law-keepers. The major resistance movements which had openly used Lyons as the hub for their activities were now operating deep underground. Klaus Barbie, who had recently arrived to lead the Gestapo's tenacious and merciless campaign against subversion, was already striking terror in the town.

Taking back the reins of the network from his father-in-law, Pineau, still badly run down by his illness and his time in prison, found himself yearning for an escape from the oppression and anxiety of working against the occupation. In spite of this, he knew he had important work to do, building up the intelligence-gathering strength of the network and trying to arrange Cavaillès' escape before the Germans took over the internment camp. Being short of the requisite manpower for such a venture, he made contact with Lucie Aubrac of the

Libération Sud resistance organization. At their meeting, he was taken aback by her furious verbal attack on him. She had been behind the plot to spring him and Cavaillès from the gaol at Montpellier and roundly chastised him for failing to use the saw and cord provided. She was equally reproachful that he subsequently abandoned his comrade when he made his escape from the train. She was eventually mollified, however, and they devised an operation involving agents from both their groups, which would succeed in its aim shortly before Christmas 1942.

By then, Pineau had received news that Arlette was safely delivered of a son who was given the name of Francis, his father's own code name in the network. London had also agreed that a Lysander flight should be allocated to Pineau's evacuation; he was still working without any radio operator of his own and was therefore severely limited in his ability to communicate his network's requirements to his controller, Passy. He was also in desperate need of a break from the front line. Heavy snowfall in the Pouilly-Fuissé area to the west of Mâcon prevented the intended landing there in the December moon, but it did give Pineau the chance to see his wife for the first time since her confinement when she came with the newly released Cavaillès to celebrate New Year's Eve with him at his Mâcon hotel.

The snow did not prevent a December parachute drop, which brought the answer to many of Pineau's prayers in the shape of radio operator, Pierre Delaye (Barbara's beloved 'Pierre-le-paysan'). He would transform the efficiency of the network, both in its communications with London and in its reception of airborne operations. His first action was on the night of 14 January, when he set up a Lysander landing ground close to the Rhône near the town of Loyettes, east of Lyons. The terrain was ideal (even if only some three kilometres from a *Wehrmacht* garrison), and it allowed Squadron Leader Hugh Verity to carry out a perfect landing and take-off on what was only his second mission. It could have been his last when, on the way out, concentrating for too long on his chart to pinpoint his position over the river Saône, he nearly collided with a tall radio mast in his path, banking fiercely away at the last moment.

Verity's outward payload had been just a sack of courier, but he knew when he witnessed three men squeezing into the rear cockpit for the return passage that progress home would be extremely slow against a strong north-westerly wind. Pineau, for it was he and two of his newly recruited agents who were the passengers, stoically endured the five-and-a-half hour flight, which included some alarming aerobatics over the Channel to shake off a German fighter. An exquisite sense of freedom rapidly replaced the cramp and knot of fear in his stomach as he stepped across the tarmac at Tangmere.

And there to meet him was the familiar figure of Tony Bertram. In his memoirs, Pineau commented,

> Anthony Bertram provided the human connection between the Resistance in France and freedom. How many of our fellow combatants have been able to draw on his slender, athletic outline for their courage and their good humour in the dusk before a departure or the dawn following an arrival at his Elizabethan manor? For so many, he represented the last silhouette of Great Britain.

Pineau considered Bertram not just a comrade-in-arms but a kindred thinker whose company he thoroughly appreciated. Bertram told him he was looking terrible but that, fortunately, he would find some red meat in England to restore his colour, thanks to the American liberty ships. Pineau's two young fellow passengers were certainly suitably delighted by a foretaste of such luxury, as the three Frenchmen sat down to Barbara's bacon and eggs on their arrival at Bignor.

Pineau found London full of American servicemen and sensed a more optimistic atmosphere among the inhabitants as he made his way to the offices of the *BCRA*. Passy had a much clearer picture of the undercover situation throughout France than he did when Pineau last visited. This was mainly thanks to the steady flow of agents and politicians arriving in London, courtesy of the special RAF and RN services. He made it clear to Pineau, however, that, while the flow of political intelligence from the *Phalanx* network was first class, its military intelligence was scarce, to say the least, and this was of some concern to their British paymasters. He promised Pineau that he would provide him with the necessary personnel to improve this branch of his activities.

When Pineau complained that people like 'Lot' the radio operator were more trouble than they were worth, Passy was quick to point out that, with only about a one in ten chance of survival, volunteers were not exactly queuing up to do the work. The pool of people he had to choose from in London was unlikely to yield choirboys. He urged Pineau to do more recruiting of his own in France and to send them to London for training. That was how he could be sure of good agents.

When he was received by General de Gaulle, Pineau was relieved to find he had a better grasp now of what resistance groups were looking for in him as a leader. De Gaulle was also clearly relieved that Pétain was perpetuating his collaboration with Germany, in spite of its occupation of the free zone. Had the breach of the armistice been a trigger for the Marshal to escape to Algeria or London and to join the allied cause, de Gaulle knew that many foreign governments and some of the later French converts to the Resistance would sooner turn to Pétain than himself as the figurehead for liberation.

The General was still not remotely interested in the difficulties faced by Pineau in running his network. He did not want to be concerned with the minutiae of such activities, and showed far more pride in the uniformed troops under his command than in the disparate groups of the underground. The Free French army were a splendid advertisement for his cause, especially to the Americans, and were fully under his control. This could not be said of the Resistance as a whole, some of whom were communists and others, like the *Alliance*, were working directly for the British and who he therefore deemed to be no better than traitors.

All of Pineau's superiors, from de Gaulle downwards, showed considerable concern for his health, however, and insisted he spend some time relaxing. Pineau scarcely needed a second invitation and found, unlike in 1942, that there were no constraints whatever on his movements around town. A Frenchman was no longer a rare or obtrusive sight on the streets of London. As well as becoming an avid concert-goer, Pineau was able to indulge his appetite for good food and wine and the company of good-looking women. On one memorable evening, he was dined out by Squadron Leader Guy Lockhart as a special thanks for getting him back to England in record time after his sabotaged landing in Burgundy. A sumptuous dinner in the company of some thirty RAF officers, as well as Lockhart's wife and sister-in-law — both blond and beautiful — was followed by dancing and drinking until five in the morning at The Coconut nightclub. The quartet (minus the thirty RAF men) would return to the nightclub on at least one other occasion and swore to a permanent friendship. Death would sadly intervene, however, when Guy Lockhart, in command of a bomber squadron, was shot down over Friedrichshafen in April 1944.

Ever the political animal, Pineau could not resist making his own study of the nuances of opinion among the French and British he encountered during his period of rest and recuperation. Those he found to be anti-Gaullist on his earlier visit, such as Louis Lévy, had, if anything, hardened their opposition, taking their lead from the many British detractors of the General. Being a socialist like himself, Lévy wanted Pineau to go back into France and start advocating allegiance among the resistance movements to a more leftist or radical leader, such as former prime ministers Léon Blum or Edouard Herriot. How easy it was, Pineau thought, to dream up postwar panaceas well away from the conflict in the safety of a London apartment. De Gaulle's Cross of Lorraine was a vital unifying symbol to those necessarily isolated from their fellow combatants and waging a clandestine war under the nose of a ruthless occupying force.

The British secret service officers with whom Pineau dined found little sympathy with de Gaulle's exclusive obsession with the interests of France. They were concerned that it would cause disunity of command among the allies come the campaign to liberate France, expected by most to be launched later in 1943. When Pineau, somewhat injudiciously, passed on to de Gaulle the opinion of one British colonel that one first-class and timely piece of intelligence was worth a whole regiment of soldiers on parade in the desert, the General exploded.

'They're just using your intelligence for their own purposes without ever recognizing that it came from a Frenchman,' he thundered. 'At least our uniforms are unmistakeably French!'

Pineau also had a chance to sit down with Jean Moulin, the man tasked with the co-ordination of all the action-oriented resistance outfits in France. Moulin doubted that the allied embarkation would take place before 1944, and impressed upon Pineau the need to keep intelligence-gathering networks strictly separate from those involved in armed action, despite what others in the *BCRA* were now saying. He foresaw that, if he were not careful, Pineau would be sent back to France with any number of additional tasks that would not only risk diluting the effectiveness of his network but were almost bound to interfere with his own operation.

Sure enough, André Philip, the socialist politician and friend of Pineau, now in exile in London, was the first to buttonhole him. Charged by de Gaulle to direct the political scene in occupied France, Philip tried to persuade Pineau to become his on-the-spot representative and hand over his intelligence role to someone else. While he was able to refuse this request, he could not possibly say no when de Gaulle himself decided that he would like Pineau to use his contacts back in France to prepare a plan to resupply the country with food, clothing and raw materials after its liberation. Fortunately, Passy had a remedy, suggesting Pineau simply 'resupply' another section of his intelligence-gathering enterprise.

Although Pineau had experienced moments of doubt in his own courage to return to a clandestine existence in France, when it was time to return to Bignor Manor for the March moon, his nerves had settled. They were further helped by a weather delay, which allowed him a whole week in the Sussex haven, every day of which he was able to enjoy a long walk in the surrounding countryside in the company of Tony Bertram. Neither Pineau nor Barbara Bertram mentions in their memoirs whether the two other men destined to fly out with

Pineau when the weather cleared were fellow guests at Bignor. It would be fair to assume they received the same accommodation arrangements as all of the SIS's other Lysander passengers, but it is a pity not to be certain, in the context of this story, that two such crucial players in France's undercover war had indeed been guests of the Bertrams. The two men in question were General Charles Delestraint, returning to France to take command of all undercover military operations, and Jean Moulin, his immediate political superior.

Moulin had already endured near catastrophe aboard a Lysander in the previous moon period when Hugh Verity had attempted to land him near Bourges on the Loire. Fog in the area forced Verity to return with his passenger to Tangmere, where similar conditions now prevailed. After several aborted landing attempts, Verity had to guess where the ground was and the aircraft fell thirty feet to the runway, shattering its undercarriage and scraping along on its nose. As he helped Moulin from the badly damaged plane, which miraculously did not catch fire, he apologized profusely for the disastrous landing. Moulin told him to think nothing of it and thanked him for a 'very agreeable flight'.

Now, on the night of 19 March 1943, Flight Lieutenant John Bridger would be flying Moulin, Delestraint and Pineau to the north of Roanne on the upper reaches of the Loire, where Pierre Delaye had selected a field for their return to the front line. The operation was successful and the men were driven away in a van by *Phalanx* agents to a small farm nearby. The next day, via a bus to Mâcon and then a train, they disappeared to their various hideouts in Lyons. It was only later that Pineau heard that the Gestapo, now hyper-alert to all Lysander operations, had arrived at the landing field just ten minutes after the plane and van had left the scene.

The month which followed Pineau's return to France was probably the most productive period in the life of the *Phalanx* network. Despite the ever-tightening grip of Klaus Barbie's Gestapo operation in Lyons, intelligence was coming in thick and fast and being transmitted or sent as courier to London in record time. This was thanks in large part to the services of an additional radio operator, 'Roger', transferred from another network in France, and to the efficiency of Pierre Delaye, who had recently recruited his own sister, Adrienne Loison, to act as liaison between him and Pineau. Since the Lysander operation delivering Pineau, another had been successfully accomplished under Delaye's direction from his favoured Loyettes terrain, when Pineau's 17-year-old eldest son Claude had been one of the three fugitives departing for Tangmere (see Chapter 9). On one occasion, thanks to the network's slick operation, the minutes of a Vichy government cabinet meeting had reached the offices of the *BCRA* in London on the same evening that the meeting had taken place. André Manuel, Passy's second-in-command, was on a mission in France at this time and, after a visit to Lyons, declared himself entirely satisfied with Pineau's outfit.

Pineau's business during this period took him to Paris for the first time in more than a year. Travel to the north was now much more straightforward, as the *Ausweis* was a thing of the past since the German occupation of the old free zone. He felt less threatened by the Gestapo in the vastness of Paris than he did in Lyons and found no difficulty in recruiting a young liaison agent by the name of Isabelle, who would identify apartments from which Pierre Delaye could transmit when he was in the capital. He also set to work among his old colleagues at the Ministry of Supply, looking for people who would help him fulfil the task set him by General de Gaulle. Although he established a small group of sympathetic informants, he almost fell foul of one the ministry's inspectors, who had in the past been a vociferous critic of the Vichy government. The man, when asked to help, became extremely nervous and accused Pineau of asking him to betray his country by assisting de Gaulle. It was fortunate that Pineau was an old colleague, he told him, otherwise he would have had him arrested on the spot.

The Côte d'Azur was another destination for Pineau where he again found less evidence of Gestapo activity than in Lyons. The *Wehrmacht* were extremely busy, however, building defences along a prime target for an allied invasion. Pineau's agents in the region were working equally hard, gleaning information on the fortifications for swift despatch to London. While he was in Marseilles, Pineau had a long meeting with Daniel Mayer, secretary-general of the clandestine Socialist Party of France. As with so many of his colleagues from the left, Mayer was already planning how France should be run come the liberation, and was particularly preoccupied by the question of how collaborators and all active or tacit supporters of Vichy should be punished. For his part, Pineau did not share this appetite for revenge and, apart from those who had actually spied for the Germans or who had turned resistance agents over to the Gestapo, it was not hatred that he felt for such people, but contempt or even pity.

There was terrible news awaiting Pineau on his return to Lyons. His father-in-law, Bonamour, had been picked up by the Gestapo at the town's main Perrache railway station on the morning of 27 April as he was about to board a train to Tournon where his wife, daughter and Pineau's children were living. It remains a mystery to this day as to who betrayed

Bonamour to the Germans, and Pineau is very careful in his memoirs not to speculate on this. It did not, however, prevent him from remarking that there was one agent in his network who seemed anything but dismayed at the arrest. This was Fernand Gane, a man who had gained an expertise in military intelligence while working for the Paris-based Polish network, *Interallié*, before its betrayal by Mathilde Carré in November 1941. Gane had eventually managed to escape to England some ten months later where, as usual, the SIS had first call on debriefing him before his eventual release from the 'Patriotic School' immigration control in London.

Colonel Passy at the *BCRA*, having been assured by Gane that he had not agreed to act directly for the British, took him on and, in a move to strengthen the military intelligence function of the *Phalanx* network, had sent him out in a Hudson operation in February 1943 to join Pineau's team. When Pineau returned from his own London trip, he found little love lost between Bonamour and Gane, the latter obviously resentful at taking orders from Bonamour, whose knowledge of military matters he believed was inferior to his own. Gane also had an unhealthy interest in money, demanding a higher wage than any of his fellow agents, and this when Pineau knew that he had been sent out from London with a large sum which he had seemingly spent entirely on himself. It would probably have shocked Pineau to know that Gane would eventually end up as leader of the network, dealing directly with the British when he chose to (in spite of what he had told Passy) and flying in the face of all that Moulin had advocated by confusing the intelligence-gathering role of the network with the use of arms and explosives for sabotage.

Bonamour's arrest had, in fact, made Pineau momentarily regret the strict separation he had dutifully upheld between intelligence and combatant networks. Knowing that his father-in-law's only chance of escape was by some form of ambush on the vehicle transporting him between Fort Montluc prison and interrogation sessions at the Gestapo's Hotel Terminus headquarters, he was equally aware that he had neither the men nor the means for such a task. Bonamour would never crack under interrogation, Pineau was sure, but he took instant security precautions all the same, not knowing what information he might have been carrying when he was picked up nor how much the informant who had turned him in knew about their operation.

Adrienne Loison was sent to Paris where her brother was working to tell him only to transmit messages in his own personal code while all other outposts of the network received similar alerts. 'Roger' the Lyons-based operator was tasked with informing London of the emergency. Pineau reluctantly moved from his Lyons lodgings (at the house of his old trade union friend and colleague, Léon Goyet) to another part of the town and made arrangements for a meeting with Arlette to break the news to her of her father's predicament. Fearing that her house in Tournon-sur-Rhône would be under Gestapo surveillance, Pineau arranged to meet his wife at a mountain inn, some two hours' walk outside Tournon. Although she was extremely distressed by the news, Pineau was reassured to some extent to hear that there was no sign of any German police at her address. The couple left their mountain retreat after a night together: Arlette to gather up the children to find somewhere outside Tournon to live, Pineau to return to Lyons to nurse his damaged network.

And there had been more damage. Roger's transmissions to London had been detected by the Gestapo and he had been caught red-handed at his radio and was now also a prisoner at

Fort Montluc. Pineau was far less certain about his ability to keep quiet under interrogation than he was about his father-in-law and, as Roger had been found at his post, there was more chance that his captors would have discovered other sensitive papers. Pineau now felt he had to act quickly. Lyons was no longer safe and *Phalanx* headquarters would have to move to Paris. Pierre Delaye was already working up there on a mission and had established a number of transmission hideouts. Pineau saw his immediate task was to get all existing courier despatched as soon as possible and to collect the network's funds, as important as its agents, and get them safely to Paris.

Calling at any of his agents' houses now presented a risk, although, if security rules had been correctly observed, Roger would not have known the address of the network's chief admin man, who kept the money in his safe. When Pineau arrived there, he found only the man's mother at home. Unfortunately, she managed to jam the key of the safe in the lock, so he left empty-handed, hoping a locksmith would arrive later that day, before Pineau's train was due to leave for Paris that evening. Two days earlier, he had left a note, signed 'Francis', his code name, at the house of Adrienne Loison. The message said that he would be calling in on her on the evening of 3 May, so that she could hand over the courier she had collected from a liaison trip to Paris. Although this was only lunchtime on 3 May, Pineau hoped he could save time by calling early, especially as he had some urgent alert messages for her to deliver to other agents in the network.

Again, even though he did not even think of it this time, this should have been a safe address for him to visit, as only he and Delaye knew about it. He had to ring the bell twice before the door opened, but the person who ushered him in was a short man he had never seen before. It took Pineau about two seconds to register something was very wrong and, in that time, a fair-haired giant had placed himself in the doorway, blocking any escape. The two Gestapo officers were clearly surprised not to find any weapon on Pineau when they frisked and handcuffed him. They burst into raucous laughter when, in answer to the inevitable first question of what he was doing at the flat, Pineau replied that he had come to collect his laundry. They were less amused when, having ascertained that he was married (he could not deny this as he carried pictures of his family in the wallet they had found on him), he would not say where they lived. His reason to them was that, having arrested him for no reason, he had every right to protect his wife from a similar fate.

The policemen contained their anger at this response, knowing that their captive would soon be facing a much more intense interrogation once they had safely transported him to their headquarters at the Hotel Terminus. Pineau, despite the shock of his capture and the realization that it was almost certain to lead to his ultimate death, used all the available thinking time he had while waiting to face the full fury of the Gestapo to build a story which might mitigate his predicament. At the very least, his inquisitors would have read his note, signed 'Francis', announcing his calling in at 6 p.m. and the two policemen would have been waiting for that visit. Seeing that they had somehow obtained Adrienne Loison's address, it was also quite likely they had learned that 'Francis' was leader of the network. If, as was likely, Adrienne had been arrested in her flat after her return from Paris, they would also have the highly incriminating courier she had brought back with her.

The only factor in Pineau's favour was that he had called at the apartment at 1.30 p.m. instead of 6 p.m. His false identity papers showed him as a Monsieur Grimeaux of humble rank in the Ministry of Supply and even before he was escorted into the interrogation room at the Hotel Terminus, he had adopted the irresolute manner of someone scarcely suited to run an underground network. He would soon learn that among the four impassive faces that greeted him was that of Klaus Barbie himself. (The other three consisted of the short, plain-clothes man who had arrested him and two well-built individuals who supplied ample physical menace to the line-up).

'We are merciless,' Barbie assured Pineau. 'You have lied about your identity and you have lied about your reason for visiting Madame Loison. You will end up by telling us the truth, sir, as all the others have. The French are all cowards. My father was condemned to two years' forced labour for sabotage under French occupation. All my life I have wanted to avenge his mistreatment. Now that I am SS and chief of police here in Lyons, I am not going to show pity to anyone.'

The contents of the ill-fated courier lay on the desk in front of Barbie and, while he leafed through some decoded telegrams, he announced that they also had possession of the network's codes and had already arrested its principle agents. This last declaration and an accusation that he belonged to an organization which carried out assassinations of German soldiers told Pineau that they did not know as much about his organization as they pretended. There were also signs that they were beginning to doubt that Pineau was the 'Francis' they were looking for, and that he was, if anything, a more minor player in the outfit.

This was the moment that Pineau decided to change his story and play up to the role they had cast for him. If they could be convinced that he only had a peripheral involvement, they would realize that most information would have been kept from him and that torture or seizing his family would elicit nothing of value. So he began to tell them what he hoped they would believe was all he knew. Yes, he confessed in a quavering voice, he had gone to the apartment to collect an envelope. He had no idea what it would contain — his instructions were to take it to someone waiting for him in a restaurant. He realized in a flash that, when asked for this person's name, he could neither make one up, as that would remove credence from his story, nor could he use the name of a real person without condemning them to a fate similar to his own. Instead, he gave the name of 'Ludovic', which was, in fact, his second pseudonym and one which he knew would appear in the captured courier. Sure enough, the board of interrogators nodded knowingly and confirmed to Pineau that this was, indeed, the code name of one of the network chiefs.

The questioning continued with Pineau having to describe the appearance and personality of this Ludovic, which he based on a film actor he admired. He explained he had met Ludovic through a colleague of his at the ministry on a visit to Lyons the previous year. He had found him particularly interested in the supply of milk and meat in France (two reports on which Pineau knew were in the courier) and had asked him to give him some statistics on the subject. Pineau denied knowing 'Barnaud', the code name for Bonamour, and prayed that they would not make the connection between the photos he carried of his children and similar ones he knew his father-in-law kept in his wallet. He also said he did not know 'Francis' but that he thought he had heard Ludovic mention him once or twice.

Then Barbie showed him a diagram the police had drawn of their network with the name 'Francis' in the middle and various other names such as 'Ludovic' and 'Barnaud' in positions that indicated very little understanding or knowledge of the organization. All the names were Christian names only and it was not difficult for Pineau to pretend that, for instance, 'Roger' was too vague for him to be able to recognize. While Barbie examined the photographs of his children, he asked Pineau to give the name and age of each one. Pineau gave their second Christian names only and reduced their ages by a year in the hope that Bonamour would have used first names when asked the same question about his grandchildren. He was shocked to be asked if he had ever thought of sending them to England. His immediate retort — 'Whatever for, at their age?' — elicited the information that the Gestapo had decoded a message about the airlift of two boys, one the son of 'Francis', by Lysander.

The other boy in the message was André Manuel's son, who had never turned up at the landing site when Claude Pineau had been flown to Tangmere. The question had particularly unnerved Pineau because it meant that Barbie had not yet convinced himself that the man before him could not be 'Francis'. The session had gone on nearly long enough for the Gestapo chief by now, however, but he had just one more question for Pineau before he would call a halt.

'Are you a collaborator?' he threw at Pineau as he started to pack up his papers. Pineau's response of 'No, I am not' made him look up sharply. 'Why not?' he asked. Pineau asked Barbie why he felt he should be, reminding him that Germany had invaded and occupied his country and that no good Frenchman had the right to be a collaborator. Barbie remarked that it was rare for people they had arrested to give such a response and that generally they claim to be the Germans' friend. Pineau admitted that he had probably made a mistake in giving such an answer but that he had promised to tell nothing but the truth. Barbie's final remark, made to his fellow interrogators in German which he did not expect the

Frenchman to understand, came as music to Pineau's ears. 'He's too stupid,' he said, 'he's not the one we're looking for.'

Pineau may have deflected suspicion enough to avoid an attempt to tear the truth out of him, but he still now faced indefinite imprisonment at the hands of the Gestapo. He would, in fact, spend the next six months enduring barbaric conditions at Fort Montluc prison in Lyons. For nearly half that time, he was kept in solitary confinement in a 12 ft x 12 ft cell, only allowed out once a day into the courtyard below for slopping out and a rudimentary wash under a tap. Conversation between prisoners was strictly forbidden during the process and no form of reading matter or means to occupy the mind was allowed at any time. Pineau never knew from one day to the next what fate awaited him and every time there was an unscheduled throwing open of his cell door, it could so easily mean a firing squad or a call to face the torturers after his true identity had been discovered.

In fact, he was twice driven back to Gestapo headquarters for further questioning. On the first occasion, he was alarmed to find his fellow passenger was Adrienne Loison, but managed to whisper to her to make out he had never met her. The interrogation was conducted this time by one of Barbie's lieutenants and took the form of asking him all the same questions as before, obviously to check the consistency of Pineau's story. The second session required Pineau to give all the minute details of his life since childhood, such as the names of his teachers at school, his grandparents' Christian names and details about his wife's family. The trick here, Pineau knew, was to keep as close to the truth as possible, rather than invent names and people, as he was bound to be asked again to verify his answers and his memory could easily let him down. In the case of his wife and family, Pineau was able to supply the details of his first wife's relations, thus safeguarding Arlette and her father as far as possible.

This final interrogation ended with Pineau signing a charge sheet stating that he had confessed to economic espionage by providing an intelligence network with information on French supplies. At the same time, he succeeded in persuading his interviewer to return the photographs of his family for sentimental reasons. By tearing them into shreds and disposing of them via his slops bucket back at the prison, he had destroyed the last piece of evidence linking him to his actual identity.

Gradually, Pineau adjusted to his seemingly eternal solitary existence at Fort Montluc. He had learned to amuse himself in his cell by counting how many times he could successfully throw a pebble into the air and catch it again in one hand — his record was over 2,000 times. He had even managed to make himself some playing cards for patience out of scraps of paper the prisoners were allowed to salvage from the rubbish bins for lavatory paper. Most important of all, he had begun to make contact with other prisoners. He would communicate with the man in his neighbouring cell by tapping on the wall — one tap for A, two for B etc — and also stole brief exchanges of information with the prisoners with whom he shared the daily ablutions routine. Among his particular group was Roger, the *Phalanx* radio operator. Any outward sign that they had known each other previously could have been lethal, but slowly, through a few shared words at the taps each day, Pineau was able to piece together what had led to his arrest. It had been Pierre Delaye, in a rare lapse of discipline, who had given Adrienne Loison's address in Lyons to Roger. When Roger was caught at the transmitter — the first time he had ever failed to post the mandatory lookout — he had the address among his papers.

It was Roger, too, who received word of Delaye's violent death on the bridge over the Rhône at Loyettes and passed it on to Pineau. With Delaye gone, Pineau reflected miserably, his network had lost its heart and he knew it could not continue to function effectively without him. From time to time, he caught glimpses of the sad face of Delaye's sister, Adrienne, at a window of the women's wing of the prison, and also occasionally saw his father-in-law, Bonamour, from a distance but never close enough to speak to. He felt immensely proud of all three members of his network at the prison, none of whom could have given anything away under interrogation.

Roger would become Pineau's chief supplier, not just of information but of other priceless items such as a smuggled pencil, a magazine and a book, all of which added new dimensions to his solitary pastimes in his cell. He would also occasionally thrust a chunk of bread or other morsel of food, which had come from parcels from his family, into Pineau's hand. The luxury of a hard-boiled egg or a biscuit was immeasurable compared with the twice-daily prison meals consisting of a few pieces of pasta or some other shrivelled object floating in warm water. However much he craved a parcel from his own loved ones, Pineau knew that it could be fatal to him and its bearer, as a link could so easily be made to his true identity. He did, however, receive some parcels eventually, without any repercussions, courageously delivered by his friend and former landlord, Léon Goyet.

It was a terrible shock to Pineau when, one day, as he observed some female prisoners being exercised in the courtyard through his cell skylight, he saw the familiar figure of his mother-in-law among them. As well as his immediate concern that her comparative frailty would not allow her to survive for long under the harsh conditions and cruel treatment of the guards came a far more fearsome question: if the Gestapo had found her at the house in Tournon, what had become of Arlette and the children? It was only several days later that the arch prison correspondent, Roger, was able to whisper in Pineau's ear that his family were safely in hiding. He also passed him a piece of cake, telling him that it came from Pierre Delaye's widow who had made it especially for them. As his cell door was shut on him, Pineau wept for the first time since his arrest, not just with relief at the news of his family, but because of the affection he felt for his valiant team of agents and their loyal next of kin.

Among other mournful observations that Pineau made from his tiny window was the regular arrival of Jewish families who had been rounded up from the surrounding area and who were herded, fifty at a time, into a wooden hut in the courtyard. After a night, during which the prison walls echoed with the sound of their children crying, they were lined up and counted before being marched off for onward transportation. Pineau would notice an almost joyous mood about these parties before their departure, when the women would have done their hair and the men busied themselves with their meagre packages of possessions. They seemed so pleased to be leaving the prison and showed little apprehension about their destination.

Pineau would also notice, while on his daily exercise, fellow prisoners who bore the recent scars of torture at the hands of the Gestapo. He would wonder, as they staggered around the courtyard, their faces distorted by bruises and lacerations and their swollen eyes almost shut, whether they had managed to keep quiet or whether they had cracked. Then, on one such occasion late in June, he saw, to his anguish, a face he knew very well. Still unblemished, it was that of Jean Moulin. The two men gave no outward sign of recognition, but their exchange of glances was enough to tell the other he had been noticed. Pineau was only too aware of what a disaster Moulin's arrest would be to the resistance movement. He also knew the man well enough, when he saw him the next day with all the marks of the Gestapo's brutality on his face, to know that he would not talk.

The following day, Moulin was no longer among those taking exercise. However, at six o'clock the same evening, Pineau's cell door opened and he was told by one of the less offensive prison guards to follow him and to bring with him his safety razor. Pineau had always been surprised that he had been allowed to keep his razor when he arrived at the prison and it was the envy of his fellow inmates. He was constantly asked for its loan and a strange ritual had grown up by which the guards allowed Pineau to use it to cut the hair of new arrivals in his wing of the prison. Pineau was happy to do this, as it gave him the chance to find out what was happening in the world outside and how far the allies were progressing in their assault on Italy.

This was not the usual time for such a session, however, and Pineau was perplexed to be led by a single guard down the stairs of his block and towards a bench in the northern courtyard where a soldier stood, his gun slung over his shoulder. Along the bench lay the motionless form of a man to whom the soldier pointed with the words, 'Shave him.' It was an extraordinary request considering the man was clearly more dead than alive, his unconscious face a mass of bruises. It was only as he approached the prone figure that Pineau realized who it was: Jean Moulin. His eyes appeared so sunken as to have been pushed back into his skull, a vicious bluish wound coloured one of his temples and his swollen lips emitted a faint rattle of breath.

Having asked the soldier to fetch him some soap and water, Pineau began his task with a trembling hand. The blade of his razor was far from sharp after its frequent use and much of the face he dared not touch, such was the damage. Just as he was finishing, Moulin opened his eyes and looked at Pineau with a flicker of recognition. 'Drink,' he whispered, and Pineau turned to the soldier who went to get some water from the nearby fountain. While he was doing this, Moulin forced a few words out that seemed to be in English but which Pineau could not understand. Pineau offered some words of comfort of his own but, after taking some water, Moulin lost consciousness again. Since the prison guard had disappeared, Pineau stayed with him as night began to fall, as though providing a vigil to the dead. Eventually, he was led back to his cell, Moulin seemingly being left on the bench for the night. By the morning, however, he was gone. Records show that, in fact, Jean Moulin endured another fortnight of brutal attention from the Gestapo. He was taken from Lyons to their Avenue Foch headquarters in Paris and eventually died while being transferred by train to Germany on 8 July 1943.

One possible explanation for the Germans' strange wish to have Moulin shaved was that Barbie was trying to improve his appearance so as to cover up some of the damage he had inflicted on the Frenchman. He may well have been afraid of the wrath of his bosses in Paris when they discovered that their Lyons subordinate had beaten all the useful life out of the man they were so keen to interrogate themselves.

During this same summer, Pineau was witness to another legendary event in the history of the Resistance. André

Devigny, a co-founder of the military intelligence network *Gilbert*, who was incarcerated in the next cell but one to his and who had suffered long days of torture at Klaus Barbie's hands, whispered to Pineau one morning that he was soon to be executed. Three days later, Devigny and his cell-mate had vanished, not victims of the firing squad (the sound of whose volleys were a regular accompaniment to life inside Fort Montluc), but escaped from the supposed escape-proof prison. The additional deprivations and reprisals meted out by the German guards following this breakout could not dull the sense of triumph shared by all the inmates left behind. (André Devigny survived the war and wrote in *Un Condamné à Mort S'est Echappé* about his remarkable escape through a loosened panel of the cell door, across the roof and over two perimeter walls, using a rope made of wire from his bedstead and torn pieces of blanket. An acclaimed 1956 Robert Bresson film, *A Man Escaped*, shot in Fort Montluc gaol itself, recreates Devigny's feat, using the original rope and other handmade implements.)

The number of prisoners increased rapidly as 1943 wore on. Pineau was no longer alone in his cell; first one man and then a second was ushered in to share the one mattress and cramped floor-space. Although he appreciated the chance to interact fully again with human beings, Pineau could not confide anything about his background with his new companions. Even if neither had been planted by the Germans, there was no knowing what could be extracted from them under torture. As summer became autumn, Pineau began to believe that he had been overlooked and that he was destined to remain in cell 113 indefinitely. Then, one day, he was told to pack and found himself escorted out of his cell and down to the ground floor where, by pure coincidence, Bonamour had also been summoned with his baggage.

Their destination was the refectory, a wooden hut inside the prison where some fifty of the more privileged prisoners were detained. Inside, it was like paradise. There were bunk beds with proper mattresses, tables and chairs and lockers for possessions. The occupants, most of them anti-Vichy politicians and journalists, showed great concern for the newcomers' emaciated appearance and immediately offered them food from what seemed to be abundant supplies. Pineau and Bonamour marvelled at their freedom to play card games, to read, to write and, above all, to converse freely with like-minded individuals. At last, Bonamour was able to recount to Pineau the circumstances of his arrest.

It seems that his landlord in Lyons had informed on him and, when he was picked up at the central station, he was carrying documents about the military, so could not deny that he was spying. For some reason, his dossier was sent not to the Gestapo but to a major in German army intelligence. Bonamour declared immediately to this major that he pleaded guilty and, since he would get nothing out of him, they might as well shoot him without wasting any more time.

The major took him at his word and drove Bonamour in his own car to the perimeter road of Fort Montluc prison. Soon, an execution squad arrived and the major asked if he was sure that he did not want to talk. Assured by Bonamour that he did not, the major remarked how regrettable that was, as it would be he who had to give the order to fire. As the soldiers lifted their rifles, the major suddenly announced that he had noticed that Bonamour was from a distinguished French family and asked if he would to do him the honour of taking lunch with him. His only plea was that he should not take advantage by trying to escape. During a sumptuous meal at one of the best black-market restaurants in Lyons, the major, who was himself a baron, told the bemused Bonamour how lucky he had been to have come across the *Wehrmacht* and not the Gestapo scoundrels whose methods brought dishonour on his country. Their ranks contained nothing but pimps, bankrupt traders and professional layabouts, people who would never have sullied an officer's uniform in the German army of old.

At the end of the meal, the major drove Bonamour back to Fort Montluc, where he apologized for having also imprisoned his wife there. Unfortunately, the Gestapo had brought her to him, so he had had no choice, but he assured Bonamour that it would not be for too long. (She was, in fact, released after three months). As for Bonamour himself, as long as no one insisted on having him shot, he should expect eventually to be sent to Germany, where he would be decently treated. Remarking on the strange paradox that, while Germans were posted to all corners of Europe, men from all over Europe were now living in Germany, he drove off, leaving Bonamour to his destiny.

Just as the Jews that had left Fort Montluc prison with such relief, Bonamour and Pineau, when their names were called one morning for departure to Germany, were full of hopeful anticipation. A long train journey would break the monotony of life in prison, and seeing out the last few months of the war in some German factory and in living quarters probably no worse than at present seemed a reasonable prospect.

Even from what they had already seen of Nazi contempt for the rights and dignity of their captives, they could not have been expected to envisage the murderous regime that awaited them at Buchenwald concentration camp. So many failed to survive the cattle-truck transportation, the slave labour in the quarries, the near-starvation, the disease, the punishments and the summary executions that it is astonishing that both Christian Pineau and Tristan Bonamour du Tartre survived eighteen months of such maltreatment. Liberation finally came to them on 11 April 1945 — they were back among their families ten days later.

Christian Pineau, (2nd from left), with fellow prisoners at Buchenwald concentration camp, just after their liberation in April 1945. (*Gilbert Pineau*)

CHAPTER 12: THE LAW OF AVERAGES

Marie-Madeleine Fourcade's Story — Part 2

Paris, 17 July 1943

> We stopped at the Arc de Triomphe to look at the most
> beautiful view in the world. I gave the capital a big,
> conspiratorial, goodbye smile; it answered with a scowl — the
> swastika flags cracking like whips in the twilight breeze.

That image stayed with Marie-Madeleine Fourcade as her
train pulled out of the Gare de l'Est the following evening. The
menace of the swastika had proved only too real for so many
of her faithful agents and now, in her eyes, she was deserting
those who, like her, had so far escaped the Gestapo's clutches
and continued to risk everything for the allied cause.

Everyone involved in that night's Lysander operation were in
different parts of the train. There were seven of them in all:
Pierre Dallas, in charge of the landing field with his three
assistants, and the prospective passengers, Marie-Madeleine,
and two of her agents, Lucien Poulard and Michel Gaveau.
Both men were being withdrawn to London for their own
security or that of the network. Poulard had narrowly avoided
arrest when the Gestapo called at his parents' house in Brest,
and Gaveau, an expert in military intelligence, had become
careless, allowing two women with no affinity with the
Resistance to share his house. Betrayal and infiltration by
German counter-espionage had become the scourge of the
network and no one outside its compass could be trusted.

Marie-Madeleine Fourcade in the uniform she wore in Germany during her tour of concentration camps in 1945 to trace lost agents of the Alliance network. (*Colin Cohen*)

As for Marie-Madeleine, nearly eight months had elapsed since she had sent three Corsican policemen in her place to Tangmere and, until this moment, she had continued to ignore the entreaties of her SIS correspondents to come out of France for a break from the constant threat of capture. Even now, it had taken all the persuasive powers of her second-in-command, Léon Faye, to convince her that face-to-face meetings with British intelligence had become essential if they were to achieve some of their aims. One of his former air force colleagues and a member of their network, Jean Carayon, had just been appointed Secretary-General of Air Defence by Marshal Pétain. While Pétain had consented to Hitler's plans to use the men under his command as anti-aircraft gunners on German rail transports, Carayon was asking for arms drops from the allies so that the same men could join the British and American forces when they landed in France. The *Alliance* network had also been approached to act as go-between in an attempt to set up negotiations for peace between a number of disaffected *Wehrmacht* officers and the British. Although highly sceptical about their ability to dislodge Hitler, Marie-Madeleine had agreed to put the proposals to Sir Claude Dansey in person.

The party left the train at the small town of Nanteuil-le-Haudouin, only about twenty-five miles north-east of Paris. Dallas had excelled himself in the eyes of the RAF by identifying a landing site which not only provided a perfect approach over open cornfields, but its proximity to the north coast of France also meant only a three-hour round trip for their pilots, about half the flying time of the network's two earlier sites. The first operation to this field had gone without a hitch for Bunny Rymills a month earlier, allowing two *Alliance* agents back into France and extracting three others. This time, it was Peter Vaughan-Fowler's turn to make the same trip and he, along with Eddie Keyser from the SIS, who had come down to Sussex for the occasion, would be keeping fingers crossed that Marie-Madeleine would be among his returning passengers. It was therefore a great relief for him to see an elegant moonlit figure picking her way across the freshly cut stubble and embracing, one after the other, the three men who had just climbed out of the cockpit behind him. As she and her two companions found space for themselves and their courier in the same cramped compartment, the grinning features of Pierre Dallas appeared beside him. He had climbed to the level of the pilots' seat and, greeting the man with whom he had carried out his Lysander training in Hertfordshire, presented him with the customary souvenirs of cognac and perfume.

Even as the white cliffs of Beachy Head glowed in the moonlight beneath the returning Lysander, Marie-Madeleine could not feel the exhilaration that a successful escape from France would normally engender in a secret agent. Too many of her friends were suffering at the hands of the Gestapo and, even though she was proud of the information contained in the cases of courier at her feet, courageously gathered by those in her network still at liberty, her sense of deserting them overwhelmed her. There was some comfort in the warm greeting she received from Eddie Keyser as she stepped from the plane. It was more than a year and a half since their meeting in Madrid, and his gentle reproach that she had caused so much worry by staying in France for so long, coupled with the celebratory fug of cigarettes and whisky in the Tangmere Cottage mess, lightened her mood to some extent.

It improved further as the car taking her and her two comrades from the airfield pulled into the drive at Bignor Manor. Instead of the harsh military barrack accommodation she was expecting, they were in a garden that reminded her of the nursery rhyme illustrations of her childhood and the shapely, auburn-haired hostess welcoming them on the doorstep completed the illusion. As they sat in the farmhouse dining room with their 3 a.m. reception pie, they were intrigued to hear the sound of whispering in the hall and several feet on the stairs. Tony Bertram was quick to shut the door, explaining how important it was that separate parties arriving from France should not meet. Such secrecy in these homely surroundings seemed incongruous to Marie-Madeleine and she was even more surprised to be asked by Keyser what name she would choose for her false identity while in England. The risk, apparently very real to the SIS, of her being identified by a spy from Germany or an ill-disposed rival French agent, was laughable to Marie-Madeleine when compared to the dangers she had just escaped.

She awoke the next morning with a start, convinced it was the Gestapo banging on her bedroom door. In fact it was Keyser, trying to wake her from her deep sleep to tell her it was time to leave for London. In the car, there was nothing he could do or say to Marie-Madeleine to stop her tears, which flowed uncontrollably for the entire journey to the capital. Once he had installed her in a flat there, he was at least able to send round a doctor who could prescribe some alleviation from her mental and physical exhaustion in the form of bromide and vitamins. The next day, the newly knighted Sir Claude Dansey called at her flat. Showing none of his renowned cynicism or ill-humour, he was at his most charming with Marie-Madeleine. Taking both her hands in his and calling her 'Poz', he said he had always wondered what this 'terrible woman' was like who had them all so scared, and expressed his relief at her safe arrival in London.

Marie-Madeleine was swift to make it clear that she intended to return to France at the first opportunity, but her visitor had different ideas. She had, he told her, stayed in the field long past the safety limits. By the law of averages, an underground leader did not last more than six months and she had been operating without a break for two and a half years. He thanked her profusely for what she had achieved, told her that she must rest and that she would have a vital part to play in the network's operations from the English side of the Channel, at least for a while.

The dining room at Bignor Manor, where all new arrivals from France were welcomed with a serving of 'reception pie'.
(*The Bertram Family*)

Of the thirty months in the field without respite, it was the last eight, during which the Nazis had taken control of the free zone, that had taken the greatest toll on Marie-Madeleine.

Every day had brought new traumas and every night horrifying dreams, too often predictive of the terrors that awaited her comrades. In one recurring nightmare, she would witness a Lysander bringing Léon Faye and her personal radio operator, Ferdinand Rodriguez, back to France and landing in a field surrounded by clumps of heather in full bloom. Unable to warn them, she could only watch as her friends disembarked, unaware of a ring of German soldiers that closed in around them. So vivid was the dream that she forbade Pierre Dallas, to his obvious bemusement, ever to select a landing site in the vicinity of heather.

Ever since her escape from arrest in Marseilles in November 1942, Marie-Madeleine had been on the run, barely a step ahead of the Gestapo as her headquarters moved from one hideout to another in the southern half of France. During a short stay back in Toulouse, she was able to see her son, who was at a Jesuit boarding school and under the protection of one particular priest who had undertaken to hide him from the Gestapo, should they find out that he was there. It was in Toulouse that she also learned Faye had made a daring escape from prison and decided that she needed somewhere more secure and central in France for the two of them to resume their direction of the network. She therefore set off for the upper reaches of the Dordogne, close to the disused aerodrome where the network's first two Lysander receptions had taken place and where numerous agents could lend protection.

Briefly based at Ussel, the headquarters then moved westward down the main Clermont-Ferrand to Bordeaux road to a hotel at Terrason before the local sector head, Colonel Edouard Kauffmann, found Marie-Madeleine and her entourage a more permanent base in a draughty château outside the town of Sarlat. They moved in just after Christmas 1942, but were on the road again a few weeks later when Marie-Madeleine became uneasy that too many people in the local sector had become involved with the headquarters' activities and they were threatening each others' security. Her instincts saved her, but only just; the Gestapo, pistols at the ready, arrived at the château ten minutes after her departure, asking the locals for a 'Mrs Harrison', a dangerous spy. Clearly, they had been given only her code name, *Hérisson* (Hedgehog) and leapt to the conclusion that they were looking for an Englishwoman.

After Sarlat, the next headquarters were established in a house in the centre of Cahors on the River Lot. This proved ideal because the house was on a hill and all the roads leading to it could be watched. There was also an escape route through the back into the countryside if a car caught them unawares. But it was still January when Marie-Madeleine took the decision to decamp once again. This time, it was at the shocking news that the German police had pounced on three of the network's sectors: Toulouse, Nice/Monaco and Pau. With so many agents undergoing torture, however much she believed in their courage, she could forgive any of them if they were to divulge her whereabouts and so another move, this time to Tulle, was essential.

By now, as news reached London of the Gestapo's inroads into the network, Eddie Keyser of the SIS was sending urgent messages, demanding that Marie-Madeleine take the Lysander flight planned for the February moon. If his belief that her arrest would effectively end the *Alliance's* operation in France, Marie-Madeleine sensed that the network could only survive its recent body blows if she remained in France and, all the time, the Gestapo were at her heels. Only Kauffman had survived a swoop on the Sarlat sector and, on the day the headquarters party had decided to leave Tulle, this time for Lyons, the local priest had enabled the local sector leader to flee from a German raid on his house by stirring up a mob of angry inhabitants who had forced the policemen into a temporary withdrawal.

In spite of its size, Lyons was hardly an ideal hiding place. By February 1943, Klaus Barbie, in his pomp, was flushing out agents with ruthless efficiency in a city that had become the unofficial capital of the Resistance, and Fort Montluc prison was filling rapidly with battered, emaciated prisoners. In the very week of Marie-Madeleine's arrival in Lyons, six key members of the local sector walked into a Gestapo trap and it was only because of her widespread and well-to-do connections that she was able to find refuge with a friend for herself, her assistant Hermine Bontinck, and radio man Ferdinand Rodriguez.

After a few days, a larger flat was found in Lyons to serve as headquarters but eventually that, too, had to be abandoned when Marie-Madeleine discovered that a former leader of the network's Paris sector had become an *Abwehr* double agent and was the likely cause of all the recent arrests. Still in Lyons, Marie-Madeleine took refuge in a private clinic while the rest of her team carried out their work in another part of town. It was while she was here that her two children, Christian (twelve) and Béatrice (ten), were brought to Lyons. They believed their mother was in London, as did many of her agents in the provinces, as she had asked that the BBC put out a message to that effect to throw her German pursuers off the scent. True to their word, the Jesuits in Toulouse had refused to hand over Christian when the Gestapo came to claim him as a hostage and hid him instead in a mountain refuge run by the Christian

Friendship organization for Jewish children. Béatrice had been with her grandmother, who was at a loss to know how to ensure her safety.

Feeling it would be unfair to let her children see her, Marie-Madeleine asked her assistant Hermine to look after them in Lyons while a route was devised for their escape into Switzerland. On one occasion, Hermine led the malnourished and bewildered pair past a window so that their mother could see them — an experience that Marie-Madeleine likened to 'being buried alive'. The children made it into Switzerland even though they had to be left entirely on their own, miles from anywhere, to crawl through the rows of barbed wire between the two countries.

Lyons finally became too dangerous after a bungled operation by the Vichy police in which nearly all of Marie-Madeleine's staff were arrested but then allowed to escape through various means. The police superintendent in charge was tortured and deported for his incompetence by the furious Gestapo, but they were unable to prevent an evacuation of the headquarters team to Paris at the end of May. The growing pressure both from London and her closest colleagues in France that it was time for Marie-Madeleine to leave the country was intensified on the Metro one day when she found herself sitting opposite the official of the Vichy government who had once issued her with a marked *Ausweis*. Although she fled from the train, he had clearly recognized her, and his inevitable subsequent report to the German police would explode any enduring myth that she was in England. The time had finally come to turn the myth into a reality.

Suitcase radio transmitter-receivers issued to agents in France became increasingly compact as the war progressed. This B2 model was a great improvement on the unwieldy sets first supplied in the early years of the occupation. (*Edward Wake-Walker*)

If such a restive trail from Marseilles to Paris appeared merely a means of avoiding capture, it did, in fact, achieve much more than that. In spite of innumerable soul-destroying setbacks, it allowed the *Alliance* network to continue to supply London with an abundant and uninterrupted stream of essential military intelligence. While a growing number of its men and women were paying dearly for their cause through torture, deportation and the firing squad, others, thanks to materials and means from London distributed via Marie-Madeleine's headquarters team, continued to work silently, pinpointing precise enemy targets for the RAF and the Royal Navy along the Atlantic coast and returning detailed questionnaires about German anti-invasion defences.

To run her headquarters effectively, Marie-Madeleine leaned heavily on a number of individuals. Although he was away for more than two months during this period, first in London, then in Algeria dealing with General Giraud who had taken over control of French troops in North Africa after Admiral Darlan's assassination, Léon Faye was a mainstay. As her chief of staff, he ensured the network continued to function in its adversity and, with his air force connections, continued to recruit new, motivated agents to take the place of others who had been captured. The *sangfroid* and ingenuity of Rodriguez ensured, even when they were moving rapidly from one town to the next, that transmissions to London were as regular as humanly possible. While Marie-Madeleine and Hermine worked feverishly on the courier reaching them from the four corners of France, encoding the information for transmission that was too urgent to await the next Lysander, Rodriguez would scour the surrounding area for suitable sites to set up his aerials, never exceeding twenty minutes in any location to avoid the detector vans.

The link with London was not only vital in the supply of intelligence, it also served to relay communications between Marie-Madeleine and all her regional teams, who were each supplied with their own radios for contact with British Intelligence. Another man whom she came to rely on was Georges Lamarque, a brilliant mathematician, who she had put in charge of all radio operations for the network. He spent months on end in transit across France and was often the first to find out and report to Marie-Madeleine the details of a Gestapo raid after a sector's radio had fallen silent.

Even before Marie-Madeleine arrived in Lyons herself, there were two other essential arms of her central operation already established there. One was a policeman, Ernest Siegrist, originally part of her Marseilles headquarters, whose speciality was forging new identity documents for new agents or those whose cover had been blown. The other was her Avia team, who ran all the parachute and Lysander operations for the network. All these people, along with the liaison agents who would carry reports back from the sectors, comprised a dogged machine which, although backfiring occasionally, continued to serve the allied cause in an extremely hostile environment.

Examples of its success were particularly marked on the west coast of France. Lucien Poulard, arriving from his native Brittany at Marie-Madeleine's Sarlat hideout with a suitcase full of reports, had just avoided catastrophe. In order to avoid a search at the demarcation line, he had got out of the wrong side of the train but found himself face to face with a German officer. He sat on the suitcase while being interrogated at the station and was astonished to find his explanation for wanting to cross the line illegally accepted. He had claimed that he was a student eager to visit the prehistoric caves at Les Eyzies and he had not the documentation to allow him to do so. One of his agents in Brittany was a policeman who would set up road blocks in order to be certain of Nazi regimental insignia for precision in his reports of enemy troop movements. Another, supplied with a radio, was able to give accurate information to London every time a U-boat set sail from Brest, making it a sitting target for the British. The information would come from a dressmaker employed in the lifebelt repair shop of the submarine base who, when crews came to collect their lifebelts, would glean which boats were about to depart.

Another sector head, Philippe Koenigswerther, whose region included Bordeaux and La Rochelle, provided information that enabled the famous Royal Navy Operation Frankton to take place. Known as the 'Cockleshell Heroes', ten Royal Marines launched two-man canoes from the submarine *HMS Tuna* near the mouth of the Gironde Estuary. Their mission was to plant limpet mines to the hulls of blockade running ships of the German merchant navy docked in Bordeaux. Five ships were severely damaged on the night of 11 December 1942 as a result, although eight of the ten commandos lost their lives, two when their canoe capsized soon after its launch and the rest by execution after they had been captured making their escape overland towards the Spanish border.

The *Alliance* network also benefited during this period from its friends in high places in Vichy. Marie-Madeleine's most senior contact there was General Camille Raynal who, among other useful sources close to the Pétain government, turned up a naval specialist, Joël Lemoigne, who had ready access to all the ports occupied by the Germans. One of his agents in the Brittany port of Lorient who could speak fluent German, thanks to his Alsace upbringing, had won the confidence of the Germans to the extent that he was the only Frenchman allowed into the Keroman U-boat base, built by the Todt organization. Loathed by his fellow French workers for his apparent avid collaboration, this engineer was entrusted with a job which gave him access to all operational orders, boat movements and the effects of their activities. British Intelligence became party to every detail. Through Lemoigne, the network was also the conduit of information about the Italian and German attempts to salvage parts of the French naval fleet of seventy-seven vessels which had been scuttled by their own crews at Toulon just after the allied invasion of North Africa in November 1942.

There was a growing tendency among some in the network to look for more active ways of undermining the German occupation, especially after the invasion of the southern zone. This was understandable, as so many of the agents were trained soldiers and airmen, but Marie-Madeleine was sometimes compelled to remind the more belligerent that theirs was an intelligence-gathering outfit and, as soon as they became involved in operations outside their normal function — such as the seaborne evacuation of General Giraud — the risk to their security became too great. Therefore, when one of her Vichy agents came up with an audacious plan to kidnap either Pétain or Laval by persuading the apparently complicit pilot of the French government's official plane to re-route a Paris-bound flight to London, Marie-Madeleine resisted the temptation to give the venture her blessing.

There was, after all, enough risk attached to the routine task of receiving the monthly Lysander flights. Her Avia team, headed by Pierre Dallas, successfully despatched Léon Faye to London on the night of 14 January from the tried and tested Thalamy airfield in the Auvergne (see Chapter 9), and received some much-needed funds for the network, their first supply since the November debacle in Marseilles. A parachute drop around the same time provided a consignment of handguns for agents to carry and accumulators that would allow radio operators to transmit in the open air, independent of mains power supplies and out of the reach of detector vans.

John Bridger, the pilot who had flown the January Lysander mission to Thalamy, complained on his return to Tangmere that the airfield was no longer ideal because it had been colonized by clumps of heather which made for a very bumpy landing and take-off. Marie-Madeleine never saw the Thalamy site herself so it is unlikely that the heather of her nightmare was drawn from this. Certainly, it did not deter either the Avia team or the RAF from planning another operation to this field for the March moon when Faye was to be returned to France. They were both deterred, however, when news arrived that the Germans were driving stakes into the field. Worse still, the Gestapo had raided the house of the local sector leader in nearby Ussel, where Rodriguez, in charge of this particular air operation (Dallas was to fly out for Hudson landing training), had installed a radio to co-ordinate the reception.

Although her master was fortunately absent when the German police descended on his house, the elderly maidservant of Jean Vinzant, the sector head, knew only too well how incriminating the radio would be for the household. She successfully smuggled it out of the house in her voluminous apron under the noses of the Gestapo agents, who were too busy searching for papers to pay her any attention. Rodriquez was therefore able to retrieve the radio and contact London to cancel the mission.

With Thalamy no longer available, the network needed another landing site and located one much nearer to Lyons, which had by now become the centre of its operations. The field lay beside the Saône, to the north of Lyons, about three kilometres upriver from Villefranche-sur-Saône. Therefore, only a few days after the aborted operation in the Auvergne, Flying Officer Bunny Rymills was taking off from Tangmere with a hunchbacked man with snow-white hair and steel-rimmed spectacles installed in his rear cockpit. This was, in fact, Léon Faye, heavily disguised, courtesy of the SIS make-up department. It turned out to be a hugely frustrating flight, especially for Faye, who, with his airman's eye, realized, as they flew over France, that Rymills's course was too far to the east. The intercom was either switched off or out of order and, although he thumped hard against the fuel tank which separated him from the pilot, Faye was unable to make himself heard. It was only when the Swiss Alps came into view that Rymills understood that he had dramatically missed his target and that the only thing to do was to return home before his fuel ran out. There was no mistake by Wing Commander Pickard on the following night and, much to Marie-Madeleine's relief, her right-hand man was returned to her after his two-month absence.

If the Villefranche landing field was convenient in its proximity to Lyons, it turned out to have a severe drawback. Although Rymills completed the April operation there without any of his earlier difficulties, soon afterwards, Marie-Madeleine was shocked to have the field pointed out to her by a talkative taxi driver who assured her that everyone locally knew what went on there. A new site was duly identified for the May exchange far away from Lyons, close to the River Cher, to the east of Issoudun in central France. It was provided with the willing co-operation of a wealthy local farmer, who plied the reception team and outgoing agents with champagne while they awaited the Lysander's arrival. After the plane had come and gone, the farmer offered to keep the documents and several million francs sent from London in his safe until the network's treasurer arrived the next day to collect them. To his consternation, when the treasurer asked for the money and reports, the farmer denied all knowledge of them and threatened to call in the Gestapo.

Desperate to save the arms and radio sets that had also been delivered by the Lysander, the leader of the operation, Henri Courmouls, fled the scene with his team and the empty-handed treasurer. When a report of what had happened reached Marie-Madeleine, she judged that the farmer was more of a crook than a traitor and ordered that an armed team return to the farm. They waited until nightfall, then cut the telephone wires and forced the doors of the house. It did not take much to persuade the farmer to open his safe and hand back his ill-gotten gains. It was following this incident and Marie-Madeleine's move to Paris that the field from which she eventually made her own escape to Tangmere during the July moon was chosen by the Avia team.

It must have seemed remarkable to Eddie Keyser back in London that the *Alliance* was continuing to produce such copious and valuable reports and still arranging regular Lysander and parachute operations while, nearly every week, he was receiving news of devastation to the network's ranks or another near miss for the headquarters team. It was little wonder that they had so much concern for Marie-Madeleine's morale and safety; her comrades seemed to be falling like flies. While she was still at the château outside Sarlat, she was distressed by the physical state of Maurice Coustenoble, one of her first and dearest agents, who had come to deliver reports from the forbidden zone in the north. It was not the bullets that had passed through his coat as he was fired at crossing the demarcation line that ailed him, but an advanced state of cancer which had him coughing blood as he spoke. His region had been devastated after the arrest of the former leader of the Paris sector, Commandant Verteré, who had apparently fallen for the Gestapo ploy of placing a stool pigeon in his cell to whom he told everything. Coustenoble's illness did not prevent him returning to his post in the north, but Marie-Madeleine would never see him again. He died nine months later from his cancer just at the moment when the ambulance in which he was being taken to safety was overhauled and stopped by the Gestapo.

Verteré was, in fact, the cause of far more damage than that reported by Coustenoble. As a senior air force colleague of

Faye's, he had been given the Paris sector in the spring of 1942 with much confidence that his influence and connections would be of great value to the network. He proposed an extraordinary cover as a member of the Nazi-sympathizing *rassemblement* political group led by the arch collaborationist Marcel Déat. It was not long, however, before his conduct began to make Marie-Madeleine uneasy. He would not take orders from Faye because he was senior to him in the air force, and showed a marked reluctance to set up radio communications with London and little interest in seeking out military intelligence. Furthermore, he showed no concern at all when a close acquaintance of his and leader of the network's Lille sector was arrested by German police, refusing to change his address or post office boxes in Paris, which the Lille man could easily have betrayed under torture.

Because of these shortcomings, Marie-Madeleine decided to dispense with Verteré's services, but maybe she should have suspected him of duplicity even then. If he was not in the pay of the *Abwehr* at that time, he certainly became so after his arrest. Claiming to have escaped from German captivity, he wrote a letter to General de Gaulle asking for his help in forming a new network. It was the *Abwehr* who sent the letter to London via one of their Lisbon channels which, fortunately, was well known by British Intelligence to be in the service of the Germans. Even if that plan had been thwarted, it did not prevent Verteré from handing over all his old contacts, which led to the execution of all the network's principle agents in Lille and a wholesale rounding up of the southern sectors.

Many of the network's longest-serving recruits, such as Colonel Bernis in Monaco and Marc Mesnard in Marseilles, were arrested along with several others, and whole regions were put out of action. As Marie-Madeleine made her frantic progress across southern France, setting up one headquarters after another, the devastation seemed to follow her. Pau fell; so, too, did Toulouse. Only Edouard Kauffman, head of the Sarlat (Dordogne) sector, escaped to join the headquarters team as head of its security. There was nothing he could do to prevent the raid at Tulle and, on the very day they arrived in Lyons, an ambush was awaiting the local sector there where, among others, two of the network's most courageous and effective female agents were led away for interrogation at Klaus Barbie's dreaded Hotel Terminus. Both women, Madeleine Crozet and Michèle Goldschmidt, endured humiliation and torture as their breasts were burnt with cigarettes and electric shocks applied to their naked bodies while they remained utterly silent. Even the German officers who signed their death warrant at the ensuing military tribunal were moved sufficiently by their courage to submit an appeal to Hitler for mercy — although the women themselves refused to add their signatures to it.

A further act of treachery put paid to another hugely valuable arm of the network, the Vichy sector run by General Raynal. The general had hatched a plan to spring Navarre, the network's founder, from the prison where he was being held in the Massif Central. When he explained to Marie-Madeleine that he intended to pay 100,000 francs to the prison van driver to smuggle Navarre out under a pile of poultry cages, she was immediately suspicious of the driver's motives because of the high price he demanded. She was also shocked that he had been allowed to deal directly with the sector head. She decided to meet him herself and was immediately put off by his voluminous girth, a sure sign of black-market dealing at the very least in a malnourished nation. When he boasted to her that his mistress was friendly with the Germans, Marie-

Madeleine became convinced of the man's duplicity but, in order to buy time to warn the Vichy team of the danger they faced, gave him a bundle of twenty halved 5,000 franc notes, saying he would receive the other half when Navarre was free.

Tragically, before her warning could get through, one of the Vichy agents found himself surrounded by the Gestapo at a station while in the company of the van driver. He drew his revolver but was shot dead through the throat. For some reason, General Raynal refused to flee his house when news of the shooting reached him and he was arrested a few days later along with nearly all his Vichy team. The outcome for Navarre was no better, as the planned escape persuaded Marshal Pétain to hand over the responsibility of his imprisonment to the Germans.

Blows landed even closer to home for Marie-Madeleine while she was in Lyons. Her radio operator, Rodriguez, had an extremely narrow escape when, having just finished a transmission from a house in a small town outside the city, found himself face to face with a detector van crew as he stepped out of the front door. By throwing the case containing his radio straight at the head of the German policeman who accosted him, he gained just enough time to make a dash for it on foot, successfully dodging the hail of bullets which followed him. With the help of his comrades back in Lyons, he managed to thwart the manhunt by escaping on a train to Paris, but his departure was a major loss to Marie-Madeleine, who had drawn great strength from his unflappable assistance.

It was only because of the incompetence of the French police in Lyons that all the activities of the *Alliance* did not come to an abrupt halt for good in May 1943. Events began with a serious car crash in which three members of the Avia team, including Dallas, were badly hurt when their car hit a wall on the way to a parachute drop. They were taken to hospital, where one of them, in a delirious state, talked about his team's headquarters and the police who were investigating the accident pricked up their ears. The trail they were able to follow led to a house in Lyons, where Faye was conducting a meeting of senior network agents who were compiling a report to send to General Giraud in Algeria to help him in his plans to attack Corsica and the Mediterranean coast. While the four apparently most senior at the meeting were taken to a nearby police station, Hermine Bontinck, Marie-Madeleine's courier and assistant, and another female agent were kept under guard in the house. In spite of the guard, Hermine was able to make a surreptitious telephone call to Marie-Madeleine to warn her of the arrests and was also able to hide some very incriminating reports in a rubbish bin. Later, she managed to give her guards the slip and escape from the apartment building, but not before asking the doorman at the street entrance to salvage the reports and keep them until a messenger arrived for them. (The female comrade she left behind ended up in prison and was eventually shot in the back of the neck by the SS at Schirmeck concentration camp).

Meanwhile, Léon Faye and the three others, which included Colonel Kauffman and an air force general, René de Vitrolles, who had taken on the task of rebuilding the network's south-east region, baffled their police captors with their indignant reaction to their arrest. The police were clearly impressed by their rank and by their assertion that they were working with the backing of Pétain's intelligence service. While the superintendent waited for orders about how to deal with them, the four men simply walked out of the police station, telling their bemused guard that they were off to find something to eat.

The guard on the three hospitalized Avia team members was no tighter. Their fellow agent, Henri Courmouls, had found a way to visit them by disguising himself as a male nurse. Although they were all still very groggy (Dallas had earlier actually been given extreme unction), he persuaded the sister in charge that they needed fresh air and took them outside in their pyjamas — never to return to the hospital.

The Gestapo backlash which followed all these escapes necessitated the headquarters' final hurried decampment to Paris, and it was here that Marie-Madeleine received the last piece of bad news before her flight to London. It would have been bad enough if it had been only that the last of her team left in Lyons, the document forger Ernest Siegrist, had been arrested along with all his equipment. This included three transmitters, a large supply of seals and blank identity forms, as well as a dagger, two revolvers and a stock of high explosive. He also had in his possession a duplicate of Faye's personal encoded notebook, which contained hundreds of addresses, passwords and codes.

What made the matter worse still was the manner of Siegrist's arrest. It happened during an operation by two members of Kauffmann's security team to move Siegrist to a new hideout, and the conduct of one of these two agents, a young Alsatian student by the name of Jean-Paul Lien, was at best incompetent and at worst suspicious. While acting as lookout, when he saw Siegrist's house surrounded by the Gestapo, instead of warning his opposite number as he went to collect him, he fled the scene, allowing both his fellow agents to be caught. There was another reason Marie-Madeleine had doubts about Lien; he had earlier been one of the two messengers sent to the house where Faye and the others had been arrested to collect the reports which Hermine had hidden before she made her escape. They had contained documents and films but, when they were returned, only the films were there. Neither incident involving Lien was enough to persuade Marie-Madeleine to take summary action against him, but she would soon bitterly regret that she did not.

London, July 1943

If Marie-Madeleine had known that she would not set foot in France for an entire year once she had landed in England in July 1943, it is doubtful if she would ever have agreed to leave her country in the first place. It became clear to her soon after her arrival in London that the only man who could prevent her return, Sir Claude Dansey, would exercise that power, albeit with kind words and assurances that it was for her own good and that of the network. He argued that with such a huge organization — there were some 5,000 agents now involved from all over France — an overall view away from the immediate firing line would put her in a better position to direct operations. He also strongly believed that the Germans' counter-espionage machine was now so efficient that her chances of avoiding capture were non-existent if she returned and the value to the Gestapo of what she knew was inestimable.

Realizing that there was some truth in what Dansey said, particularly about the size of the network and the security problems posed by expecting all regions to report to a single headquarters in the field, Marie-Madeleine asked Léon Faye to come over with the August Lysander flight. Her aim was to discuss with him ways to decentralize the organization, which had just received a further blow with the arrest of a number of agents, including Henri-Léopold Dor, all of whose names had appeared in Faye's notebook found with Siegrist.

When Faye arrived in London, she found that Dansey was equally loath to let him return to France and suggested that they hand on-the-spot control to Paul Bernard, a Parisian banker and economist who Marie-Madeleine had for some time earmarked as a future chief should anything happen to her or Faye. By then, Marie-Madeleine had become convinced that Faye would be in great danger if he returned, but she succumbed to his furious protest that he could not desert the men and women he had persuaded to fight alongside him and she gave him permission to go.

Although Marie-Madeleine enjoyed a far easier relationship with Dansey than those who worked with him or for him in the SIS, there were still some considerable obstacles which, if not deliberately put in her way, nonetheless made the task of monitoring and directing her network problematic. It was not helped by the officious attitude of the officer who had taken the place of Eddie Keyser as her link with the SIS. Known to her only as 'Tom', he may well have been the same individual as Gilbert Renault's Major 'J' and Passy's 'Crayfish'. Marie-Madeleine got the impression he was withholding information radioed to London from her own agents, and his insistence on repeatedly searching the cases of two newly recruited agents due to fly into France annoyed them so much that they resigned from their mission.

Worse still, as her time in London wore on, Dansey began to give the distinct impression that the *Alliance* was losing its importance to him. Excuses about bad weather and a scarcity of pilots were given to Marie-Madeleine to explain the lack of available Lysander operations throughout the autumn and winter. Records show, however, that 161 Squadron continued its service to other intelligence networks and the SOE with unprecedented frequency during those months. It was possible that, with the betrayals that continued to devastate the *Alliance*, Sir Claude felt that any contact with its agents in France was too risky even for the RAF. Marie-Madeleine had to be content with increasingly intermittent radio contact from her agents and a house at 10 Carlyle Square with a direct telephone link to British Intelligence. Dansey did listen to her protests about the obstructive 'Tom' and replaced him with a far more sympathetic officer, code-named 'Ham', but it was only when Kenneth Cohen returned from a posting overseas in the early days of 1944 that Marie-Madeleine found someone within the SIS who was willing to re-open her physical links with France. Up until then, her life in London had been largely one of perpetual impotent anguish, punctuated occasionally with moments of immense pride at the continuing achievements of her beleaguered network.

One such moment came early on during her London vigil when she had gone down to the Bertrams' house anxiously to await the arrival of Faye and Rodriguez with the August moon.

'Barbara did her best to cheer me up by chatting away gaily,' she recalled in her memoirs, 'but my thoughts were in … turmoil. Then Bertram called to say that "it was time to put the kettle on for tea." That meant that all was well and at last our passengers appeared.'

Among the impressive quantities of courier that arrived with them and which Marie-Madeleine and Faye wasted no time in opening and examining was one meticulously detailed report which had them both transfixed. It had been compiled by Jeannie Rousseau, a female agent of the *Alliance's* sub-network, the *Druids*, which their indefatigable radio chief, Georges Lamarque, had formed using disaffected members of the disbanded Vichy youth organization, *Les Compagnons de France*. Rousseau, who spoke German like a native, had an officer contact who worked in the island laboratories of Usedom in northern Germany, where new weaponry was developed. Her resulting report was the first in-depth intelligence available to the allies about the development and deployment of the V-1 flying bomb and the V-2 rocket — both of which would prove to be lethal barbs during Nazi Germany's death throes.

If Faye's arrival had brought such valuable information to the allies and such comfort to Marie-Madeleine, his and Rodriguez's return to France would bring nothing but despair. To her horror, and in her firm belief in the power of premonition, Marie-Madeleine caught a glimpse of a vast expanse of heather as she travelled through the Surrey heathland on her way from London to Bignor Manor to see the two men off. Her recurring dream about Faye's arrest had become real, yet she knew everyone would think she had finally cracked if she were to try to stop the operation.

In fact, the moon on the night of 13 September was so bright that Flight Lieutenant Robin Hooper failed to see any of Pierre Dallas's signals at the field and had to return with his outward bound passengers. This did nothing to dispel Marie-Madeleine's certainty that she was sending her friends to their doom and, two nights later, the BBC broadcast the message that 'whale fishing is a dangerous occupation' to denote that the operation was on again.

'This time I watched Eagle go in the absolute conviction that it would be for ever,' she later wrote, 'and my heart filled with the appalling knowledge that there was nothing more I could do. In the friendly but now deserted lounge, I sat for hours listening to Barbara's knitting needles clicking away in time with the ticking of the clock.'

Tony Bertram's call from Tangmere to say, 'tea for our new friends' must have given her at least some hope, as it meant that the exchange had taken place and that Maurice de McMahon, who had fled the Gestapo in Paris and had been hiding in Switzerland, and Philippe Koenigswerther, head of the still-functioning Bordeaux sector, were on their way to Bignor. When they arrived, they were far from euphoric. The three-night wait for the plane had played havoc with their nerves, especially as they had the feeling all the time that they were being watched.

And, of course, they were right. Jean-Paul Lien, alias 'Lanky' and one of the network's Lysander reception committee that night, had another code name that was much more precious to him. To Oberleutnant Merck of German counter-espionage, he was V-Mann E 7226. Lien did not only have a code name conferred on him by his *Abwehr* masters — he would soon be receiving the Iron Cross with Sword and two million francs in return for the betrayal of his countrymen. It was a small price for Oberleutnant Merck to pay considering the riches in arrests that it had afforded him, ensuring his own safety from a winter posting to the Russian front whence so many of his fellow officers would never return.

The Gestapo waited until Faye, Rodriguez and the entire Avia team were on the train to Paris early in the morning of 16 September before they moved in for the arrest. Meanwhile, another team of plain-clothes men were swooping on the *Alliance's* headquarters in the capital. If not for a botched operation where the German police thought they had mistaken the number of the apartment after they had rung the bell and descended to the floor below, the entire headquarters staff, including its acting head, Paul Bernard, would have been caught. As it was, they escaped down a drainpipe at the back of the building, but could not stop the arrest of all the Paris radio operators and security team.

It was several days before Marie-Madeleine got to hear the news that she had been dreading, when Bernard succeeded in passing a message to a radio operator in the Le Mans sector. Over the next few days, the news only got worse. Colonel Kauffmann in the Massif Central and his team were arrested along with many other agents based in the Lyons area. Transmitters were falling silent in all parts of France — Autun, Brest, Rennes and Normandy had fallen into Gestapo hands. By now, it was very obvious that all the arrests could only have happened with the assistance of an infiltrator with access to the heart of the network. When Marie-Madeleine was briefing Philippe Koenigswerther about the devastated network he was due to rejoin after his course in England, he immediately told her who he believed was the traitor. Lien had apparently been pumping him for information about his sector during their three-day wait for the Lysander. Koenigswerther was sufficiently suspicious then to give him false information; the fact that the Bordeaux sector was one of the few still intact was proof enough to him that Lien was the informer.

It was only in late November when Marie-Madeleine herself accepted that Lien was a double agent. Until then, the only thing she knew for sure was of the arrests in the train and that Lien had been picked up with all the others. She was still even hoping that Faye was not among them, having followed her instructions to make his way from the landing site separately from the others. Her hopes were finally dashed when one of her former agents, now working in London as the archivist for the *BCRA*, handed her a radio message he had come across in the files. It had come from a small Lyons network more than a month previously and gave definite news of Faye's capture and confirmation that Lien had been freed soon after the arrest. It is not clear why the message was sent by a separate network, but it appalled Marie-Madeleine that it would have been seen by both the SIS and de Gaulle's secret service and yet no one had thought of passing the information on to her. Certain knowledge of Lien's duplicity a month earlier might well have saved a number of her agents now behind bars.

In spite of such administrative shortcomings, Marie-Madeleine was able to disperse much of the bitterness which existed between de Gaulle and her organization during her time in London. Not only did the General object to the fact that all the *Alliance's* intelligence was fed directly to the British, who were selective about what they passed on to the *BCRA*, he also believed that the *Alliance* was working for his arch rival, General Giraud, who had been put in command of all French forces in North Africa after Darlan's assassination. It was true that Faye had negotiated with Giraud when he was in Algeria and set up a communication link with him in return for official French military status for the network. But Marie-Madeleine understood quite well that her agents in France, like so many others in the resistance movement, were Free French at heart and that de Gaulle was the more able leader.

She abhorred the rivalry between the Gaullists and the Giraudists and the lack of unity among those fighting the occupation. One of her own agents in France had sacrificed himself to the Gestapo by overrunning his radio transmission to London to pass on details of planned police raids on Communist Resistance fighters. When she discovered that the communist representative in London had not been provided with any radio link with France to warn his men, she was mortified that her agent's courageous act had been in vain. For all these reasons, when de Gaulle assumed overall command of French Forces at the end of 1943, Marie-Madeleine willingly agreed to a suggestion by British Intelligence that they arrange a legal agreement for the *Alliance* to become part of the *BCRA* while maintaining its direct links to the SIS.

From the SIS point of view, direct links with the *Alliance* proved still to be extremely valuable in spite of Dansey's apparent waning faith in the network's viability after the damage wreaked by Lien. Paul Bernard, now properly in charge since Faye's capture, soon made it clear to Marie-Madeleine that they were carrying on in spite of there being no regular means of delivering courier and exchanging personnel and material. Everything now depended on the radio operators who were still free and, throughout November and December of 1943, the airwaves were busy with news of German shipping movements from Bordeaux, the effects of allied bombing on Toulon, aircraft strength at Tours airfield, the numbers of submarines in dock at Saint-Nazaire and the size of infantry reinforcements stationed at the mouth of the Rhône. A number of the sectors, all now acting more or less autonomously, were also getting wind of Hitler's planned assault on London with V-1 missiles and sending information about launching installations along the English Channel coast.

Late in November, Philippe Koenigswerther did eventually make it back to France, but only by threatening to shoot the commander of the Royal Navy launch that had brought him to Cap Fréhel on the north coast of Brittany if he did not let him swim ashore. It had been the second attempt to land him in France and, as with the first time, there was no sign of the reception committee's signals. Utterly frustrated by the prospect of returning again to England, he drew his revolver and was allowed to plunge into the sea. Koenigswerther made it to shore and discovered when he found his comrades that the navy had been half a mile to the north of the agreed rendezvous and that he had just swum and waded through a minefield. This was the network's only successful exchange of any type between August 1943 and late January 1944 (another sea operation near Saint-Raphael on the Riviera), but at least it meant that Bernard received a much-needed package of two-and-a-half million francs and all the details of Lien's treachery.

By now, though, through infiltration, torture and improving radio detection, the Germans had broken down nearly all the network's defences. Koenigswerther's activities back in France lasted less than a week before he was captured after a shoot-out with a detector van crew in Bordeaux. The hugely informative Nantes sector was overpowered at the same time, with the Germans capturing the entire consignment of the only successful parachute drop of late 1943. These two coups effectively silenced the network's entire flow of information from the Atlantic side of France. By the end of the year, Marie-Madeleine was all but ready to give Paul Bernard the order to cease all undercover work, such was the dearth of equipment and money getting through to him. Finally and crucially, however, a successful parachute drop of transmitters and money was able to take place on the night of 6 January 1944. It was recovered by agents from one of the few remaining functioning sectors, run by the former French air force captain, le Comte Helen des Isnards, based at Aix-en-Provence. An attempt a few days earlier had failed when the RAF Whitley involved was lost with all its crew.

March saw the resumption of Lysander operations on the *Alliance's* behalf, thanks to the direct involvement of Kenneth Cohen. The first nearly killed the pilot, Flying Officer Duggie Bell, and the two returning agents when the plane's engine failed and nosedived into a field within a mile of the Normandy coast. With pilot and one agent badly injured, the trio managed somehow to avoid detection in a highly fortified part of France and made it to a railway station and the eventual comparative safety of Paris. A further Lysander exchange, not far from Angers close to the Loire, not only gave Flying Officer Bell a passage home, it re-established human contact between London and the *Alliance* in France, which had been lacking for six months.

Among the reams of hitherto undelivered courier that had arrived with this flight — the payload can scarcely have been safe, as there were four passengers as well — was information from the still-intact Normandy sector, which must have delighted those planning D-Day. The art master at the lycée at Caen, Maurice Dounin, had travelled the entire Normandy coast from the mouth of the river Dives eastwards of Caen to the beginning of the Cotentin peninsula on his bike and on foot, and sketched an extraordinary map. When unrolled, it reached fifty-five feet in length and depicted every fortification, gun battery and beach obstacle the Germans had constructed.

Any joy that Marie-Madeleine felt for such productive reconnection with her comrades in France was very soon dispelled by the next piece of harrowing news. Only two days after the Lysander operation, Paul Bernard was arrested by the Gestapo in Paris and began a session of beatings and half-drownings by interrogators at 84 Avenue Foch. He had been denounced by a newly recruited agent and, although he showed an extraordinary ability to stay silent before his torturers, it seems they had already acquired much of the information they required by other means. Most of the principal agents in the northern sector of France had been captured in a massive swoop, which included the map-maker and twenty others from Normandy, all of whom were summarily shot on the day after the D-Day landings of 6 June.

The question now arose about who was to command what remained of the network in the field and, as a temporary solution, Marie-Madeleine divided the network into four independent commands, splitting southern France between two existing sector leaders and giving the shattered north to a Normandy agent, Jean Sainteny, who had missed the Gestapo swoop while on a Lysander course in England. Meanwhile, Georges Lamarque would continue to lead his nationwide subnetwork, the *Druids*. Now, more strongly than ever, however, Marie-Madeleine was determined to return to France to resume overall control. All was not yet lost, as every time the Nazis struck, more volunteers seemed to be stepping forward, buoyed perhaps by the expectation of an imminent allied invasion. Both the April and May moons had seen successful Lysander operations for the network and there was still a regular radio exchange with the Mediterranean and south-west regions. The only major recent setback had been the arrest of four valuable agents, including Jeannie Rousseau of the *Druids*, in the north Brittany town of Tréguier, prior to an attempted sea evacuation to England.

By June, Marie-Madeleine had been able to use the *Alliance's* newly forged association with the *BCRA* to lobby for her to return to France. Although agreement reluctantly came in time for the June moon, with all attention focused on the momentous Operation Overlord of 6 June, it was not until the following month that she was destined to set foot once again in occupied France. Dansey was still certain her chances of survival were minimal and insisted she wore a convincing, if unflattering, disguise with a hairnet, spectacles and false teeth. He even gave her a rabbit's foot mascot and told her that, if she were caught, she was to tell the Germans that the *Alliance* was dead and that she was now working for him, sending back reports about the communists in France. They would know who he was and it might just save her.

Marie-Madeleine disguised by hairnet, spectacles and false teeth for her return to occupied France in July 1944. (*Colin Cohen*)

On the night of 5 July 1944, as Marie-Madeleine stumbled through the darkness somewhere just to the east of the forest of Fontainebleau, she stooped to pick up a small handful of French soil and fondled it between her fingers. Her last sight of England had not been the familiar surroundings of Bignor Manor and the Tangmere cottage but the headquarters of 161 Squadron at RAF Tempsford. Both Kenneth Cohen and 'Ham' had been there to wish her well and see her board a Hudson with seven other passengers, including her fellow *Alliance* agent Raymond Pezet, to whom Marie-Madeleine was married according to her false identity papers. The plan was for the pair to find their way southwards through France and make contact with Capitaine des Isnards, whose relatively intact south-eastern sector had become the powerhouse of the network, keeping up a stream of information from its transmitters while so many others had fallen silent.

The journey from just south of Paris to Aix-en-Provence took more than three days, some of it on foot, some by hitching lifts in a variety of road vehicles and some by trains severely disrupted by Resistance sabotage and allied bombing. They were welcomed by des Isnards with the news that the letter box he had been using for getting written reports to London had just been blown. Once Pezet had taken his leave — he was to join the Avia team — des Isnards took Marie-Madeleine to the hideout he had prepared for her, a flat in a small house not far from the Cours Mirabeau. He assured her that no one but he and the proprietor knew of the place and showed her some sixty pounds of correspondence and reports that had accumulated and been stored there awaiting her attention.

He also reported that Georges Lamarque had been in Aix, hoping to see her to give details of recent disasters in Paris. Most of the agents of the newly re-activated sector had been rounded up, including its leader, Jean Sainteny. The allied invasion had only increased the ferocity of the Gestapo interrogation methods. Probably as much through fear as through vengefulness, the Nazi secret police had shed all vestiges of justice, executing many of their prisoners as soon as they had extracted all they could from them. The only ray of light was that Sainteny himself had, despite the effects of torture, managed to saw through an iron bar in his prison and escape.

For the next week or so, Marie-Madeleine worked feverishly at sorting and encoding the mountain of reports due for transmission to London. Among them, she came across details of the *Wehrmacht* plot to assassinate Hitler which, only a few days later on 20 July, would so narrowly fail in its execution. She wondered if Dansey and his superiors would treat the report with as little credence as they had the previous *Wehrmacht* proposal she carried with her from France a whole year earlier. Nearly every day of that week, des Isnards collected Marie-Madeleine from her apartment and drove her in his car to his farm, just outside Aix on the road leading towards Mont Sainte-Victoire, where he directed his operations. Here, Marie-Madeleine would have lunch, hand over the messages for transmission and meet many of the *Alliance's* newest recruits, who were preparing for the imminent allied landing in the south. She did not intend to be among them for long. Once a parachute drop of arms and supplies she had arranged with London had taken place, she would head north again to help her beleaguered comrades in Paris.

But fate, in the shape of a dozen heavily armed Germans bursting through the unbolted door of her apartment one evening, was to intervene. They had come in search of des Isnards who had just left, having warned Marie-Madeleine that the town was to undergo a thorough search the next day and arranging to pick her up with all the mail in his car in the morning. With convincing indignation, she persuaded the Germans that it must have been another apartment in the building that he had visited and, while all but a single guard went to knock on other doors, she managed to throw a pile of messages that had been on a central table under a nearby divan. The posse soon returned to Marie-Madeleine's flat having found nothing elsewhere, but her continued play-acting eventually convinced their leader that she was genuinely scared of the maquis terrorists of whom this man was reportedly one. When a search of the flat revealed nothing, the men were about to take their leave until one of them, for no apparent reason, stooped to look under the divan.

The effect of his discovery was electric. Suddenly, the men began attacking every fixture and piece of furniture in a frenzy to uncover more evidence. They finally succeeded in their search when they tore apart some carpet hassocks into which Marie-Madeleine had sewn all the sheaves of mail that she had been processing. Their fury and indignation, fuelled by some cognac they had found, was such that Marie-Madeleine was convinced she was about to be lynched or shot. Fortunately, their leader restrained the men by force and dragged her into a corner of the room. Her refusal to say who she was and cool insistence that she would only answer to the senior Gestapo officer in the region had made him wonder if she were, in fact, a double agent and that there might be a share for him in the rewards she was due for penetrating a French network.

While refusing his proposition to that effect, Marie-Madeleine played along with the suggestion that she might be on the Germans' side, still insisting she needed to see the man in charge. This would buy her time, especially as the man in question was out of town and would not be back until 9 o'clock the next morning. It meant she had until that time to think of a way to avert the disaster that otherwise awaited her and the entire network, as the Gestapo chief would have no doubts as to her identity the moment he set eyes on her.

She was taken by her captors to the local Miollis military barracks, where she was locked into a soldiers' punishment cell on the ground floor of the gatehouse and left there for the night. Allowed to keep her bag, she felt inside for the cyanide. Was that the best solution? It would prevent her giving anything away under torture, but it would not save des Isnards or countless other agents. What else could she do? Escape?

There was a large window to the cell, whose glass casements had been replaced by a horizontal thick wooden board which blocked four fifths of the opening, leaving a narrow space at the top. By putting her slops bucket upside-down on her bed and standing on it, she could see out into the street through protective vertical bars which were set a few inches beyond the board.

Remembering stories from her childhood in the Far East of burglars who broke into houses naked and covered in oil to slip through the tightest gaps, Marie-Madeleine set about her desperate plan of escape. Removing all her clothes and with a few banknotes and a flimsy, rolled-up dress clenched between her teeth, she pulled her meagre frame up and over the board until she was standing on the windowsill, tightly pinned between board and bars and totally exposed to the darkened street outside. Hoping that if her head would fit through the bars, the rest of her would follow, she tested the nearest gap, but it was too narrow. Praying that there might be some inconsistency in their spacing, she tried again further along the window. This time, with much pain, she was able to force her head through. At this precise moment, a German motor convoy swept into the street and screeched to a halt right in front of her window. With excruciating pain to her ears, Marie-Madeleine jerked her head back inside the bars and stood there pinned, naked and utterly vulnerable. The military convoy had lost its way and the man at its head began demanding directions from the sentry to the barracks, which stood a few yards to Marie-Madeleine's right and which she had not even noticed before. When the convoy eventually moved off again, she once more squeezed her head through, but this time it was followed by her neck, her right shoulder and her right leg. Her hips were the most painful of all but, with them free, she found herself on the pavement. The sentry had heard something, though, and shouted and flashed his torch in her direction. Its beam missed her lean frame flattened on the ground beneath the window and, in a few seconds, she took off into some rough ground across the street and, hearing no sound of a pursuer, put on her dress.

Marie-Madeleine now had only one thought: she must make it to des Isnards' farmhouse before he set out to collect her from her flat where the Gestapo would undoubtedly have set a trap. In the rapidly growing dawn light, she first made her way to a stream on the eastern edge of Aix to wash as much scent from herself as possible, in case they came looking for her with dogs. Then, on a route that took her straight back past the barracks and the sentry, she began her barefoot journey to the farmhouse. On the outskirts of the city, she found German soldiers putting up road blocks — her escape would by now have been discovered — but she managed to skirt round the checkpoint by joining peasants gleaning in the fields beside the road. To her utter relief, when she finally staggered in through the front door of the farmhouse, des Isnards and his wife were still in bed. Bursting into their bedroom and announcing that she had saved them, she promptly collapsed.

Although Marie-Madeleine would never again come quite as close to her death as she did in Aix-en-Provence, her dangerous fight against the German occupation of her country continued right up to the moment that American forces finally pushed the German army back across its own borders in late December 1944. With des Isnards' sector well and truly blown by Marie-Madeleine's arrest, he and his team escaped into the hills to the east of the city to join the maquis. Here, he and Marie-Madeleine (once she and her lacerated feet had recovered from the flight out of Aix) re-established contact with London and thus a flow of intelligence from the south of France.

Still determined to get to Paris, where she hoped to assist with its speedy liberation, Marie-Madeleine assumed first the identity of a local peasant to escape from the hills, then of a widow in full black mourning clothes to allay suspicion on a Paris-bound train from Marseilles. It was Georges Lamarque's *Druids* who facilitated her return to the capital, as their sub-network still had active headquarters in both Marseilles and Paris.

By the time she arrived after another tortuous journey through the chaos of devastated roads and railway lines, General Patton's army was not far from the outskirts. One of the first of her old comrades she came across was Jean Sainteny, brandishing the prison bar he had removed to gain his freedom. She was keen to see him safely delivered out of the reaches of the Gestapo and agreed that he should attempt to breach the battle lines to the west on a motorbike, taking with him courier for London and details of the enemy's positions for the American commander-in-chief. So delighted were the allies with Sainteny's intelligence when he reached their lines that he agreed to return to Paris to come back with more information about the Germans' resolve to defend the capital or to lay waste to it. Soon after his second successful mission, bringing news that most of the *Wehrmacht* forces were making a rapid retreat eastwards towards the Rhine, the Second French Armoured Division made its triumphant entry along the Champs Elysées on 24 August.

Still Marie-Madeleine kept up the fight. She now travelled east towards Verdun in an ambulance with a fellow agent, their story being that they were collaborators following the German withdrawal and offering medical help to the wounded. The more intelligence she could supply the advancing allies, the sooner she hoped they would be over the German border. So many of her captured comrades who were still alive were incarcerated somewhere in Germany, and their only hope of survival was a rapid advance on Berlin. Verdun proved to be a fertile sector for newly recruited agents and, although she could not gain radio contact with London via the radio hidden in the ambulance, Marie-Madeleine was able to send a number of couriers back through enemy lines with information about which roads were mined and where the machine-guns were installed.

News that Verdun had finally been liberated came to Marie-Madeleine early in September, after she and her team had been forced to retreat from their village hideout to an open-air headquarters in the Hesse forest. But if she was happy to be caught up in the hysteria of victory celebrations that immediately ensued in a nearby village, she could not but ask herself, 'What is victory to us when those who won it are missing?' Victory, in any case, was still a long way off and the last eight months of war would prove fatal to so many of her missing friends. It would be Christmas before the Germans were forced out of eastern France and, all the while, agents of the *Alliance* continued to operate ahead of the advancing American lines, sending back reports of the enemy's strengths and weaknesses. Marie-Madeleine remained on the front line herself for most of that time, returning on several occasions to Paris where she was delighted to meet up with Kenneth Cohen and 'Ham'. On one of these occasions, a ceremony was organized by the British when Cohen proudly presented her with the OBE; on another, she was reunited with her children, brought back from Switzerland.

With the armistice eventually signed on May 8 1945, far from any scene of jubilation, Marie-Madeleine embarked on a final sombre duty to her lost comrades. This was a tour of all the prisons in Germany where records showed that members of the *Alliance* had been imprisoned. There had been a few blessed reprieves for individuals such as Ferdinand Rodriguez (who accompanied her on her grim tour), Navarre, Paul Bernard, Colonel Charles Bernis, Marc Mesnard, Henri-Léopold Dor, Madeleine Crozet, Michèle Goldschmidt and Jeannie Rousseau. But the further she ventured into Germany, the more the heavy toll of executions became apparent. At the fortress of Bruchsal, she came across the cell where her beloved Léon Faye had been imprisoned and saw the chains that had been used to lash him to the foot of his bed. Faye was later taken to Sonnenburg (now Słońsk) across the Polish border, where he was killed in a massacre of 800 prisoners.

In some places Marie-Madeleine visited, the bodies of her friends were still lying at the spot where they had been shot. For those where the executioners had not succeeded in reducing the evidence of their deeds to ashes, Marie-Madeleine undertook to return the remains to their families in France. In all, of the 1,000 agents in her network who had fallen into the enemy's hands, 438 were never seen alive again. Among these were Lucien Poulard, Pierre Dallas, Ernest Siegrist, Joël Lemoigne, Camille Raynal, Philippe Koenigswerther, Georges Lamarque and Edouard Kauffman.

To all those that did survive, Léon Faye sent a message, scrawled with a manacled hand and hidden behind the radiator in his prison cell before he was shot. It read:

I ask you to serve our unhappy country so that it may enjoy peace again and happiness, songs, flowers and flower-covered inns. Close the prisons, drive out the executioners. Like so many other countries, France will have to tend, cleanse and heal cruel wounds and rebuild vast numbers of ruined places. But she is the only one whose moral unity was broken. Pulled and torn in all directions, she is a dyke bursting under the weight of water. That is the most serious and urgent task. Everything must be done to get out of this impasse. Later, historians will judge. For the moment, the important thing is union, not reprisal, work and not chaos. Act to this end, my dear friends, that is my last wish.

EPILOGUE

As we have seen, the allied invasion of Normandy in June 1944, and the subsequent landings in the south of France a few weeks later, changed the nature of the task for undercover agents operating in France. The emphasis shifted from getting information about enemy defences back to London to assisting internal insurrection and sabotage against the retreating German army, as well as providing the advancing allies with intelligence from behind the enemy lines. Tangmere began to lose its tactical significance as northern parts of France were liberated, and larger transport planes such as the Hudson were now required to ferry greater numbers of personnel onto and away from the Continent.

With much of the business of 161 Squadron now emanating directly from its RAF Tempsford headquarters, Bignor Manor was no longer required as a staging post. Barbara Bertram, however, had proved herself so indispensible in the process of caring for agents in transit that she and her two boys were moved to a large Queen Anne house at Wootton, not far from Tempsford, to carry on her work. Supplied now with a staff of at least three French servicemen, including a cook, her work was considerably less hands-on and she, Tony and the boys all luxuriated in their own bedrooms. As Barbara put it:

'There was now comfort and space and leisure, but the old love and intimacy was gone.'

There was even time for Barbara to be allowed to visit Tempsford, where she was given a flight in a Lysander, an experience she found most uncomfortable in a 'machine that went crab-wise like a tiresome horse'. By the time France was liberated, there were no French left in the house with whom to celebrate the event, and the Bertram family went quietly home to Bignor to resume a life they had not lived for more than three years.

The pages which follow give a brief account of what happened to them in the years following the war, together with a number of the other leading characters in this story.

Anquetil, Bernard — Gilbert Renault's first radio operator, tracked down by detector van in Saumur and executed by the Gestapo in October 1941.

Aubrac, Lucie — After persuading Klaus Barbie to allow her husband Raymond out of Fort Montluc prison for a marriage ceremony (she was heavily pregnant), she succeeded with members of her network to kill his guards and free him. The couple escaped to London in a 161 Squadron Hudson operation in February 1944.

Bacque, Robert — Head radio man for *CND* and professional tennis player, whose treachery led to the final downfall of Renault's network. He is reported to have died in Ebensee, Austria, in May 1945.

Barbie, Klaus — 'The butcher of Lyons', responsible for the torture and death of some 4,000 French citizens while regional head of the Gestapo. Soon after the war, he was recruited as an agent of the US intelligence services and, with their assistance, escaped first to Argentina, then Bolivia. He lived there until 1983, when he was finally arrested and extradited to France to be tried for his war crimes. He was given a sentence of life imprisonment in July 1987 and died four years later of leukemia at the age of 77.

Bardonnie, Louis de la — Renault's earliest recruit, playing a central role in the early days of his network. Released from his arrest by the Vichy police in the spring of 1942 for lack of evidence, he spent the rest of the war on the run from the Gestapo, his wife filing for divorce to save her and her large family from deportation. All survived the war and the family resumed their wine-growing existence on the slopes of the Dordogne.

Bathgate, Flying Officer Jimmy — Lysander pilot of 161 Squadron who was shot down over France and killed on 10 December 1943.

Beaufils, Georges — Representative of the communist underground movement who struck up a friendship with Gibert Renault, which led to communist involvement in de Gaulle's Free French. He served in the French army after the war, but never severed his contacts with the Soviet Union. In 1977, now a civilian, he was arrested for passing secrets to Russia and was imprisoned for four years. He died in 2002.

Bernard, Paul — Banker and economist friend of Marie-Madeleine Fourcade whom she appointed to lead the *Alliance* network during her year in London. One of the very few of the network's agents to survive capture by the Gestapo. The Germans had mistakenly implicated him in the July 1944 plot to assassinate Hitler and he had been taken to Berlin to face interrogation. He escaped during allied bombing of the city. After the war, he established and ran an air navigation company.

Bertram, Anthony — Conducting officer for the SIS. He was awarded the *Légion d'Honneur* and the *Croix de Guerre avec palme* immediately after the war, such was the regard in which he was held by the French. He continued to write, especially about art, including books on Paul Nash (1955) and Michelangelo (1964). He died in August 1978.

Bertram, Barbara — Hostess to the French at Bignor Manor.

After the liberation of France when her duties at Bignor were over, Barbara was invited to a lunch in London, where the head of the Free French intelligence service presented her with a silver cigarette case with the Cross of Lorraine inlaid in gold. In June 1945, Barbara went to live in Paris, Tony having been given a job there with the British Council. There, sometimes by pre-arrangement but others through chance meetings in the street, in cafés or the Metro, they became reunited with many of the surviving agents who had passed through Bignor Manor. After the tragic death of their son, Nicky, in 1947 when they had returned to Bignor, Barbara converted to her husband's Roman Catholic faith and they both began a devout observance of its doctrines. Their third son, Jerome, now a Catholic priest, was born in 1950. After Tony died in 1978, she toured the USA on an open Greyhound bus ticket, exhibiting her embroidery. Based back in Sussex, she delivered more than 500 talks about her war experience to Women's Institutes up and down the country. She died aged 97 on 24 January 2004.

Bell, Flying Officer Duggie — Lysander pilot who survived a crash in France in March 1944. After the war, he went on to fly V-bombers for the RAF's strategic nuclear strike force.

Bla — see Davies, Arthur Bradley

Bonamour du Tartre, Tristan — Father-in-law of Christian Pineau and deputy leader of the *Phalanx* network. He survived deportation to Buchenwald concentration camp along with his son-in-law.

Bontinck, Hermine — Courier and assistant to Marie-Madeleine Fourcade, who escaped her arrest in Lyon and who would marry the network's radio supremo, Ferdinand Rodriguez, after the war.

Bouryschkine, Vladimir — MI9 agent whose attempts to get to France by Lysander were twice thwarted in December 1942.

Finally parachuted into France in March 1943, he was arrested on a train to Pau three months later while attempting to smuggle American airmen out of France across the Pyrenees.

Boutron, Commandant Jean — Survivor of Mers-el-Kebir who smuggled Marie-Madeleine Fourcade across the Spanish border to Madrid. He escaped France aboard a British submarine in November 1942 and joined de Gaulle's Free French navy in London.

Bridger, Flight Lieutenant John — Lysander pilot who went on to fly Halifax bombers. In April 1959, he was flying an Avro Super Trader IV cargo plane, carrying top-secret rocket components from the UK to Woomera rocket range in Australia when the plane crashed into Mt Süphan in Turkey. Everyone on board was killed.

Bridou, Jacques — Marie-Madeleine's brother who eventually made it back to London via the Pyrenees and Spain after his escape alongside his sister from their arrest in Marseilles. Fighting with the French army in the Italian campaign, he was badly injured by a mine in July 1944.

Brossolette, Pierre — Hero of the resistance movement, instrumental in uniting different political factions under de Gaulle, who jumped to his death from the fifth floor of Gestapo Paris headquarters at 84 Avenue Foch.

Carré, Mathilde — Double agent involved with the Franco-Polish espionage network *Interallié*. Tried in Paris and sentenced to death in January 1949, her sentence was commuted to twenty years in prison three months later. She was released from prison in 1954 and died in 1970.

Cartaud, Pierre — Traitorous member of *CND* who was responsible for the network's devastation in 1942. According to Miannay (see bibliography), he was accidentally killed by the Germans in May 1944.

Carudel, André — Agent trained in Lysander reception who was a professional jockey in peacetime. He became a good friend of the Bertrams and, in one of their postwar reunions, challenged Tony to join him on the gallops the next morning. In the sobriety of dawn, both saw better than to carry through the experiment.

Cavaillès, Jean — Christian Pineau's right-hand man in his *Libération Nord* resistance movement. After his escape from internment in December 1942, he was flown by Lysander to London, where he was tasked by the *BCRA* to set up an action-oriented network in northern France alongside his intelligence-gathering organization, *Cohors*. Becoming increasingly occupied with his action group, he was eventually betrayed and arrested August 1943. Condemned to death by a German military tribunal, he was executed by firing squad in February 1944.

Cholet, André — Paris radio operator for the *CND*, arrested in the round-up caused by 'Phoebus's' betrayal in March 1942. He was executed along with a number of other fellow radio operators on 13 May 1942.

Cohen, Kenneth — Co-ordinator of much of the SIS's intelligence work in France. He became chief controller of Europe and director of production for the SIS after the war and was appointed CMG (Companion of the Order of St Michael and St George) in 1946. He retired in 1953 and was created CB (Companion of the Most Honourable Order of Bath). For the next thirteen years, he served as European adviser to United Steel Companies. He died in September 1984.

Courtaud, Olivier — Renault's radio operator parachuted into France in May 1942. He was arrested in June 1943, deported and eventually freed in June 1945.

Coustenoble, Maurice — One of Marie-Madeleine's earliest recruits and mainstay of her network in the northern occupied zone. Escaped capture by the Gestapo but died of cancer in November 1943.

Crémailh, André — Paris radio operator in Renault's network, arrested with several others in March 1942. He would eventually be released from Fresnes prison through lack of evidence, partly due to the courage of his fellow agent, André Cholet, who swore under torture to Crémailh's lack of involvement.

Dallas, Pierre — Leader of the Lysander reception of Avia section of the *Alliance*. Captured along with Léon Faye in September 1943 and shot on the rifle range attached to Heilbronn barracks in Germany in August 1944.

Dansey, Sir Claude — Head of the French sector of the SIS. He retired from the service at the end of the war and died in June 1947.

Davies, Arthur Bradley — Fascist traitor who infiltrated the SIS and who caused havoc to the *Alliance* network. Two conflicting versions of his eventual fate exist: either he was executed at the hands of Léon Faye in 1942 or he escaped to Algeria with his wife and children to live out the war in safety.

Decker, Jean — Gilbert Renault's uncle who ran a letter box in his photographic shop in Saumur for his nephew's network. He was arrested in November 1941, deported and died in a concentration camp.

Delattre, Robert — Renault's aerial operations specialist and radio operator, arrested in Paris in May 1942, imprisoned in Fresnes and died there from his mistreatment.

Delaye, Pierre — Barbara Bertram's 'Pierre-le-paysan' and highly effective agent for Christian Pineau's network. He was gunned down and killed by a radio detection squad at Loyettes on the Rhône in May 1943.

Delestraint, General Charles — Sent to France by de Gaulle in March 1943 to take control of all undercover military operations. He was captured, along with Jean Moulin, on 9 June 1943, interrogated by Klaus Barbie and eventually sent to Dachau concentration camp where he was executed in April 1945, days before the camp was liberated.

Déricourt, Henri — Enigmatic agent of the SOE who was tried but acquitted for working for the Germans and who might even have been a triple agent for the SIS. Even the circumstances of his death have unanswered questions attached, but it seems he was killed in an aircraft accident over Laos in November 1962.

Dewavrin, André (Passy) — After his return from his dangerous mission in France in the spring of 1943, Passy was awarded the *Croix de la Libération* by General de Gaulle and then sent to Algeria to take command of the combined secret services of General Giraud and the *BCRA*. In February 1944, he returned to London as chief of staff to the general commanding the French army in England and the undercover forces in France. In August that year, he was parachuted into Brittany and took command of 2,500 French troops engaged in the liberation of the north coast port of Paimpol. In May 1945, he was again in charge of France's secret services but, with de Gaulle's departure from power, he left his post in February 1946. He was then accused by the government of embezzlement of state funds and imprisoned for 200 days before his eventual release without trial. In 1953, he began a life in commerce, first in the banking sector, then in the textile industry. He died in Paris in December 1998.

Duclos, Maurice — Following the destruction of his intelligence network and his escape to England in March 1942, he took charge of the sabotage section of the *BCRA*. He took part in a number of missions into France, destroying dams on the River Saône, railway lines and enemy telecommunications prior to D-Day. He then fought alongside General Montgomery's Special Forces after the allied landing, seeing action in Normandy, Belgium, Holland and Germany. Among his decorations were *Compagnon de la Libération* and the *Croix de Guerre*, as well as the OBE and Military Cross conferred by the British. After the war, he settled in Argentina and died in Buenos Aires in 1981.

Farley, Flight Lt Wally — Killed in April 1942, when the Halifax he was flying on an operation to Austria with two agents aboard flew into Blauberg Mountain in Bavaria.

Faure, François — Spent fourteen months in Fresnes prison after his arrest in Paris in May 1942. He then spent the next twenty-one months in concentration camps, first at Natzweiler-Struthof in Alsace, then in Dachau. He survived and was freed on 29 April 1945. After the war, he returned to his family furniture business and died in June 1982.

Faye, Commandant Léon — As a prized prisoner of the Nazis, he was taken to Gestapo headquarters at 84 Avenue Foch in Paris after his arrest in September 1943. From there, he, the SOE heroine Noor Inayat Khan and another British agent, John Starr, nearly succeeded in escaping together across the roofs of surrounding buildings, but were eventually trapped in a cul-de-sac as they reached street level. He was later among 800 massacred at Sonnenburg concentration camp.

Fleuret, Jean — Sector head and abundant source of intelligence for Renault's network, based in Bordeaux. He survived deportation, but his wife and son did not.

Fourcade, Marie-Madeleine — After the war, she became secretary-general, then president of the Resistance Action

Committee, putting herself at the service of the families of those from her network who were killed. With her second husband, Hubert Fourcade, she had three more children and, also with his help, worked as a fervent Gaullist to bring the General back to power in May 1958. She became a member of the European Parliament with a keen interest in the cause of the Afghan resistance movement. She died in 1989.

Fourcaud, Pierre — Pioneer intelligence agent for the Free French, he spent a year in prison after his arrest by the Vichy police in August 1941. He then managed to escape and after an epic 1,245-kilometre bicycle ride across France, he found his way back to London via Cassis, the Balearics and Gibraltar. He was sent back out to France in February 1944 to co-ordinate the efforts of the maquis in the Savoie region. Arrested three months later, he was seriously wounded when he was shot at whilst trying to escape. The Germans brought him back to health in order to interrogate him, but he escaped from Chambéry prison in August 1944 and was back in London three weeks later. He continued to work as a colonel in the French intelligence service until 1956. He died in 1998.

Hankey, Flight Lt Stephen — Killed attempting to land his Lysander in fog on his return from a mission in December 1943.

Hodges, Wing Commander Lewis (Bob) — Continued a successful career in the RAF after the war, becoming Air Chief Marshal in 1971, and was Air Aide-de-Camp to the Queen until his retirement in 1976.

Hooper, Flight Lieutenant Robin — Returned to his career in the Foreign Office after the war and served as Ambassador to Greece from 1971 to 1974.

Lamarque, Georges — Captured by the SS during the parachuting of supplies to his intelligence-gathering group behind the retreating enemy lines in eastern France on 8 September 1944. He had refused to escape, knowing that the Germans would carry out reprisal killings among local inhabitants. He and an assistant were taken immediately to a nearby field and shot.

Lien, Jean-Paul — He was tried and executed for his treachery in October 1946. With the liberation of France, he had joined the French army and it was only because, in March 1945, Ferdinand Rodriguez happened to recognize him in a bar on the Champs Elysées in an officer's uniform that he was eventually arrested and brought to justice.

Lockhart, Flying Officer Guy — Died on the night of 26/27 April 1944 when, as captain of a Lancaster bomber, he was shot down over Friedrichshafen.

Loustaunau-Lacau, Commandant Georges — Survived his captivity at Mauthausen concentration camp. On his return to France, he shocked public opinion by sharply criticizing what he saw as victimization of Marshal Pétain by those trying him. Loustaunau-Lacau then found the state prosecutors turning on him for his pre-war involvement with the ultra right-wing organization, *la Cagoule*. He was imprisoned in 1947, but was released when the case against him was withdrawn six months later. Undaunted, he continued a political career and was elected member of the National Assembly for the Basses-Pyrénées in 1951. He died in Paris in February 1955.

McBride, Flying Officer Jim — Died on the same night as Stephen Hankey, attempting to land his Lysander in fog at Tangmere in December 1943.

McCairns, Flying Officer James ('Mac') — Was killed in 1946 on a training flight at RAF Finningley when his Mosquito lost hydraulic power.

Méric, Marie-Madeleine — see Fourcade, Marie-Madeleine

Moulin, Jean — De Gaulle's envoy and arch co-ordinator of the resistance movements in France. Arrested in Lyons in June 1943, he died less than a month later from the brutal and fruitless attempts of Klaus Barbie and Gestapo interrogators in Paris to extract information from him.

Murphy, Squadron Leader Alan ('Sticky') — Pioneer special duties Lysander pilot, killed in 1944 after his Mosquito was hit by flak over the Netherlands.

Navarre — see Loustaunau-Lacau, Commandant Georges

Nesbitt-Dufort, Flight Lieutenant John — Pioneer special duties Lysander pilot who survived further wartime postings which included test-flying, night-fighters, and commanding a mixed Spitfire and Mosquito wing in Norway. After the war, he was involved in the Berlin Airlift of 1948-9, and later flew air freighters in the Middle East. He died in 1975.

Passy, Colonel — see Dewavrin, André

Phoebus — Head of *CND*'s Paris radio operation who denounced all members of his team when captured by the Gestapo in March 1942. In spite of this, he was executed two months later alongside the men he had betrayed.

Pickard, Wing Commander Percy ('Pick') — Commander of the special duties squadron, who was later killed during the celebrated air raid on Amiens prison in February 1944.

Pineau, Christian — Having survived sixteen months at Buchenwald concentration camp, he returned to France and, after only a month of recuperation, was appointed by Genral de Gaulle as Minister of Supply in May 1945. He became an elected member of the National Assembly in 1946 and served the French government continually in a number of senior posts, including Minister of Public Works and Transport, Finance Minister and Minister for Foreign Affairs when he signed the Treaty of Rome on behalf of France in 1957. He left politics in 1958 and pursued a career in business until 1970. He died in Paris in April 1995.

Christian Pineau (front row, third from left), as French Minister for Foreign Affairs, signs the Treaty of Rome with the Foreign Ministers of West Germany, Italy, Belgium, Luxemburg and the Netherlands on 5 March 1957. (*Gilbert Pineau*)

Renault, Gilbert (Rémy) — Spent most of his time after the war as an author, writing prolifically about his experiences and those of others working for the Resistance. He also worked with General de Gaulle in his postwar movement to reunite the French people (the RPF) but lost all favour with the General when he published an article in 1950 which sought to reconcile the followers of Marshal Pétain with those of de Gaulle, saying that, in 1940, France had needed the 'shield' of Pétain as much as it did the 'sword' of de Gaulle. He continued to defend the memory of Pétain until his death in July 1984.

Robert, Jacques — One of Gilbert Renault's key agents who went on to form his own Lyons-based network, *Phratrie*, after the disintegration of the *CND*. The Vichy police arrested him in April 1943, but he escaped four days later and returned to London by Lysander in June. There, he helped to train agents of the Jedburgh contingent, who were to be parachuted behind the enemy lines at the same time as the D-Day invasion in teams of three (one French, one English and one American in each team) to harness the help of the maquis. Robert himself was parachuted into France on 27 June 1944 and took command of a guerrilla group that fought for two months in the Corrèze and Creuse regions. After the war, he became commercial director of Mercier champagne until, in 1956, moving onto a series of other industrial directorships. He died in February 1998.

Rodriguez, Ferdinand — The only *Alliance* agent to escape with his life among all those arrested in September 1943 following Lien's betrayal. A prisoner at Sonnenburg concentration camp along with Léon Faye, he was saved from execution at the eleventh hour thanks to his British citizenship and to an exchange with a German spy held by the British in Iran, negotiated by War Office administrative captain Gareth Maufe. Rodriquez married Hermine Bontinck, Marie-Madeleine Fourcade's assistant and liaison agent after his release.

Rymills, Flying Officer Frank ('Bunny') — Special duties Lysander pilot who went on to command a Halifax squadron, dropping supplies to the Resistance and towing gliders during the Normandy invasion in 1944. He retired from the RAF in 1963 and became a successful pig farmer in Suffolk.

Vaughan-Fowler, Flight Lieutenant Peter — After leaving 161 Squadron, he went to fly Mosquitoes before being called back to special Lysander duties, flying from bases in Italy and Corsica to southern France just before the allied landings in 1944. He continued a career in the RAF after the war and retired in 1975. He died in 1997.

Verity, Squadron Leader Hugh — He worked in the air operations branch of the SOE after 161 Squadron, involved, in 1944, in deception measures for the Normandy invasion, which included flying large numbers of sorties over the northernmost beaches of France to give the impression the landings would take place there. He continued with a career in the RAF until his retirement in 1965. He died in November 2001.

BIBLIOGRAPHY

Andrew, Christopher, *Her Majesty's Secret Service* (Penguin Books, London, 1987)

Bertram, Barbara, *C'est On, C'est Off* (unpublished monologue)

Bertram, Barbara, *French Resistance in Sussex* (Pulborough, Barnworks Publishing, Pulborough, 1995)

Bertram, Barbara, *Memoirs* (Oxford, 2001)

Boyd, Douglas, *Voices from the Dark Years* (Stroud, Sutton Publishing, Stroud, 2007)

Cointet, Michèle, *Marie-Madeleine Fourcade. Un Chef de la Résistance* (Perrin, Paris, 2006)

Farmer, Alan, *The Second World War* (Hodder Education, London, 2004)

Fourcade, Marie-Madeleine, *Noah's Ark* (translation by Kenneth Morgan from the original *Arche de Noé*), (E.P. Dutton & Company, Inc., New York, 1974)

Groussard, Colonel, *Chemins Secrets* (Bader-Dufour, Paris, 1948)

Helm, Sarah, *A Life in Secrets* (Little, Brown, London, 2005)

Jeffery, Keith, *MI6, The History of the Secret Intelligence Service, 1909-1949* (Bloomsbury, London, 2010)

Langley, J.M., *Fight Another Day* (Collins, London, 1974)

Miannay, Patrice, *Dictionnaire des Agents Doubles dans la Résistance* (le cherche midi, Paris, 2005)

Nesbitt-Dufort, Wing Commander John, *Black Lysander* (Jarrolds, London, 1973)

Passy, Colonel, *Mémoires du Chef des Services Secrets de la France Libre* (Éditions Odile Jacob, Paris, 2000)

Pineau, Christian, *La Simple Vérité* (René Julliard, Paris, 1960)

Read, Anthony and Fisher, David, *Colonel Z, The Secret Life of a*

Master of Spies (Hodder and Stoughton, London, 1984)

Rémy, *La Ligne de Démarcation* (Presses Pocket, Paris, 1966)

Rémy, *Mémoires d'un Agent Secret de la France Libre*, Volumes 1-3 (Éditions France-Empire, Paris, 1959)

Rodriguez, Captain F.E., *L'Escalier de Fer* (Editions France-Empire, Paris, 1958)

Verity, Hugh, *We Landed by Moonlight* (revised edition) (Crécy Publishing Ltd, Manchester, 1995)

West, Nigel, *MI6, British Secret Intelligence Service Operations, 1909-1945* (Weidenfeld and Nicolson, London, 1983)

WEBSITES

http://genealogie-simard-boudarel.over-blog.com/article-4925626.html

http://ghmistral.free.fr/resistance.htm

http://maquisardsdefrance.jeun.fr/recits-temoignages-f4/missions-des-lysander-de-la-raf-dans-le-berry-t4373.htm

http://rha.revues.org/index1783.html

http://rha.revues.org/index2123.html#ftn12

http://www.archivesnationales.culture.gouv.fr/chan/chan/AP-pdf/580-AP-25-32.pdf

http://www.francaislibres.net/liste/fiche.php?index=64108

http://www.historyofwar.org/

http://www.memoresist.org/

http://www.pilotfriend.com/

http://www.youtube.com/watch?v=I1OM2JWaMdk

Sapere Books is an exciting new publisher of brilliant fiction and popular history.

To find out more about our latest releases and our monthly bargain books visit our website: **saperebooks.com**

Printed in Great Britain
by Amazon